KU-590-843

An Introduction to Moral Philosophy and Moral Education

Most introductions to moral philosophy, in one way or another, delineate the field and introduce the reader to various moral theories and arguments. *An Introduction to Moral Philosophy and Moral Education* is different in that it eschews the traditional, historical approach and the use of names and schools of thought as organizing devices. Focusing on the ideas themselves, it keeps jargon to a minimum and with a wealth of examples from drunkenness to torture, from cell-phones to tax evasion, this compelling book brings philosophy and everyday reality firmly together.

This book seeks to present and argue for a moral theory which draws on most of the major theoretical positions to some degree, but it also spells out the limits and boundaries of such a theory. In doing so, it exposes a number of common confusions and misunderstandings about morality, and presents a strong argument for some indisputable truths in relation to the moral sphere.

Divided into four parts, the book covers the key issues within moral philosophy:

- Part I provides a lucid and powerful account of the nature and limits of moral theory, sharply distinguishing it from religion.
- Part II outlines a positive moral theory by exploring the defining principles of morality and the reasons for being moral.
- Part III distinguishes moral values from others such as ecological, health and safety, and sexual values.
- Part IV is concerned with the implications of our moral understanding for moral education.

While the book concentrates on argument and ideas, a commentary to each chapter provides historical context and contemporary reference points. It will prove an invaluable resource for students of both education and philosophy.

Robin Barrow is Professor of Philosophy of Education at Simon Fraser University, Canada.

Withdrawn

ACCESS. NO. TO55020

CLASS NO. 370.1

Other books by Robin Barrow

An Introduction to Moral Philosophy and Moral Education

Robin Barrow

Routledge
Taylor & Francis Group

LONDON AND NEW YORK

First published 2007 by Routledge
2 Park Square, Milton Park, Abingdon, Oxon OX14 4RN

Simultaneously published in the USA and Canada
by Routledge
270 Madison Ave, New York, NY 10016

Routledge is an imprint of the Taylor & Francis Group, an informa business

© 2007 Robin Barrow

Typeset in TimesNewRoman by
Keystroke, 28 High Street, Tettenhall, Wolverhampton
Printed and bound in Great Britain by
TJ International Ltd, Padstow, Cornwall

All rights reserved. No part of this book may be reprinted or reproduced
or utilized in any form or by any electronic, mechanical, or other means,
now known or hereafter invented, including photocopying and recording,
or in any information storage or retrieval system, without permission in
writing from the publishers.

British Library Cataloguing in Publication Data
A catalogue record for this book is available from the British Library

Library of Congress Cataloging in Publication Data
A catalog record for this book has been requested

ISBN10: 0–415–42102–0 (hbk)
ISBN10: 0–415–42103–9 (pbk)
ISBN10: 0–203–94622–7 (ebk)

ISBN13: 978–0–415–42102–7 (hbk)
ISBN13: 978–0–415–42103–4 (pbk)
ISBN13: 978–0–203–94622–0 (ebk)

For Alexandra and Natasha, with all my love

Contents

Acknowledgements

I am especially indebted to Devi Pabla for her help in the preparation of this book. Thanks are also due to Professor Jack Martin, Professor Tasos Kazepides, Professor Ruth Jonathan, Dr Ieuan Lloyd, Professor William Hare, Professor Howard Woodhouse, and Dr Patrick Keeney for their comments and advice. I should also like to thank my editor, Anna Clarkson, and all her staff at Routledge: it has proved a pleasure to work with them on publishing both this and a previous volume.

Introduction

To flee vice is the beginning of virtue, and the beginning of wisdom is to have got rid of folly.

(Horace, *Epistles*, 1.1)

Most people who choose to study moral philosophy perhaps do so in the hope that they will acquire a better understanding of what being moral is all about. Just as those who attend history of art courses hope to increase their understanding of what those who appreciate, judge, and criticize art are doing rather than to become artists themselves, so students of moral philosophy want to get inside the business of moral thinking and understand what makes a sound moral argument, rather than to improve themselves morally. They do not necessarily expect to learn all the answers to moral questions or to become more adept at making moral judgements. But they do expect to understand what morality is, just as those who study law, engineering, or the Roman Empire expect to come to grips with those fields and to appreciate the problems peculiar to them and the appropriate procedures for dealing with them.

Most introductions to moral philosophy, in one way or another, delineate the field and introduce the reader to various moral theories and arguments. They don't usually try to tell the reader directly what needs to be done to lead the moral life. Even though many examples considered may be drawn from real life, the understanding acquired overall doesn't translate automatically into a practical guide to living in the world. And whereas many art students come to look at art in a new way as a result of their studies, many philosophy students may be unaffected in their personal lives by their understanding of morality. They are often no more discerning about daily moral problems than anybody else. At least part of the reason for this may be that introductory texts and courses tend to cover a wide area of ground and are reluctant to pursue a particular line or advance a specific theory at the expense of others. The emphasis, even when the organization of the material is neither historical nor based on distinct schools of thought, nonetheless tends to be on the differences and rivalries between theories and ideas. Monographs that are not written at the introductory level do frequently take a position, but it seems to be widely felt that this would be inappropriate in a general introduction to the subject.

The time has come to challenge this assumption and to introduce the business of moral philosophy by arguing for a coherent gathering together of all that can be said with pretty much certainty about morality; to show that there is much that is not contested to any serious degree, and to suggest that much of what is contestable may be inevitably so – the consequence of the way things are rather than of any deficiencies in moral philosophy. With this in mind, this book is designed to be different from most other introductions to moral philosophy. No doubt authors commonly have a tendency to regard their own work as distinctive, whether or not with good reason, so I should be careful. But I can at any rate spell out some of the features that differentiate the approach adopted here.

The main objective of this book is to introduce the reader to an argument about the nature of morality and, consequently, to an understanding of what makes people and actions good and bad, or right and wrong, and to an understanding of how to determine in principle what one ought to do. For reasons that will be fully explained, it does not provide a check-list of good and bad behaviour, and it is therefore completely distinct from self-help books and other guides to conduct. But, while it is not dogmatic and definitive in that manner, it does clearly pinpoint and distinguish between the kind of thing that is in itself and always good, the kind that is generally but not always good, the kind that is not good but may be justified, and the kind that cannot in the nature of things be categorically classified as good or bad.

Quite understandably, introductions are reluctant to be too specific or to ally themselves clearly with some particular author, theory, or position, precisely because they are introductions to the field, and the field is broad. Introductory books generally don't take sides or build up one consistent point of view, because they see their job as being to survey the subject and they therefore want to introduce various rival theories, a number of philosophers with different views and approaches, and a host of distinct, sometimes incompatible, ideas. Here I have taken an unusual tack. I have for the most part deliberately avoided reference to any philosopher by name in the main text. For those whose primary interest is in the history of ideas or who want to associate ideas and arguments with particular people, a brief, largely bibliographical commentary at the end of each chapter provides information about historical and contemporary relations between people and ideas, but the main emphasis in the body of the book is on the ideas and arguments themselves, regardless of their source or backing.

The tracking of names at the same time as the arguments is perhaps merely a potential distraction from focusing on the reasoning itself. But the equally common practice of introducing moral philosophy by way of a number of rival theories and distinctive labels can be positively misleading in that the unwary will conclude that one has to choose between various packages such as utilitarianism or intuitionism, teleological or deontological theories, and virtue or feminist ethics. The fact of the matter is that one can perfectly well be a feminist and committed to virtue ethics, and neither approach will provide a complete and adequate account of morality in itself. There are insights to be found in the work of those who call themselves feminist philosophers, and of those who subscribe to virtue ethics, but also of those who think in terms of situational ethics, Marxism or practically anything else.

The notion that one must, for example, adopt either a teleological or a deontological theory and that species of the two are in inevitable conflict is bizarre, and is at least partly to be accounted for by the fact that they are invariably introduced as contrasting positions. This particular issue will be explained and explored below, but for the moment suffice it to say that any sane understanding of morality must contain elements of both positions. Similarly, while for purposes of study it can be convenient to focus on utilitarianism today and intuitionism tomorrow, the truth is that there is nothing in the world to stop one being both a 'utilitarian' and an 'intuitionist'. Indeed, if one looks at a specialist monograph on something such as utilitarianism, the first thing that becomes apparent is that there is no such thing as utilitarianism; rather, there are many species of what may be categorized as utilitarian theory, and without too much distortion some of these could equally well be classified as something else, and other theories which are not categorized as utilitarian might reasonably be so. This is to say that our classification of moral theories, while it has many uses, can be seriously misleading, if what we want to do is understand morality, since that in fact requires drawing on all sorts of position generally presumed to be antithetical to one another.

Another reason why focusing on individual thinkers, historical evolution, or the standard classification of moral theories may be unwise is that it may lead one to infer that morality is a domain that can in principle be fully explained. It seems to me urgently necessary to knock that idea on the head: life is messy and complex and often presents insoluble problems, particularly in the moral sphere. But this has an important corollary which is regularly ignored: if it is agreed that some problems are insoluble, then the fact that a given theory cannot solve a particular problem is not necessarily to be held against it. Yet it is almost routine to argue against utilitarianism, for instance, by considering examples in which it appears that the committed utilitarian wouldn't know what to do. I shall be arguing that we need to be eclectic in piecing together our understanding of morality, putting aside any idea that some individual or school of thought might have got it entirely right, but also recognizing that part of the reason why that cannot be the case is that a convincing theory, far from wrapping everything up, must account for the fact that a lot of the time there is no definitive or correct answer to the question, 'What is it morally right to do in this situation?'

One particular claim, then, is that paradoxically a convincing moral theory should not explain everything. This is an aspect of a wider point that is also too often ignored: we need to have a clear idea of what a moral theory is for, or what it is supposed to do. There is a marked tendency, for instance, for critics of a given theory to point out that it does not give unequivocal guidance or that it is difficult in practice to reason in the way the theory requires. But that is to presume that a theory is designed or should be able to help us make decisions in practice. This, I shall argue, is seriously misplaced.

Some of the distinguishing features of this book, then, are that it eschews the historical approach and the use of names and schools of thought as organizing devices. It keeps jargon to a minimum and focuses on the ideas themselves. It seeks to present and argue for a moral theory which draws on most of the major theoretical positions to some degree, but it also spells out the limits and boundaries of a moral theory, not least the point that a moral theory cannot hope to solve all moral problems either in practice or in principle. If it purports to do so, something is wrong.

What the moral philosopher tends to see as problematic in moral matters is similar to but not entirely co-extensive with what may worry the proverbial man in the street. The latter, one may suggest, is perplexed or concerned about four things in particular. First, that as a matter of fact there appear to be widespread differences of opinion as to what specific behaviours are morally right and wrong, not only throughout the world and at different times, but increasingly within our own society. Second, there is disagreement (or at least uncertainty) as to what it is about an action that makes it moral or immoral. If bullfighting is morally unacceptable, why is that? Third, assuming we have an answer to that question, which is to say a clear idea of the criteria by which we judge conduct to be moral, how do we prove or demonstrate that those are indeed the criteria? How does one establish the truth of a moral claim? Fourth, there are a number of problems and questions to do with maintaining moral behaviour in practice: even if there is no difficulty in knowing what ought to be done, there are all sorts of obstacles and temptations that may get in the way of it being done.

The philosopher as such is not directly concerned with the fourth problem, although there are philosophical questions that need to be asked about such things as weakness of will, intentions, and, of course, moral education. But certainly the question of how in practice to achieve a more moral society goes beyond philosophy. Nor, as I shall hope to make clear, is the philosopher necessarily worried by the point that there is widespread disagreement about what is moral and what is not. This observation, the truth of which is undeniable, does need to be explained or accounted for, but it need not be seen as problematic. But the questions of by what criteria we are to judge an action to be moral and how one can substantiate or prove one's answer to that question are both central to the philosopher's concerns as well as problematic to ordinary people.

There are a number of other quite common assumptions about morality that are seriously misleading, if not mistaken. These will be discussed in more detail below, but I list some of them here for convenience. (Some of these are of course related to one or more of the four basic concerns just noted.)

1   The view that to describe or give an account of morality is to describe a specific code of conduct. The view that morality can be defined in terms of particular prescriptions or proscriptions such as do not drink, do not lust, and do not steal; or love your neighbour, keep your promises, and pay your taxes.
2   The view that a person's moral quality is to be judged solely by reference to their actions or behaviour.
3   The view that what is morally good is so because it is sanctioned by God, the Big Chief, or Nature.
4   The view that there can be no grounding for morality, if it is not embedded in some religious faith.
5   The view that there is no objective moral truth, but that whatever you believe is good (or, perhaps, your society believes is good) is good.
6   The view (usually a confusion rather than a stated position) that morality can be identified with the legal, the socially acceptable, or the prudent.
7   The view that a moral theory must provide clear guidance for action.

Common to all these assumptions is the implicit presumption that, to be successful, our thinking about morality must end up by providing clear and certain direction for action. This is such a common presumption, and yet so false, that it must be dealt with here and now. To be sure, in some areas of inquiry, such as in certain parts of the natural sciences, we look for, expect, and often achieve unequivocal and indisputable truths. But not all areas of inquiry operate in the same way or can expect the same degree of certainty. The historian, for example, cannot conduct the kind of laboratory experiment that the scientist can, and for that and other reasons his conclusions are often less secure or more debatable than those of the scientist. But that does not necessarily make them less true. Judgements in aesthetics, such as that Berlioz was a very good orchestrator or that the symphonies of Shostakovich do not have the quality of those of Sibelius, are even harder to establish than historical judgements, but it does not follow that there is no question of truth. In these musical examples I would actually say that the first is true and can be defended as such, whereas the second may be a claim that there really is no way of resolving. But in either case there is a distinction to be made between a coherent and relevant argument in support of the judgement and an irrelevant or incoherent one. Whether or not we can settle the question of the superiority of one composer over another, we can certainly distinguish between talking sense and talking nonsense about the issue. The points to be emphasized are that different subject matters or areas of inquiry demand different ways of trying to establish truth and may allow of different degrees of certainty. But the certainty of our knowledge should not be confused with the question of truth: something can be true, even if we are unable to prove it. My argument overall is that there are certainly some things that are true about morality, and some of these we can demonstrate in the sense of providing reasoning to show that there is no good reason to deny their truth. That may be the extent of the certainty we can hope for here, but it would be sufficient to conclude that what we have to say should be regarded and provisionally accepted as the truth about morality. It should also be recognized that within any given field some questions are easier to answer than others. For all our relative certainty in science, we are not really very sure about the nature of black holes; conversely, while it may be very hard to determine whether abortion is morally justifiable, it is absolutely certain that to gain credit as a moral agent you must, among other things, act freely rather than under coercion.

If the seven common assumptions listed above are all highly questionable, the following represents a list of seven questions that are among the proper concerns of the moral philosopher and, once understood, probably of equal concern to any thinking individual.

1   How is morality to be defined? What makes something a moral rather than a non-moral question? (This is a question distinct from and prior to the question of how we determine that this is moral and that immoral, or how we distinguish the good from the bad. It is a question about how we distinguish the moral from other domains. It is parallel to the difference between asking how we are to distinguish the aesthetic realm from others, and asking how we are to determine which paintings are aesthetically pleasing.)

2   How do we ground our thinking about morality? What can be regarded as incontrovertible and thus give us a base from which to explore the moral domain further? What can we accept as basic and given, or in some sense proved or established?

3   What can we see follows by reasoning from these fundamental premises?
4   What argument can be presented against the view that smart individuals will act to their own advantage, by exploiting the moral commitment of others? That is to say, how do we deal with the view that there is no good reason for me to be moral, provided that most other people are?
5   What argument can be presented against those who say that morality consists in doing what God demands?
6   What argument can be presented against those who say that morality consists in doing what those in power demand?
7   What can be said about various excuses such as 'I acted out of fear', out of 'self-interest', or 'out of commitment to an ideology'?

These questions will be explored in the following chapters in some depth. But it may be useful in the remainder of this introduction to make a number of initial observations relating to them.

Moral theory or moral theories are sometimes treated as if they have to provide guidance for daily activity, as if they have to provide an answer to every question and problem that may arise in the moral sphere, and as if they must at least point the way to a practicable ideal. On these grounds philosophers may variously scorn or reject a theory by showing that in certain circumstances it would not be clear what individuals should do according to the theory, that they would not in practice be able to reason according to the theory, or that there is no way that the ideal could be realized in practice.

Although I do not want to get involved with particular theories and labels, this can be briefly illustrated by reference to utilitarianism, one version or reading of which maintains that happiness is the supreme good and that our moral duty is to act in ways that provide the greatest happiness for the greatest number of people. Now there are all sorts of difficulty with that bare summary, and there are innumerable writings that pursue and develop issues within it. But the kinds of objection that I am suggesting are irrelevant to the question of the plausibility of the theory are claims such as that a utilitarian could never in practice calculate what would provide the greatest happiness, that he could not even in principle do this (because there is too much that he could not know or predict), and that the theory might lead us to be unclear which of two things should be done, or might justify acts that we feel intuitively to be wrong. The point is not that these four kinds of objection are necessarily false as statements (sometimes utilitarianism cannot tell you clearly what to do) but that they do not constitute objections to or evidence of the shortcomings of this or any other theory.

A moral theory is not a survival kit, or a guide to moral decision-making, or even a theoretical model of practical morality. It is an attempt to understand the moral ideal or the quintessence of morality, just as an aesthetic theory is an attempt to lay down the principles of ideal beauty in form; it might well be that in terms of a full understanding of a particular theory of aesthetics, we would have to conclude that no actual work of art known to us was perfect, but that would in no way invalidate the theory. Thus, moral theory is an attempt to delineate an ideal world in terms of the principles and precepts that would define it. So the fact that in the world as we have it there are problems about aiming for the greatest happiness of the greatest number is irrelevant. What the utilitarian is saying (in simplified terms) is that a perfect moral society would be one that, among other things, ensured the full happiness of every individual. That is the ideal, and this view is to be contrasted with others such as the view that the perfect society would involve people worshipping God, keeping promises whether it made them happy or not, expressing their individuality, or advancing something mysterious called the common good.

The essence of a moral theory, any particular moral theory, is a set of principles, and these are not, cannot be, endlessly negotiable or varying. There may be societies that are not interested in or do not have any morality, but if they are concerned about morality at all, and if we are not engaged in a simple linguistic confusion in that they, for example, use 'morality' to refer to what we call 'legality', then it must be presumed that there is some common ground. Another society may have very different particular moral rules, but if we are talking about the same subject, there must be something we have in common. For example, I shall be arguing in the body of this book that certain principles including that of fairness define morality; for the moment let us just assume that this is so. So the presumption is that there are certain principles that define the sphere of morality, such that we can say things like, 'Morality is about fairness', and, consequently, any society that claims to be moral has to show some recognition of these principles. In this limited sense, morality is universal and absolute: morality the world over and throughout history is, among other things, concerned with acting fairly, and acting fairly is one necessary or absolute demand, if conduct is to count as moral as opposed to non-moral. For we are not here defining the good as opposed to the bad, but delineating one aspect of the moral as distinct from other spheres such as the prudential, the self-interested, the profitable, or the aesthetic. The principles that define morality will give rise to or point to various other goods and virtues. But whereas the principles define morality at any time and place, the rules, practices, and values that they give rise to may obviously be affected to some extent by time and place. Anything that counts as a moral viewpoint has to be concerned with fairness, but what is in fact fair may well be affected by particular local circumstances. Consequently, at a lower or more specific level of conduct there is room not only for some legitimate differences between cultures, but also for some arbitrary decisions within a society, some uncertainty, and some incompatible differences between societies.

This is not problematic for moral theory, because we should not judge the quality or truth of a theory by its ability to give absolute and definitive guidance. But what it does suggest at the outset is that freedom and tolerance may also be an essential part of any genuine moral theory, since they are necessary in proportion to the degree of our legitimate and unavoidable uncertainty. If we cannot be sure whether euthanasia is acceptable or not, then clearly it cannot be right either to prohibit or to prescribe it: we must, on moral grounds, learn to live with the uncertainty and divergence of opinion.

This line of reasoning suggests that the essence of moral theory lies in providing general guidance by its principles rather than in providing specific rules of conduct. However, it is arguable that some principles clearly give rise to further, more particular values. For example, if we value truth, then we are inevitably drawn to valuing sincerity and honesty, and they may lead in turn to a broad commitment to keeping promises, telling the truth, and not cheating, until finally we begin to consider issues such as treachery, buying examination answers, how we treat each other in personal relationships, and filing honest tax returns. By this stage there may be a great deal of variation between cultures, and argument and uncertainty within a culture. But that does not weaken or invalidate the theory in any way, because what may be precisely the right way for two particular people involved in an intimate relationship to conduct themselves, for example, goes beyond moral theory. It is of course governed by moral theory, but what one should actually do depends on other things besides our commitment to fidelity, sincerity, and so forth, and there may be no clear answer to the specific question, 'What ought this person to do in this situation now?' The important thing here is not to turn away and blame moral theory or dismiss it as inadequate, but to face up to the facts: this is often the way life is – messy. And while moral theory may not always be able to tell you exactly what to do, it can definitely tell you that certain ways of behaving would be wrong, and it does tell you what principles you need to consider in making your decisions.

When it comes to grounding a moral theory or anchoring it, so that we recognize that the claims made are not merely arbitrary, but have to be acknowledged by us all, it would be helpful if we could advance beyond a common tendency to see things in stark contrast as either given in nature or devised by humans. As a matter of fact, very little is simply given in nature and unaffected by our way of looking at the world, as we may say the movements of the tides are, and very little is simply the arbitrary invention of humans. There is a sense in which and a degree to which morality may be said to be given in nature, and a degree to which it is clearly not. But the admission that to some extent morality is man-made does not mean that it is an arbitrary construct or that it could have taken some completely different form.

Love, to draw a possible though undoubtedly rough parallel, is a natural phenomenon in the sense that people just are biologically attracted to one another, and to that extent love is a real thing that does not exist only because we thought of the idea of loving relationships and then set about forming them. But this love will involve emotions and mental attitudes of caring, wanting, needing, jealousy, etc. These emotions, though again the experience of them is an indisputable phenomenon, a fact about human nature, depend partly on our minds or sets of beliefs for their realization. In this respect, therefore, aspects of loving may truly be said to be in the mind rather than in the world. At yet another level, very obviously the form that loving takes, the rituals, practices, expectations and so on are devised by humans, with the result that while all societies are likely to acknowledge love, and in so doing to refer to essentially the same phenomenon, some of what counts as love and the evidence for judging people to be in love may be quite different. Love is therefore culturally variable in one quite straightforward sense, but it is no less real for that and, at any given time, we either are or are not in love as a combined result of our genes, our upbringing, and our circumstances. 'Why should I fall in love?' is a meaningless question; telling people that it is time to fall out of love is futile.

Morality is somewhat similar. In its finer detail it is shaped by us, but it arises out of a sentiment that seems as much a part of being human as loving does. A combination of our genetic inheritance and our upbringing disposes most of us towards being moral. It could have been otherwise, just as, no doubt, we could blunt our instinctive yearning for love; but it isn't otherwise. In most cases some sense of duty, some concern for what one ought to do, is given, and that sentiment can be readily harnessed to an understanding of the fundamental principles of morality. 'Why should I be moral?' thus becomes a question on a par with 'Why should I fall in love?' or 'Why should I have friends?' No reason, if you don't happen to have any sense of duty, feel any love, or want any friends; if, however, you have the sentiment, the question is pointless.

As to why people have a moral sentiment, or when it first emerged historically, it may be difficult to say, but by and large they do have it, if only because it is cultivated during upbringing. Here a distinction of some importance needs to be made: while there is room for argument about why I as an individual should be moral, the case is quite different if we focus on society as a whole. Quite apart from the fact that morality is by definition a good thing, there are clear, incontrovertible, and overwhelming reasons why a society should be moral. Without morality neither the individuals within it nor society as such can feel secure or ultimately survive. So the difficulty has never been that of convincing a society of the value of being moral; the difficulty, such as it is, is persuading the individual who sees that he can get away with taking advantage of the morality of others, that he should not do this. (I think the answer to this, in simple terms, is that while there may be an argument that shows that he should be moral, there is no way to make him choose to go along with the conclusion of the argument, other than by holding the fear of some penalty or disapproval over him.)

While there may be certain genes that incline most of us to moral or at any rate socially acceptable behaviour generally, and while some may therefore grow up with a moral disposition regardless of upbringing, most of us grow up inclined to be moral because we are brought up to be so, just as most people who appreciate the arts do so at least partly because they have been brought up to do so. Thus, if an individual has in fact got moral sentiments and asks why he should be moral in a purely intellectual sense, he can be answered by the sort of reasoning put forward in this book. If, however, the question is asked by one who in fact lacks any moral sentiment, disapproval, coercion, or threat of punishment may be the only response. If that is broadly correct, of course, it underlines the extreme importance of moral education to both the individual and society.

There is a long tradition that sees morality in terms of the Golden Mean, and there is something to be said for orientating oneself by reflecting on the fact that bravery is a virtue situated midway between timidity and recklessness, good temper a virtue between placidity and irascibility, and liberality a virtue between meanness and prodigality. But while it is true that any excess is by definition a failing and that almost any disposition or state of mind can be indulged to excess, this approach has only limited value as a rough and ready reckoner. After all, it is not the case that one can be too generous in moral terms (though one may be too generous for one's own good), too compassionate, or too kind. Nor can all virtues and vices be categorized in terms of the mean: no degree of intolerance is strictly speaking morally acceptable; closed-mindedness, partiality, meanness are always in themselves bad. This of course is because these are examples of terms that are by definition bad, as are unkindness, dishonesty, intemperance, insincerity, hatred, treachery, cheating, lying, and cowardice. The question in all these cases is what counts as intolerance, cheating, cowardice, etc.; nonetheless there is something important about the fact that we all recognize these many words that by definition refer to wrongdoing: it reminds us that for all our concern about establishing the truth of moral claims, there is a surprising degree of self-evidence and hence agreement on the subject. Certainly there can be argument about whether this or that counts as an instance of treachery, cowardice, or unkindness. But equally there are examples where there can be no reasonable doubt and therefore where we can categorically conclude that wrong is being done.

Broadly speaking, in the pages that follow I shall argue that there is both much more agreement in the moral sphere than the philosophical focus on difficulties sometimes acknowledges, and yet room for much more legitimate openness than the man in the street may realize. A true moral understanding suggests that there is truth in ethical matters but that what we can confidently say that people ought to do is more circumscribed than some might wish. Neither the dogmatism and fanaticism or even conviction, nor the relativism and subjectivity, both of which, though quite incompatible, are so prevalent today, have any justification. The key to ethical conduct is an unwavering commitment to a set of particular principles that define morality, combined with a recognition of the limits of what the principles can dictate.

Commentary

There are many introductions to moral philosophy or ethics which focus, variously, on the history of moral philosophy, ethical theories, contemporary moral thinking, or practical moral problems. Many of them would make a virtue of not providing definitive answers and make claims somewhat along the lines of Ray Monk's review of Mary Warnock's *An Intelligent Person's Guide to Ethics*: 'the chief value of this book [is that] it does not present final answers to every dilemma. How could it? What it does, rather, is show what it is like to think through moral questions with care [and] seriousness'. This is as it should be, inasmuch as not all moral problems can be solved and it must be part of the function of an introductory text to get people to focus on the quality of the thinking, regardless of the conclusions. But it does seem important to me both to distinguish between a true dilemma (a problem which is by definition insoluble) and areas where there is a degree of disagreement but not necessarily a problem that is insoluble in principle, and to put more emphasis than is usually given on such broadly accepted conclusions as there may be.

The following list of introductory texts, for the most part published between the late 1980s and the present, and still available, excludes those that are focused on a particular historical individual or school of thought (e.g. Hegelian ethics), that link morality with religion (e.g. Christian ethics), or that are devoted to a single dimension of putative moral experience (e.g. environmental ethics). A few, such as Richard Norman *The Moral Philosophers: an Introduction to Ethics* and Raymond J. Devettere *Introduction to Virtue Ethics: Insights of the Ancient Greeks*, are predominantly historical.

The remainder for the most part have a contemporary slant. It is worth noting the apparent interchangeability of the words 'moral' and 'ethics' in these titles, which I shall comment further on in Chapter 3 below: Bernard Williams *Morality: an Introduction to Ethics*, Scott B. Rae *Moral Choices: an Introduction to Ethics*, Edward Bentham *An Introduction to Moral Philosophy*, Gerald J. Williams *A Short Introduction to Ethics*, Simon Blackburn *Ethics: a Very Short Introduction*, Montague Brown *The Quest for Moral Foundations: an Introduction to Ethics*, Ray Billington *Living Philosophy: an Introduction to Moral Thought*, Tom Regan *Animal Rights: Human Wrongs: an Introduction to Moral Philosophy* (Regan's interest in animal welfare perhaps makes this a book with a particular focus, but it nonetheless provides a general introduction), Donald Palmer *Why It's Hard to be Good: an Introduction to Ethical Theory*, and Philip Wheelwright *A Critical Introduction to Ethics*.

Interestingly, a survey of books currently in print reveals nothing in the way of a study of moral philosophy specifically related to moral education (as this book seeks to provide) and very little in the way of moral philosophy and moral problems in education. (As this book goes to press, I have advance news of Colin Wringe *Moral Education: Beyond the Teaching of Right and Wrong*, which it appears may be the exception that proves the rule.) Almost all titles that have even a tangential connection with these areas are either focused on ethical issues to do with leadership and administration or, more rarely, may be classified as 'how to' books on teaching to develop moral habits. There is little that is recognizably philosophical in either of these last categories. (The exception that proves the rule here is William Hare *Controversies in Teaching*.)

Utilitarianism is a school of thought that will be referred to by way of example once or twice in this book. One of its first conscious proponents was Francis Hutcheson (1694–1746) who wrote 'that action is best which procures the greatest happiness for the greatest numbers' in his *Inquiry concerning the Original of our Ideas of Virtue or Moral Good* (which is included in his *Philosophical Writings*). Among the most celebrated of the utilitarians were Jeremy Bentham (1748–1832), *The Principles of Morals and Legislation*, and John Stuart Mill (1806–73), *Utilitarianism*. Useful recent studies include Anthony Quinton *Utilitarian Ethics*, Donald H. Regan *Utilitarianism and Co-operation*, Amartya Sen and Bernard Williams (eds) *Utilitarianism and Beyond*, R.G. Frey (ed.) *Utility and Rights*, Geoffrey Scarre *Utilitarianism*, and David Braybrooke *Utilitarianism: Restorations; Repairs; Renovations*. (Although I am myself the author of *Plato, Utilitarianism and Education* and *Utilitarianism: a Contemporary Statement*, this book is not predicated on the truth of utilitarianism.)

One of the more notable philosophers to have taken a strong intuitionist line was W.D. Ross *The Right and the Good* and *Foundations of Ethics*. His historical precursors include Bishop Joseph Butler (1692–1752), author of *Five Sermons*, and Richard Price (1723–91). W.D. Hudson *Ethical Intuitionism* provides a useful survey.

'Virtue ethics' is a relatively recent label, although for many this idea can be traced back to Aristotle. The essence of this approach is that the question 'What ought I to do?' is the wrong one to ask. I should rather inquire into what kind of person I should be and focus on what virtues go to make a good character. But while this is obviously a good question to pursue, there seems no reason to take it as the only question for a moral philosopher, and indeed it is difficult to see how one could answer it without also being involved with other traditional questions in moral philosophy. Whether feminism can legitimately be seen as a monolithic and coherent school of thought is highly questionable, let alone whether there is such a thing as a feminist ethical theory (as distinct from various particular takes on morality from a variety of feminist perspectives). Useful in respect of virtue and feminist ethics are contributions by Greg Pence ('Virtue Theory') and Jean Grimshaw ('The Idea of a Female Ethic') in Peter Singer (ed.) *A Companion to Ethics*.

There will be further comment on teleological and deontological theories (as well as on utilitarianism and intuitionism) in the body of the text below.

The claim that a 'moral theory should not explain everything' is important. While nobody actually believes, let alone says, that if there is a moral truth, then there must in principle be the possibility of absolute clarity in thinking and the resolution of all problems, this seems to be the unreflective, unexamined inference commonly made. Similarly, while nobody, to my knowledge, has ever explicitly stated that a moral theory, if it is to be plausible, must give us the answers and tell us in practice what to do, that does seem to be the implication of the way in which philosophers generally discuss, criticize and reject various attempts, historical and contemporary, to formulate a moral theory. As against these tendencies, I am suggesting that, in principle and not just in practice, the true account of morality will lead us to recognize a number of insoluble problems.

I suppose that the proverbial 'man in the street', besides being de-gendered, is nowadays somewhat dumbed down, like many other things. I mean, of course, that the concerns I refer to are very possibly those of many thinking people who happen not to have any specialist background in philosophy. I refer to 'philosophical' questions, although it may be observed that I haven't actually defined 'philosophy' or 'philosophical'. The word has of course many meanings and uses. G.E. Moore (1873–1958) is said to have responded to the question of what philosophy as a formal specialist discipline is by pointing to his bookshelves and saying, 'It is what all these books are about'. As A.R. Lacey's *Dictionary of Philosophy* says, it is 'an embarrassment for the professional philosopher that he cannot produce a succinct, or even agreed, definition of his profession. "What is philosophy?" is itself a philosophical question' (p. 176). The kind of philosophy I am concerned with (what some would call analytic philosophy) is primarily concerned with understanding concepts or analysing ideas, and its most obvious characteristic is that unlike most (but not all) other forms of inquiry it does not itself make use of any empirical test. The key questions are of the form 'what do we mean by' or 'what are the defining characteristics of' love, beauty, moral goodness, friendship, etc.

The seven 'quite common assumptions' that are 'misleading if not mistaken' are not, by the way, generally speaking philosophers' mistakes. But the view that there is no objective moral truth is nonetheless held by some philosophers and the view that ' a moral theory must provide clear guidance' also seems to be held, if unconsciously, by some, and these are, as I argue in the body of the text, importantly mistaken views.

The point about different subject matters giving rise to different degrees of certainty was first made by the Greek philosopher Aristotle (384–322 BC), tutor to Alexander the Great, in his *Nicomachean Ethics*. This basic insight was built upon in an important paper by P.H. Hirst, 'Liberal Education and the Nature of Knowledge' (in Reginald D. Archambault (ed.) *Philosophical Analysis and Education*), in which he argued that certain basic disciplines were to be differentiated by, among other things, the manner in which claims had to be tested for truth, as the manner of establishing a mathematical claim is quite different from that of establishing a scientific one. The question of how to deal with the view that there is no good reason to be moral particularly exercised Aristotle's fellow Greek and one-time tutor, Plato (c 429–347 BC), in the *Republic*.

The distinction between the principles that 'define morality at any time and place' and the 'legitimate differences between cultures' at a 'lower or more specific level' is central to an understanding of morality and will form the basis of the solution to the problem of relativism which seems, unnecessarily, to bother many people a great deal. It also has indirect consequences for the importance of seeing tolerance and freedom as values that are imposed upon us by the human situation. It is partly because there are limits to what we can be sure about in the moral domain that tolerance and freedom are virtues. It may be said that at this point, and more generally throughout the book, I am trying to cut moral theory down to size, while stressing the importance and the unremitting and unqualified nature of the streamlined theory that remains.

The distinction between the 'natural' and the 'man-made', which will be discussed in more detail in Chapter 3 below, is another important one, as is the distinction between the 'contingent' and the 'arbitrary'. A contingent fact is a fact that might have been otherwise. It is a contingent fact that you are reading this now, since, although it is indisputably the case that you are, you might well not have been, had I not written it, had you accepted an invitation to go out today, had you been sick, etc. But the fact that it is contingent does not mean that it is entirely arbitrary. There may be many very good reasons and a clear and full explanation of why you are reading this now. Our decisions may be contingent, but they are not necessarily arbitrary.

The analogy with love is risky, as is the more fully explored analogy with a library classification system introduced below (Chapter 3), and as indeed are all analogies, since it is a moot point how comparable any presumed analogous items are. Nonetheless, I like it and think it may be useful. In the main text, I simply observe that being in love may reasonably be seen as partly a consequence of human nature and partly a consequence of the way in which we think. (D.J. Enright *Injury Time: a Memoir*, referring to an article in the *Independent on Sunday* of October 2000, remarks: 'by leaving out details such as the rustle of a condom packet, writers of romantic fiction, it is claimed "create negative attitudes towards the use of contraception and perpetuate the myth of being 'swept away' by romantic love"' (p. 148)). It is worth adding reference here to Plato's influential Theory of Ideas or Forms, according to which the Idea of, say, love is more real, because more perfect and timeless, than any actual instance of love. Some contemporary philosophers such as Iris Murdoch, *Metaphysics as a Guide to Morals*, still fully embrace such a view, but almost all varieties of conceptual analysis owe something to Plato's position. Also to be stressed is that, besides being affected by 'nature' and 'ideas', many of our beliefs and patterns of behaviour are partly the product of social conditioning.

The question, 'Why should I be moral?', understood in a slightly different way, will be returned to. The remarks relating to why a society should be moral are akin in tone to some of the writing of Thomas Hobbes (1588–1679), who famously referred in his *Leviathan* to the life of man in a state of nature as 'solitary, poor, nasty, brutish and short'. But there is also a more moderate expression of the view that society as a whole, and most of us as individuals, benefit from a set of agreed rules or a social contract. This is represented by such works as John Locke's (1632–1704) *A Letter Concerning Toleration*, Jean-Jacques Rousseau's (1712–78) *Social Contract*, and John Rawls's *A Theory of Justice*. This line of moral and political reasoning is to be sharply distinguished from the thinking of Immanuel Kant (1724–1804) whose perception of moral virtue and duty is based upon the inherent rightness of certain acts without explicit emphasis on social advantage. In line with my lack of enthusiasm for concentrating on any one school of thought at the expense of others, or for pitting them against one another as rivals, I shall be drawing on all of these philosophers (and others) in one way or another.

Recent publications on genetics are many. I draw particular attention to Matt Ridley *Nature via Nurture*, which provides a lucid summary of our understanding to date and a very clear-sighted view of what it does and does not entail, particularly in respect of the human mind and individual autonomy. When I say that by and large people have moral sentiment 'if only because it is cultivated during upbringing', I do not mean that our moral sentiment is therefore merely arbitrary. Rather, I am suggesting, as Iris Murdoch used to argue that education didn't make you happy but gave you the understanding and awareness that enable you to be happy, that while moral sentiment might arise in some regardless of upbringing, and while it is not something that could arise in a frog or a horse, its development in most humans is ensured by circumstance; but the form it takes is not arbitrary.

The doctrine of the mean is most particularly associated with Aristotle (*Nicomachean Ethics*), but the broad theme of 'moderation in everything' is very classical. 'Nothing in excess' was one of the inscriptions on the temple at Delphi in Greece, while the Roman poet Horace (65–8 BC), who saw 'measure in everything' (*Satires* 1.1), and who provided the epigraph for this chapter, was also a champion of the Golden Mean (*Odes* 2.10).

In saying 'partiality, meanness are always in themselves bad', for the first but not the last time, I use a variant of the phrase 'in itself'. There has been some writing on the notion of intrinsic value or the valuable in itself (e.g. I.M. Gregory and R.G. Woods 'Valuable in Itself'), but, while the distinction between the intrinsically valuable and the extrinsically valuable, or something that is valued for its own sake, not for the sake of something further, is very important, I don't think that we need to regard the concept as particularly complex or awkward. It is, however, perhaps worth spelling out just what is meant by saying that something is good in itself. If we say that kindness is good in itself, we mean that considered simply in itself, without reference to either consequences or circumstances, it is a good thing. There may be occasions when, for one reason or another, one should not be kind or when there will be trouble as a result of one's kindness; nonetheless, considered in and of itself alone, kindness is always good. It is inherently valuable and preferable to both unkindness and indifference, although indifference might be regarded as morally neutral and even unkindness might in extreme conditions be morally justified. By the same token, even kindness may at times be inappropriate or impossible and therefore it is not always good to be kind – but kindness in and of itself is always good. Contrast this with something like exercise which, though it may be good for you, is morally neutral. Something that is intrinsically good may, of course, also have extrinsic or extraneous value, as kindness may be valued because it leads to popularity, a good reputation, or social harmony as well as being good in itself.

When I say that there is 'self-evidence' about, e.g., the wrongness of treachery, I mean both that it is self-evident that treachery is bad and also that certain acts are self-evidently treacherous. What is problematic is that it is not always clear whether a given act constitutes treachery and some treachery, though inherently wrong, might nonetheless be justifiable given certain conditions.

Part I

Understanding the nature and limits of moral theory

BISHOP BURTON COLLEGE
LIBRARY

1 Integrity: a shared moral value

Part I is concerned with clearing the ground and laying the foundations for a moral theory. Some of the difficulty in understanding what morality does and does not involve is the result of misunderstandings and misapprehensions about the nature of morality and what a moral theory can and cannot do. Chapter 1 focuses on some common ground in the form of commitment to integrity. The next three chapters introduce a number of basic distinctions and errors. In particular, the relationship between morality and religion and nature, the contemporary tendency to think in terms of 'rights' and 'procedural justice', and the object or purpose of morality are considered.

The most obvious problem with morality is that people disagree about what behaviour is or is not moral. One culture finds stoning adulterers to death morally shocking, another finds it morally incumbent. Within the same culture some think animal vivisection is morally defensible, others think it morally defensible to harm, even kill, people who are associated with vivisection. Some members of the same family or circle of friends support abortion as morally acceptable, others regard it as morally indefensible. But, if disagreement is the most striking difficulty, the more insidious danger, and ultimately the most worrying, is that many people feel that there is no grounding for morality. Moral claims and judgements, it is widely believed, cannot be proved or demonstrated to be true. They used to be linked to religion, but, for many, religion no longer has the grip it used to have. In addition, various factors, such as a sense of fatalism, the perception of great differences between people's values, and perhaps simply an increased selfishness and materialism, may contribute to a widespread feeling that morality is dead. It is a rather old-fashioned concept, and what our pious ancestors saw as matters of objective right and wrong are really matters of opinion, preference, even mere taste.

I believe that this idea that morality cannot be firmly grounded and that moral claims are mere matters of opinion is quite mistaken. To introduce one of the themes that will run through this book, we are confusing the fact that many moral problems are difficult, and some indeed are insoluble, with the notion that there can be no truth on moral questions. But these are quite distinct points. It may be difficult, sometimes impossible, to decide what is the wisest or best thing to do in a non-moral sense, as, for example, when I have to decide whether to take up an appointment abroad. But the fact that it may be impossible for me to know in advance whether in terms of material gain, satisfaction for me and my family, career success, etc., it would be a smart decision shows neither that there is no wiser or worse choice in this case, nor that other choices about other matters are similarly problematic. And whether it is or is not possible to determine the most advantageous course to pursue in this example, it still remains the case that there are appropriate and inappropriate ways to examine the issue. In exactly the same way, while it may be conceded that there are moral disagreements, some of which cannot be resolved, this does nothing to establish that no moral questions can be answered, or that there are not appropriate and inappropriate ways to reason about morality, or that there is no moral truth. The question of whether something is morally true must be distinguished from the question of how certain we may be about it or whether we can know it.

That it is a mistake to deduce from the fact of moral uncertainty and disagreement that there is necessarily no moral truth having been noted, it should also be emphasized that the sense that there is a widespread suspicion that there is no moral truth is not particularly well founded. One indication that most people, whatever they may say to the contrary, do in fact have a basic belief in a moral truth that transcends mere opinion is that they believe in and respect integrity. The word itself may or may not be used, but remarks of the type, 'He lacks integrity' or 'I wouldn't trust him', are commonplace and generally delivered with the implication that they state a matter of fact, and one that is objectionable. While we may argue about whether freedom or equality is ultimately more important, and disagree about the rights and wrongs of abortion, the limits of free speech and the virtues of monogamy, most of us agree that we ought to live our lives with integrity and that those who lack integrity are to that extent to be criticized for a moral failing.

Stated baldly in this manner, this may not at first sight seem a very significant point. After all, a dictionary will typically define the word 'integrity' in some such terms as 'abiding by moral principles', and clearly, on any view, morality involves abiding by rather than disregarding moral principles. So integrity is morally good by definition. But the claim does have significance, partly because integrity involves more than simply 'abiding by' moral principles and partly because in focusing on integrity as a moral concept we take the emphasis off various other things that are mistakenly regarded as necessary or crucial parts of morality. In addition, the prime concern here is to point out that people who might be inclined to say that morality is just a matter of convention seem nonetheless to recognize its demands when it is couched in terms of integrity. There are at least some who will say, without much sign of shame, 'I don't see myself as a very moral person', but who would not want to say, 'I see myself as lacking in integrity'.

The person of integrity does not simply 'abide by' moral principles in the sense of acting in accordance with them. At the very least, he acts in accordance with them because he recognizes that they have some authority over him. I do not show integrity merely by keeping my word, or by keeping my word because I am frightened that you will take revenge if I don't. Indeed, a judgement that somebody has integrity is usually made precisely when they keep their word despite being threatened, bribed, etc. Only if I keep my word because I recognize that it would be wrong not to do so, do I deserve to be commended for behaving with integrity. Furthermore, one expects both consistency and determination from a person of integrity. The fact that on a certain occasion I act in a certain way because I believe it to be morally right does not establish my integrity. I need, at least, to show that I can be counted on to act in such a way consistently and regardless of temptations and pressures to do otherwise. And it goes without saying that my commitment to acting on principle must be sincere, which means in turn that the person of integrity needs to have self-understanding. People who see themselves as acting on principle, but who in fact are motivated by something else such as hope of praise or respect, or out of fear, do not have integrity, even though they obviously think they do. (There is a secondary meaning of the word 'integrity' which is 'wholeness' and derives from the meaning of the original Latin word. Although I shall not pursue the matter, there is, I think, something of the idea of wholeness also associated with the moral concept of integrity: a person of integrity should have a wide-ranging, coherent moral viewpoint and not simply adhere to one or two isolated principles.)

Equally important is the fact that the person of integrity, in acting on the basis of moral principles, is by implication not acting in accordance with a calculation of advantage to self or others, is not motivated by some particular goal, and is not simply following rules. There is an important difference between telling the truth because it is to your advantage to do so and telling it because you believe that you ought to do so regardless of the consequences; and so there is between telling the truth on principle and simply obeying a rule to tell the truth. Following a rule because it is a rule to be obeyed is different from believing in a principle. The rule follower will always follow it, regardless of the circumstances. But, as I shall argue, the principle that truth-telling is good does not necessarily lead to the conclusion that the truth must always be told. (That indeed is the essential difference between a principle, which guides, and a rule, which demands.)

In short, behaviour of integrity is to be distinguished from rule-bound behaviour; it involves conscious, sincere, and consistent adherence to principles out of recognition that the principles ought to be upheld. To this we may add 'regardless of consequences', provided we distinguish between ignoring the claims of other principles and all other types of consequence. If in principle one ought to tell the truth, the woman of integrity will do so even if it makes her unpopular etc. However, she might not tell the truth, if some other moral principle has an equally strong or stronger claim on her. Thus she might not tell the truth if the consequence of doing so would be that she caused great harm to others and she also subscribes to the principle that one should avoid harming others.

This brings us to the heart of the matter. Since integrity is a moral notion, the principles in question cannot be any old principles such as 'Look after number one' or 'Never give a sucker an even break'. They must be moral principles. So the idea of integrity by no means solves all our problems. I have introduced it because it lacks some of the connotations of words like 'virtue' and 'morality'. As I say, most people seem at ease with integrity; they may say that morality is dead, but they don't say that integrity doesn't matter. They may find the idea of proclaiming themselves 'moral' or, worse, 'virtuous' a little pompous and overweening, but they would surely be prepared to defend their integrity. To be contrasted with integrity is another word in fairly common use: hypocrisy. And, similarly, while we are all probably guilty of a little hypocrisy from time to time, most of us share the conviction that there is something wrong with saying one thing and doing another. Despite the too easy assumption that there is no universal common moral sense, I don't know of any culture, historical or contemporary, that doesn't share the insight that being two-faced, though it might conceivably be justified on some occasions, is in itself morally repugnant. And when people are two-faced or hypocritical they invariably seem to feel a need to explain away or justify their hypocrisy by appeal to some unavoidable constraint or some other moral imperative. Nobody, in other words, denies that integrity is morally commendable or hypocrisy to be morally condemned; nobody has yet been known to argue that there is simply nothing wrong with hypocrisy (although some have argued that it can be engaged in for some higher good). There is, despite claims to the contrary, a common perception of and a common commitment to morality, when conceived in terms of integrity.

To recognize this is of importance; but while reflection on the notion of integrity draws our attention to the fact that there is some permanent, unchanging core to morality, and, furthermore, that people, generally speaking, recognize this despite the fashionable tendency to dismiss morality as a matter of subjective judgement, it cannot in itself define morality since the person of integrity acts on moral principles; and it cannot in itself answer such further questions as whether the martyr for any cause, if consistent, sincere, and principled, can claim moral integrity. (Since a person of integrity acts on moral principles, those principles themselves cannot be defined in terms of integrity, and acknowledging that we all recognize the goodness of principled behaviour neither tells us what the principles are nor establishes that nothing else matters except acting on principle.) Nonetheless, the idea of integrity provides a useful starting point in reminding us that there is widespread agreement that sincere and consistent principled activity is to be valued and commended. That such behaviour is desirable seems to be one fact about morality.

The first question addressed was: do we have any common moral sentiment or sense? Is there any reason to assume at least some common core to a moral viewpoint? The answer was, broadly speaking, yes. The second question is: how, given the world in which we live, can any of us find it in ourselves to sustain faith in morality?

Towards the end of the Second World War a certain man was arrested by the Gestapo. He found himself being interrogated by two men whom he knew quite well. With one he was on friendly terms, with the other he had a polite relationship. He was accused by these men of certain things of which he was in fact quite innocent, and he was brutally tortured. He was imprisoned for several months and routinely beaten up. By the end he had lost an eye and was crippled and sexually impotent for life. When he was released, he was informed by his torturers that he would not find any trace of his wife or children. Nor did he.

Several months later, impoverished, ruined, and alone, the war now being over, he happened to pass his two jailers on the street, talking and laughing cheerfully and looking in the pink of health. They were never called to account either for their treatment of him or for any other of their grotesque and brutal acts during the war.

The point of telling this story, merely one of thousands that can be told about man's inhumanity to man, is to highlight the question of how anyone in the world in which we live is supposed to sustain any faith in a moral universe. How can one believe in goodness in a world in which we do what we do to each other? How can one believe in a just world, when the vile and the vicious so often thrive? How can one believe in morality, when immorality so often and so clearly gets away with it? This man may have suffered rather more than many of us, but he, the millions who have been cheated, betrayed, raped, and killed, and we, who may, if we are lucky, merely have seen the dishonest prosper and the honest go unrewarded, all have this in common: what we know from history and what we see around us suggests that 'God is dead'. Whatever else may be said about the world, an honest appraisal does not lead one to believe that it is an ordered place in which good will necessarily triumph. And when it does there is a feeling that this is a matter of chance. For we sense increasingly that life is a matter of randomness or chaos rather than something that is rationally, let alone benignly, ordered. It should be noted that this question of whether the world is an evil place, or whether moral conduct in practice triumphs or gains recognition and reward, is logically distinct from the question of whether there are moral truths (and what they may be); after all, as we are often reminded, we are supposed to pursue a moral life for its own sake and not for reward or fame. However, it remains true that the perception that the world is on balance an evil place in which the bad often triumphs over the good is a powerful factor in suggesting to people that morality is not worth pursuing and need not be taken too seriously.

Although my opening example is taken from recent history, there is nothing new about the problem. Plato, 2,500 years ago, wrestled with exactly the same issue in his *Republic*: how to convince people that they should follow the path of morality, even when to do so was manifestly not to their immediate advantage on earth and when the idea of reward in an after-life was disallowed? On the latter point more will be said later. Here it is sufficient to say that the questions of whether there is a God and, if so, what he requires of us are distinct from the question of whether there are certain principles of conduct that ought to be followed because they are binding on us. Like Plato, I shall avoid both the easy (but unconvincing) claim that virtue will find its reward in heaven and the patently false claim that it is necessarily (or even very often) rewarded on earth.

Nor shall I hide behind the cliché that virtue is its own reward, although that claim could be said to be true in a sense. It is its own reward inasmuch as there may be no other reward, and it is certainly true that one ought to act morally because moral behaviour is by definition behaviour that we ought to engage in. But to argue that one ought to be moral because morality is what we ought to pursue is obviously circular. The question in that case becomes 'Why should I do what ought to be done?' in the sense of 'What is going to motivate or make me do it?' Nor shall I appeal directly to nature, although, as we shall see, nature does need to be considered in various respects. But I shall attempt to argue neither that there are certain tendencies that are natural and therefore ought to be indulged, nor that certain rights are natural or given in nature. Some might argue, for example, that, because we as a species are competitive, it is right that we should be so. But quite apart from the question mark over whether the factual claim is true (might not an equally good case be made for the intrinsic co-operative spirit of humans, notwithstanding the horrors we are capable of?), I accept the view widely endorsed by philosophers that one cannot derive an 'ought' directly from an 'is': to argue that because something is the case it ought to be, or that it is morally good, is fallacious. The language of rights is always problematic; but the notion that some rights are natural in the sense of given in nature clearly begs the question. It would be nice to think that we all have a natural right to freedom, but to claim that we do, meaning that nature has somehow dictated that we ought to be free, makes no discernible sense. (This issue will be explored in more depth in Chapter 4 below.)

My premise is that the world seems to be a random one. Our problem is to come to terms with the random nature of events. We seek to impose order on our collective behaviour because we need to, partly (probably) because it is in our nature to do so, and partly (certainly) because it would be foolish not to. So morality is devised by humans, but it is not arbitrary; it is not just a code of conduct comparable to a code of table manners, which could take more or less any form; it is not a code comparable to a driving code where it doesn't matter at all whether we drive on the right or the left, provided we all do the same. It is an attempt to devise principles to govern our conduct so that we can maximize our potential – so that we can most fully live and develop ourselves, including our capacity to create art, to develop the mind, and to control nature, so that we can survive as a species and so that we can flourish as individuals. Morality, while there is no disputing that it is about the quality of our conduct, makes no sense without a presumption that we are looking for principles to enable us to live and to live well. This, at any rate as presented here, is not itself a moral rule so much as a statement about the object of morality. For while moral behaviour is enjoined on us for its own sake, there may still be a further point to it, just as the pleasure of listening to music is its own reward but the point of making music is to contribute to making life worth living. We could not wish misery on ourselves as an ultimate goal and there is no percentage in wishing it on the world. There is nothing to be said for a world of brutality, of nihilism, or of excessive and selfish individualism. This is not a moral point; it is the backdrop that explains why we need morality. Everybody knows that once a moral system is in place, an individual can take advantage of it and, relying on most others abiding by it, can convince himself that he does not need to abide by it. But that is not the same thing as saying that we collectively could wish upon ourselves an immoral or even a non-moral world. And while some people do take advantage of others without remorse, or do *prima facie* wrong things that they nonetheless seek to justify, as no doubt the two Gestapo men justified their behaviour to themselves, it is hard to imagine anyone, even they, saying with pride something like 'I beat up small children'. What such people do is plead mitigation or try to justify their action by telling some story which they may or may not believe, such as 'I thought he was guilty', 'I thought he didn't count', 'I was frightened', 'I obeyed orders'. All of which goes to suggest that people in fact do have a sense of moral shame. The only exception would appear to be the very, very small number we classify as psychopaths, and their existence no more proves the subjectivity of moral reasoning than the existence of blind people proves that sight is not to be trusted.

Morality, then, is not simply given in nature; it is devised by us but within some considerable constraints. We can only devise a theory that takes account of the way the world is and who we are. Since morality is a set of principles to govern human life in general, the question becomes what principles, for whatever reason (because we shall shortly see that different principles are backed by different kinds of reason), should ideally govern our conduct, so that we can flourish, develop, advance our interests, survive, and achieve. In just the same way as a library classification system has to meet the aims of the library or marriage customs the aims of such a relationship, a moral theory has to meet these human aims.

The ultimate answer to the question of why we should be moral is because it is to our advantage as humans. To the individual who asks why he should not take advantage of the system, the answer is partly because you will usually pay the price, but it is also partly because you will lose out on the inspiration of this idea; you will miss the beauty, the quality, the magnificence in this aspiration of humans to live morally, just as those who turn their backs on love and friendship miss part of the potential joy and wonder of life. It is not wrong in any moral sense to live a life without love or friendship or without any developed aesthetic awareness, whether or not this is the result of choice. But to live without these things is to lead an impoverished life, a lesser life, a life that quite simply doesn't yield all that it might have done. It is to miss out on sources of great potential satisfaction that carry with them the possibility, even likelihood, of opening up further kinds of rewarding experience. So one may say to such a person: 'Don't turn your back on this; do what you can to gain the advantages available.' One way of looking at education is to say that this is what it tries to do: open up avenues of potentially rich experience for people. In the same way, it may be argued that to live the moral life brings with it a certain satisfaction. Some would say that this is to import the idea of extraneous reward as a motive for being moral. It seems to me that it is not, that satisfaction in living the moral life (or in having a developed aesthetic sense or having good friends) is not an extrinsic reward in the way that winning popularity or a cash prize is. In any case, however we classify it, it is surely reasonable to argue to those who are inclined to opt out of the generally beneficial and desirable moral system that in so doing, apart from risking penalties of various kinds, they may very likely be trading in a real and rich personal satisfaction for a far from certain material gain.

Commentary

Simon Blackburn *Ethics: a Very Short Introduction* has a useful chapter on some of the factors that may contribute to the 'widespread feeling that morality is dead'. Entitled 'Seven Threats to Ethics', it considers 'the death of God', 'relativism', 'egoism', 'evolutionary theory', 'determinism and futility', 'unreasonable demands', and 'false consciousness'. I shall focus mainly on the death of God (arguing, however, that for many God is far from dead but that this is irrelevant to morality), relativism, and 'unreasonable demands' (by which phrase Blackburn refers to what I categorize as mistaken ideas of what moral theory can and should do).

The reference to the distinction between truth and certainty, and, throughout the book, similar distinctions between precision, knowledge, and belief, strictly speaking take us into the realm of what is called 'epistemology' or the philosophy of knowledge, which obviously overlaps with most other branches of philosophy (e.g. aesthetics, the philosophy of science) as well as moral philosophy. For a standard introduction to this topic, see Roderick Chisholm *Theory of Knowledge*. See also A.D. Woozley *Theory of Knowledge: an Introduction*. A. Phillips Griffiths (ed.) *Knowledge and Belief* provides a set of classic papers.

The distinction between principles and rules is important to understanding moral conduct. Some readers may feel that, overall, I perhaps over-emphasize rule-bound conduct: the popular view of our society, at any rate, may be thought to be one in which very few people treat any rules as binding. A moment's reflection, however, will remind us that millions of individuals (particularly, but not only, many religious and politically committed individuals) both within and outside our society are indeed living their lives in accordance with a set of unyielding rules. It is quite common to find moral philosophers arguing against relativism, but it is more appropriate, perhaps, to see a plausible moral understanding as lying midway between the equally erroneous claims of relativism (in which, in a sense, anything goes) and those of dogmatic, rule-governed behaviour.

I note that Mel Thompson *Ethics* also mentions integrity as a central ethical concept. Above, I claim that everybody shares the insight that hypocrisy or 'being two-faced, though it might conceivably be justified on some occasions, is in itself morally repugnant'. Should I perhaps have left out the word 'morally', which might seem to beg the question, and just have said that more or less everybody recognizes it as objectionable or repugnant? That would probably do for my purpose here, which is mainly to draw attention to certain common sentiments of approval and disapproval; but in fact I suggest that our revulsion in this case is of a distinctive moral kind: we do not simply shy away from two-faced behaviour. We think that it is wrong. That said, the qualification that it may be justified introduces another crucial distinction between something that is simply wrong and unacceptable and something that, though in itself wrong, is justified by circumstance. (See Chapter 3 below.) This distinction, which is obviously linked to that between intrinsic and extrinsic value referred to in the Commentary on the Introduction above, is another distinction the failure to recognize which is the source of much confused moral thinking. Even though being two-faced is in itself morally bad, it is possible to conceive of a situation in which it might be justified. A more accurate and precise delineation of the situation would be that, considered as a characteristic of one's personality, being two-faced is always bad and cannot be justified or approved in the case of any individual, but while individual acts of dissembling or being two-faced are also intrinsically bad, they might in certain cases be justified. (A quotation from a character in Jill Paton Walsh's novel *Debts of Dishonour* (p. 256) seems to take a different view on hypocrisy: 'Don't be a hypocrite, Martin. Never mind moral issues; when the chips are down we just have to look out for ourselves.' This suggests that for the speaker the very taking of a moral stance may indicate hypocrisy. But I presume that even in a case like this the speaker, while drawing a distinction between self-interest and the moral, nonetheless feels that to be hypocritical about this distinction is somehow even more morally degenerate. Oscar Wilde put his finger on the conundrum with characteristic wit in *The Importance of Being Earnest*: 'I hope you have not been leading a double life, pretending to be wicked and really being good all the time; that would be hypocrisy' (Wilde 1999: 378).)

The conclusion to the first part of this chapter is deceptively simple, for it gives us a fact about morality, namely that sincere and principled conduct is a necessary, though not a sufficient, condition of morality.

The story of the man arrested by the Gestapo is a true one, told to me by a friend of the man to whom it happened. It was the German philosopher Friedrich Nietzsche (1844–1900) who famously proclaimed the 'death of God' (meaning that there are no objective moral criteria to guide us). The thinking of the author of *Beyond Good and Evil* and *Thus Spake Zarathustra* is complex. Ronald Hayman's brief essay *Nietzsche: Nietzsche's Voices* and Michael Tanner *Nietzsche: a Very Short Introduction* are helpful. For Nietzsche's educational philosophy, see David E. Cooper *Authenticity and Learning*.

Plato's *Republic* was regarded by Jean-Jacques Rousseau as the finest educational treatise ever written and it is certainly the first extant. Formally, its subject matter is the ideal state and the nature of justice within both the state and the individual. But as one of his two longest dialogues (so-called because they are usually written in the form of a conversation between Socrates and others), it touches on a wide variety of issues, such that A.N.

Whitehead referred to the entire history of Western philosophy as a series of footnotes to Plato. (The question of the relationship between religion and morality will be taken up in the next chapter.) For a basic but thorough philosophical introduction to the *Republic*, see R.C. Cross and A.D. Woozley *Plato's Republic: a Philosophical Commentary*. Robin Barrow *Plato, Utilitarianism and Education*, focuses on moral and educational philosophy, while the same author's *Plato* provides a somewhat less idiosyncratic view.

The relationship between nature and morality will be considered in the next chapter, with specific attention being paid to 'natural rights' in Chapter 4 below. The view that one cannot derive 'ought' from 'is' is associated primarily with the Scottish philosopher David Hume (1711–76) in *A Treatise of Human Nature*. But G.E. Moore's *Principia Ethica*, with its inscription 'everything is what it is and not another thing' from Bishop Butler, is another famous text upholding the idea of the irreducibility of the Good. See W.D. Hudson (ed.) *The Is/Ought Question*.

Reference to the 'object of morality' brings to mind an impressive book of that title by Geoffrey Warnock. It is also worth pointing out that the basic idea that morality is connected with living well in a broad sense is very Greek. The reference to 'psychopaths' (perhaps I mean 'sociopaths'?) is not idle or throwaway. I am suggesting that truly amoral people, that is those without any moral sentiment or conscience at all, are both very few in number and to be classified as some kind of clinical aberration (though not necessarily therefore to be forgiven). The point of interest is that the vast majority of us, for practical purposes people in general, notwithstanding the divergences in our moral behaviour or our moral failings, share a basic moral understanding. We do wrong, but we know that we do wrong and, variously, resort to excuses, mitigating circumstances, forces beyond our control, etc., to justify ourselves. (That no one willingly does wrong was a central tenet of Plato's moral philosophy.)

The analogy with library classification will be considered in more detail in Chapter 3 below.

2 Religion, nature, and intuition as possible sources of moral truth

Most people appreciate that a moral obligation is an obligation that is binding regardless of such things as reward, popularity, or threats. If I have a moral obligation to tell the truth, then I ought to tell the truth – not because I will be punished if I don't, or respected or rewarded if I do, but simply because that is my duty. I ought to tell the truth for its own sake. There may be various rewards, whether material or spiritual, associated with it, and there may on occasion be factors that put pressure on me to do it, but, nonetheless, to say that telling the truth is a moral obligation implies that it is something that should be done regardless of extrinsic reward or compulsion.

Consider the claim that lying is morally wrong. This has been generally accepted throughout history by a great variety of societies and cultures and would be formally acknowledged more or less universally today. Most readers will subscribe to it, whereas there would be considerable disagreement over whether, for example, suicide is wrong. This is not to say that there may not be strong differences of opinion on such further questions as whether and when telling a lie may be justified, or whether there is a difference between a lie and a 'white lie'. But, for the most part, we are on common ground in treating the proposition 'Telling lies is morally wrong' as true.

But on what grounds or in virtue of what do we make this claim? Why is it morally wrong to tell a lie? The first thing to get clear is that the 'why' is not asking for a causal explanation, as is the case when I ask, 'Why has the car stopped running?' ('Because it has run out of petrol.') The 'why' in this case is asking for a justification rather than a cause: 'For what good reason do we maintain that the truth should be told?' There is a big difference between the claim that one ought not to tell a lie and a host of other non-moral claims about lying such as that 'It doesn't pay', 'It is conventionally frowned upon', 'It will make people distrust you', 'In certain situations it is illegal', and 'It will make you unpopular'. The latter claims may all be true, but whether they are or not is a matter of empirically checking the facts of the matter. This may be more or less difficult to do in practice, but in principle it is simply a matter of looking to see whether it is or is not the case that people come to distrust liars or that certain lies are illegal. But the moral claim cannot be checked in this way. We can, by direct or indirect observation in some form or another, establish whether people *think* that telling lies is wrong, but that has no direct bearing on whether it *is* wrong. The fact that people think the earth is spherical is no part of the proof that it is, and the existence of flat-earthers doesn't in any way alter the truth that the earth is not flat. In the same way, what particular people think is moral or immoral is not in itself any part of an argument to establish what is moral. The question 'Why is it morally wrong to tell a lie?' is a way of asking what we mean by saying that it is wrong. What are the reasons that lead us to say that telling lies is something that ought not to be done, regardless of personal advantage?

Historically, the distinction that I have drawn between intrinsic and extrinsic reasons, or doing something for its own sake and doing it for reasons of further advantage, took time to make. In very early societies, no doubt, codes of behaviour were based more or less entirely on perceived self-advantage combined with some kind of coercion or threat from the more powerful members of society. What was done was done for fear of the Big Chief, so to speak, and there was little or no distinction between what ought to be done and what needed to be done in order to survive or avoid trouble. In such a situation there is a clear explanation of why people behave as they do, but the behaviour, regardless of what it is, is not to be classified as moral. This is because part of what we mean by moral behaviour is behaviour that we engage in because we recognize an obligation to do so, regardless of personal advantage, safety, etc. Therefore, we cannot allow that the reason why the truth ought to be told is simply that the Big Chief commands it. Morality is not to be defined in terms of whatever the Big Chief says; and we would need some reason (which has never been convincingly given) to conclude that whatever the Big Chief demands just happens to coincide with what ought to be done.

This brings us to one of the most long-lived and pervasive, but ultimately untenable, attempts to answer the question 'Why is it morally wrong to tell a lie?' or, more broadly, 'Why should I do what is morally right?', and that is the view that God ordains it. I ought not to tell a lie because God commands that I should not. Unfortunately, this will not work. In the first place, we should not ignore the enormous problem involved in establishing that God (of whatever particular religion) exists, and, if that could be satisfactorily done, in establishing that his commandments are indeed those that have been handed down to us. While there are philosophers who are believers, and while there may be a few who are personally convinced by particular arguments that God exists, there are very few indeed, if any, who accept that there are arguments that can withstand public scrutiny and establish beyond legitimate dispute that God exists; and there are positively none who would assert that objective argument has determined that the God of any particular religion exists and that his precise commandments are known to us indubitably. Faith in God is still possible, and the presumption that the dictates of one's own Church should be adhered to is not inherently unreasonable, perhaps; but the notion that we have established or could establish that there is a God, let alone that we know precisely what he wants, is very wide of the mark.

But even if we do nonetheless subscribe to a particular religion, we have not solved the problem of grounding morality or justifying our fundamental moral assumptions. For (and this applies equally to the Big Chief) either we must presume that God commands us to tell the truth (or not steal, or whatever) because he in his wisdom sees that telling the truth is good or moral, or we are implicitly claiming that what is morally good is whatever God commands (i.e. that 'good' means 'commanded by God'). The first option is more straightforward, but it doesn't get us anywhere: if God commands X because he sees that X is good, this leaves unanswered the question of why it is good. What is it about X that God discerns such that he can recognize it as good? For unreflective religious believers this may be neither here nor there: they feel a need to do what God tells them to do. But this is plainly unsatisfactory for those of us who are trying to understand what it means to say that something is our moral duty.

The second option doesn't in the end achieve anything either. If 'morally good' simply means 'commanded by God', then we need an answer to the question 'Why should I do what is commanded by God?' We can hardly reply 'Because God is good' (since that would appear to mean that God is commanded by God, which is meaningless). We therefore seem forced to the conclusion that we should do what God commands because he is all-powerful and will either destroy us if we don't or, more benignly, reward us if we do. But now we are right back with a version, albeit an all-powerful one, of the Big Chief. It may be prudent to do as God demands, and therefore to tell the truth, but that is not the same thing as saying that telling the truth is morally good.

The fact of the matter is that morality and religion are logically distinct and we must not confuse them. There have been religions which are not recognizably moral in any way, and there can be morality without religion. (For surely not even the most devout reader is going to deny that the atheist still faces moral choices.) There are religions (Christianity is one) that are closely tied up with moral viewpoints, but that is a contingent fact – a fact about the world that might have been different. The question of how or in what sense we have certain moral obligations or what it means to say that certain obligations are moral is not going to be answered by an appeal to religion. Indeed, part of what we are trying to do is distinguish between, for example, legal, prudent, self-serving, and religious motives for action on the one hand, and moral motives on the other.

Throughout history there have also been attempts to ground morality in nature: to argue that what is moral is what is natural. But this too has proved to be a blind alley. The first problem here, comparable to the problem of deciding whose God we are talking about or what the attributes and commands of God may be, is determining what is natural. There is more than one dimension to this problem: not only do different people see different behaviours as natural, there is also a problem about what counts as natural in principle, and the difficulty of disentangling what was literally given in nature and what, though seemingly natural now, was in fact created and developed over time by cultural pressures. Thus, at the simplest level, people have long argued, and still argue today, about whether humans are naturally 'aggressive' or not, about whether they are naturally monogamous or not, and about whether they are naturally social or not. A further problem is that regardless of whether such characteristics should be seen as natural or culturally induced, virtually all of them admit of exceptions: is the woman who has no instinct to bear children unnatural? Assuming we accept that the general female desire to bear children is in their genes rather than the product of social pressures and conditioning, then in one sense women who do not want children are indeed unnatural. On the other hand, in terms of their own genetic inheritance their wishes may equally be seen as natural.

So what do we mean by 'natural'? Do we mean innate, perhaps in the sense of dictated by genetic inheritance, do we mean universally true, or what? The question of whether homosexuality is natural or not, for example, is sometimes treated as the question of whether it is genetically based. It can hardly be argued that it is natural in the sense of universal, in the way that some maintain a sense of self-interest is natural in that everybody has it, but sometimes it is argued that homosexuality is as natural as heterosexuality inasmuch as both are equally a matter of choice or, on another view, equally a matter of response to environment. Then again, it is sometimes seen as a question of whether homosexuality, regardless of how it comes about, is as valid a 'norm' as heterosexuality, which comes close to treating 'natural' as a synonym for 'morally acceptable'. Certain traits that may be universal and that appear to be innate may in fact be the product of centuries of environmental pressure and conditioning; thus, they are internalized but they are not necessarily innate proclivities in the sense of being part of the essence of being human. Just as various other species of animal have been tamed and domesticated over the centuries, so perhaps man has been socialized into the political instincts that Aristotle attributed to nature. In one sense a dog is 'naturally' domesticated, but in other senses it is clearly not – its domesticity is in fact rather unnatural.

There is no need to pursue these points here: they merely serve to remind us that the very question of what counts as natural is not straightforward. But even if it were, could we then look to nature to tell us what is moral? Is being moral the same as acting naturally?

There are those who have argued that it is. One variant claims that what is taken to be moral, what is generally regarded as good, is simply behaviour that suits the powers-that-be, whoever they may be. This argument, however, does not ground or justify morality so much as deny it. It amounts to saying that rules about not telling lies, not stealing, and so on are useful to the rulers and have no other sanction, the consequence of which view must be that, if you can get away with it, you may as well break the rules. In saying that the view denies morality, I am not suggesting that it can therefore *ipso facto* be rejected. But I do reject it nonetheless. It could be true – that is to say, it could be the case that there is nothing more to morality than a set of rules imposed by authority with a view to keeping the authority in authority. But it is one of the purposes of this book to argue that, while it is almost certainly true that some so-called moral rules have no more warrant than this, there is nonetheless such a thing as morality which goes beyond this.

Another variant suggests that what is moral, i.e. what one ought to do, is what comes naturally, and that what is natural is for the strong to dominate the weak. This is at least recognizable as an answer to our question: it seeks to tell us that the justification for morality is to be found in nature. As we have seen, in the same way that it is not clear what the Big Chief or God demands of us, so, quite apart from arguments about what 'natural' means, it is not clear how we are to determine what is natural in any given sense. Is it in fact so obvious that it is natural for the strong to dominate the weak? Many have argued, on the contrary, that it is social and amicable tendencies that are natural to humans. But the crucial problem here is that there is no apparent reason to accept the premise that what is natural is what is good. Certainly for many it is counter-intuitive to accept that because beating up the weak is natural it is morally right. There seems to be a clear gap in the argument here: the fact that something is the case does not in itself make it right that it should be so. If it did, there would be bizarre consequences: because I loathe and despise you, it is right that I should. Because AIDS is rampant, it is right that it should be. But much more significant is the point that there is nothing recognizable as an argument here at all: it is a mere assumption or assertion that what is ought to be.

I used the phrase 'counter-intuitive' in the previous paragraph, and at some point we have to consider intuition, for some have argued powerfully for the view that 'intuition' is all we have. In answer to the question 'Why should I tell the truth?' it is said: we cannot answer that by producing reasons that justify its moral worth; rather we have to recognize it as self-evidently good in itself. The fundamental moral truths are and can only be intuited, rather as, some would say, ultimately beauty can only be discerned: we can, of course, talk about a painting or a musical composition, but in the final analysis you are either moved by a Beethoven symphony or you are not; similarly, you either recognize that friendship is a good thing or you don't.

There are some obvious immediate objections to the intuitionist account, one of which is that intuitions vary. Some people intuit that homosexuality is wrong and some that it is not, and likewise with a number of other topical issues such as cloning, abortion, euthanasia, and prostitution. It is also true that to talk of intuition as if it were not only infallible but also given in nature is problematic, for reasons already given when discussing nature: for most of us, much of the time, what we 'intuit' is at least partly a consequence of what we have been taught to see rather than being what we see 'naturally'. There is nothing necessarily wrong with that, for, as we have seen, what is natural is not necessarily good, and an 'intuition' that is based on knowledge is surely to be preferred to one based on ignorance. But it does make it difficult to accept that the solution to our problem is simply to say that we know what is right by intuition.

However, those points admitted, something needs to be said to keep the idea of intuition alive, because it is an important and inescapable part of moral understanding, although it needs to be said that what matters is a cultivated intuition accompanied by various further kinds of understanding, as distinct from a so-called 'natural' instinct. What needs to be acknowledged here is that, like it or not, there are some things in human affairs or about the human condition that just do have to be sensed, rather than demonstrated, rationally explained or justified. I would find it not just difficult but rather odd to attempt to answer the question 'What is good about friendship?' Of course, I could explain to those who don't know what 'friendship' means what it involves, and I could outline some of the benefits it may lead to. But surely, regardless of all that, we recognize friendship as, other things being equal, a desirable thing in itself. (This does not rule out the possibility of a poor, unrewarding, or dangerous friendship, or even of a rich and deserving enmity. The quality and the consequences of a good thing may be impaired, as there can be a selfish love or a love that leads to tragedy. But love itself is still inherently a good thing.) The same may be said of happiness, kindness, or beauty. These are noble and inspiring ideas and if you can't see that, something is wrong. And while the fact that intuitions do vary is quite a serious practical problem, it should be pointed out again that physical sight, in common with the other senses, likewise varies and may lead to contradictory reports, but nobody thinks that sight is therefore never to be relied upon. Besides, and most importantly, while at the level of specific actions in particular situations our intuitions often differ, it surely is correct to say that some things at a more abstract level are more or less uniformly intuited, in the sense of recognized as inescapable truths by more or less everybody: the notion that in principle it doesn't matter at all if one breaks a promise (as distinct from the notion that sometimes it may be justifiable to do so) does not seem to make sense: if you understand what promising is, you must see that, in principle, other things being equal, promises are to be kept. This is not because of any particular consequences, but because otherwise there isn't any point in the business of promising. In other words, it may be possible to argue that no promises should be made, but it is incoherent to engage in promise-giving and not see that in itself a promise should be kept.

I have referred to 'advantages' and stressed the difference between extrinsic and intrinsic advantage, between advantages that happen to follow from an act, as I may gain favour by my generosity, and advantages inherent in the act. I have also presumed that in trying to understand why we should not tell a lie, or any other moral demand, we should not be looking to extrinsic advantage. But this over-simple distinction now needs to be complicated somewhat, because there is one strand of moral thinking which has to be partially incorporated into the final picture and which on the face of it is very much bound up with consequences or, in a sense, extrinsic advantage.

In introducing a utilitarian element to the discussion, I have to guard against a commonly accepted view of what it involves that is, in my view, in various ways inadequate and that consequently may lead to a misunderstanding of what I wish to say here. To the proverbial man in the street, a 'utilitarian argument' probably means something like 'an argument in which the end justifies the means'. A dictionary may define 'utilitarian' as 'useful', in line with 'utility' meaning 'usefulness', and define the theory of utilitarianism as 'the theory that the criterion of virtue is utility' or as 'the theory that the highest good lies in the greatest good of the greatest number'. Many introductory textbooks will say that the theory is concerned with the 'greatest happiness of the greatest number', and classify it as both a consequentialist theory (meaning that it assesses the moral worth of an action by reference to its consequences) and as a teleological, as opposed to a deontological, theory (meaning that it judges acts by their tendency to promote an end, rather than positing certain acts as morally right in themselves, regardless of consequences).

None of this is necessarily or exactly wrong, but it can be very misleading and certainly doesn't capture what I regard as the most important aspect of utilitarianism and something that is also an inescapable part of any acceptable moral theory. To get at this crucial aspect I have to introduce another semi-technical distinction between act- and rule-utilitarianism. Act-utilitarianism presumes that we should judge each act in terms of utility (whatever precisely we determine that to mean); rule-utilitarianism presumes that we should follow certain rules that are judged in terms of utility, and follow them even when on particular occasions it does not serve the principle of utility to do so.

When utilitarianism is considered as a moral theory, 'utility' should not be equated with 'usefulness'. The central tenet of utilitarianism is happiness. The word is not ideal for a number of reasons, but there isn't any doubt that the theory in most of its variant forms is concerned with ensuring as much happiness or contentment, or perhaps as little misery and discontent, in the world as possible. In simple terms, it sees morality as behaviour that is conducive to the ideal of a world in which there is no suffering. It seems absolutely and indisputably clear to me (although it must be acknowledged that it is disputed by some) that a utilitarian must, on utilitarian grounds, be a rule-utilitarian. Put simply, if act-utilitarianism were adopted, every individual would on every occasion be in the position of having to decide what course of action would promote the most happiness (or least suffering etc.); this would be a recipe for disaster. We are all clearly better off if in some areas we have some rules; granted that means that sometimes in following the rule we cause more grief than we might have done, nonetheless overall we are better off. If there is no rule and no presumption about people telling the truth, life will be unpredictable, chaotic, and, as a result, in various obvious ways very unsettling and unnerving (i.e. not conducive to satisfaction and contentment), not to mention the fact that whether people do or do not tell the truth would be entirely dependent on their assessment of the consequences of their choice, and every misinformed choice would of course contribute to a decrease in the sum of happiness. But the main point is that one fairly obvious thing that humans in general need for their security and comfort are some agreed rules.

If we are talking about rule-utilitarianism in the terms that I have outlined, then the claim that it is a teleological theory is true in that it is focused on the end of happiness, but misleading in that it ignores the fact that, having made the rules, utilitarians see a need to follow them because they are rules; in the same way, it is not straightforwardly consequentialist, because one is supposed to tell the truth in any situation and not simply when the consequences of so doing will be increased happiness.

The aspect of utilitarianism that I wish to suggest needs to be incorporated into any understanding of morality is its recognition of the significance of something like happiness as a criterion of moral evaluation. I have already acknowledged that the word is not ideal, nor perhaps are any of the alternatives, for one reason or another; 'well-being' is favoured by some because it does not carry the connotations that happiness, contentment, freedom from suffering, etc., do. Some prefer 'contentment' to 'happiness' because it seems less specific; on the other hand some argue for a conception of happiness that goes beyond certain sensations and incorporates some idea of personal fulfilment. I shall not pursue this issue in detail and will tend to refer to happiness, well-being, or absence of suffering, different as they may be, indiscriminately. But my suggestion is that a part of the grounding for any plausible moral theory must be concern for general well-being. Yes, there may be rules that ought to be followed regardless of the consequences on particular occasions. Yes, there may be some other elements and principles that define morality besides well-being. Yes, there is still room for debate about what constitutes well-being or happiness. But surely at least a part of the reasoning that explains and justifies the claim that one ought to tell the truth or perform any moral act is that this is for our collective well-being.

In the past some philosophers have been drawn to what are called social contract theories and in recent years there has been revived interest in modification of such theories. The essence of these theories is not generally the historical claim that contracts were in fact made between citizens, but rather that moral theories or moral laws can be seen as what self-interested individuals would agree to in terms of co-operation, sometimes given what they may be presumed to know, sometimes assuming that they don't know anything of moment. I am not specifically thinking in terms of a contract in what I have written here so much as of a few broad and common perceptions which lie behind our sense of why we should or should not do certain things. But it is nonetheless plausible to see morality as a set of principles that, whatever other reasons may be given for recognizing them, represent the sort of rules that enlightened people would choose to adopt if starting a community from scratch.

Reducing morality to power, I have argued, is a mistake; it is neither the whole truth about what has happened historically nor plausible as an account of what we understand morality to be. Turning to God is no use either; even if there is a God, our sense of morality must be something distinct from our commitment to God (or else there is no such thing as what we sense to be morality). Nature is a dangerous guide; even if we knew clearly how to distinguish the natural from the unnatural, there is no reason to equate what happens naturally or what we are naturally inclined to do with what is good or what ought to be done.

Intuition notoriously cannot be relied upon in any field and the specific theory of utilitarianism, at least as commonly interpreted, cannot be accepted as the answer to our problems. But it can be said that a part of the answer to a moral question such as 'Why should I tell the truth?' is to be found in our intuitive sense of the absurdity of wishing for a world in which there is no premium on truth-telling and, more particularly, in our recognition that a moral obligation to tell the truth in general is in our collective interest, not in specifically material terms or for a reward in an after-life, but in terms of our general well-being.

Already we are beginning to build up an understanding of certain characteristics of the moral domain; but before we attempt to consider directly what the fundamental and defining principles of morality are, some remaining preliminary distinctions and cautions need to be introduced.

Commentary

The introduction of God brings us to the philosophy of religion. John Hick *The Existence of God* collects a number of fundamental arguments from the history of the subject. Terry Miethe and Antony Flew *Does God Exist?* is in the form of a debate between a believer and a non-believer (though the latter, Flew, is reportedly beginning to change his mind in old age). Richard Swinburne *The Existence of God* argues that on the balance of probabilities there is a God. Useful collections of papers are: Basil Mitchell (ed.) *The Philosophy of Religion*, Thomas V. Morris (ed.) *The Concept of God*, and John Hick and Arthur McGill (eds) *The Many-faced Argument*. Of interest on the specific question of apparent contradictions within an established religion is Alexander Waugh's entertaining *God*. It goes without saying in this multicultural age that the focus on Christianity in these references and in the body of the text is merely for illustrative purposes. Incidentally, according to *Brewer's Dictionary of Phrase and Fable*, the word 'God' comes 'probably from an Aryan root, gheu – to invoke; it is in no way connected with "good"'.

In relation to arguments about nature and morality, the concern about the relationship between 'ought' and 'is' expressed in the previous chapter may first be recalled. A.P. d'Entreves *Natural Law* is a good introduction to the subject, as is the more specific D.J. O'Connor *Aquinas and Natural Law*. See also Stephen Buckle's essay on 'Natural Law' in Peter Singer (ed.) *A Companion to Ethics* and further references in the Commentary on Chapter 4 below on natural rights.

Aristotle's view that humans are political animals is to be found in the *Politics*. He means that a social instinct is implanted in us by nature and he connects this with our capacity for a unique type of language that allows us to express a distinction between the just and the unjust. The argument that 'what is generally regarded as good is simply behaviour that suits the powers-that-be' is attributable to a character named Thrasymachus in Plato's *Republic* on one interpretation. (It might also be said to have a place in Nietzsche's philosophy.) But Thrasymachus has also been taken to be presenting the different argument that it is natural and hence morally right for the strong to dominate the weak (which is also one popular though hardly fair summation of Nietzsche's position). The difference can be expressed as that between thinking that 'might is right' and that 'right is might'.

In addition to the references for intuitionism given in the Commentary on the Introduction above, see Jonathan Dancy, 'Intutionism', in Singer's *A Companion to Ethics*, and W.D. Hudson *Modern Moral Philosophy*. Aristotle has some interesting things to say about friendship in the *Nicomachean Ethics*, while the argument I introduce to the effect that it doesn't make sense to presume that it doesn't matter if you break a promise is Kantian in spirit. On the distinction between act- and rule-utilitarianism, in addition to references already provided, see the debate between J.J.C. Smart and Bernard Williams *Utilitarianism: For and Against*, and on happiness see Robin Barrow *Happiness*, Elizabeth Telfer *Happiness*, and Nel Noddings *Happiness and Education*.

There are hints of social contract theory as early as Plato's *Republic*, but the key texts remain those already cited in the Commentary on the Introduction above, particularly those of Rousseau and Rawls.

3 Some distinctions and some mistakes

One impediment to understanding the nature of morality is a failure to recognize some fairly basic distinctions, and in this chapter I shall review some distinctions that are commonly ignored and some mistakes that are commonly made, with the consequence that quite false conclusions are drawn about various particular moral theories and moral philosophy in general.

But to begin with, let me draw attention to a distinction that I shall not be making, namely between 'morality' and 'ethics'. Etymologically, incidentally, there is no distinction, 'ethics' coming from the Greek *ethikos* and 'morality' from the Latin *moralis*, both meaning 'concerning habits or customs' (and thus misleadingly suggesting that morality is for us identical with mere custom). Many dictionaries of philosophy or primers therefore treat the two words as synonyms. But today, perhaps increasingly, some people tend to use 'ethics' in respect of theorizing or as a synonym for what used to be called 'moral philosophy', while using 'morality' to apply to practical moral problems and situations: 'Is happiness the greatest good?' is thus seen as a question in ethics, 'Should I tell the truth at this point?' as a moral question. But, as against that, 'practical ethics' is more often to be found than 'practical morality' as the description of the kind of philosophy course or book that is focused on actual and contemporary problems. Some distinguish between relatively specific codes and more abstract or general theory by referring to the former as 'moral' codes and the latter as 'ethical' theories. On yet another hand, an 'ethic' is often the preferred word to describe a particular rule or code of conduct, as in 'Our professional ethic demands this'. It is also arguable that the distinction is partly geographical or cultural in that at one point 'ethics' seemed to be more widely favoured in North America and 'morality', 'moral philosophy', etc. more favoured in Britain.

There is certainly a case for saying that we should mark the distinction between specific codes of practice for, e.g., business or one of the professions on the one hand and principles that ought to govern life generally on the other; the former might then regularly be referred to as 'business ethics', 'academic ethics', or 'medical ethics', and the latter as 'morality'. Unfortunately, though the difference is important, since professional ethics are by no means necessarily co-extensive with morality, current usage is so varied as to make it rather futile to attempt to lay down the law on this matter. And this is the case more generally: usage is too variable, and in some cases too entrenched, to make it profitable to try and use the words to mark out clear and distinct concepts. Perhaps, slowly but surely, the word 'ethics' is becoming more commonly used (and it is certainly beloved of publishers, as is witnessed by the far greater number of contemporary books with 'ethics' in the title than those with 'moral' or 'moral philosophy'). Be this all as it may, as far as my usage is concerned, 'ethics' and 'morality' are more or less interchangeable, though I prefer to think of myself as a 'moral philosopher' than as an 'ethicist'. But the important point for the reader is obviously to recognize that within these pages, on this particular issue, nothing hangs on which word is used. This may be described as a book about ethics or morality, it is an introduction to ethics, ethical theory, or moral philosophy, and it refers to and attempts to deal with a variety of ethical or moral problems, dilemmas, and demands. (It is also, of course, a book about 'moral education', and here there seems little doubt that that is the apt phrase. For whatever reason, people do not seem to talk very often of 'ethical education' or 'education in ethics'.)

Another distinction which needs to be mentioned, but which will be 'more honour'd in the breach than the observance', is that between behaviour and actions. Strictly speaking, 'behaviour' refers to what we do, our physical performance, while 'action' includes implicit reference to unstated intentions and beliefs that may explain and cause the behaviour. Thus to raise a hand is a behaviour, but it becomes an action when it is understood as a cry for help, a greeting, etc. In practice, it is hard to maintain this distinction much of the time, simply because common usage generally refers to behaviour rather than action, whatever the context and the precise meaning intended. Thus, typically, people don't talk of moral acts or actions so much as moral behaviour, even though, strictly speaking, that is by definition incorrect, since moral conduct is generally agreed to imply conscious volition. And I shall often ignore the distinction. But, unlike the ethics/morality distinction, this does relate to a very important conceptual distinction. It matters that we are aware of the difference between talking about the observable physical performance or the behaviour, and the meaning of the behaviour, which is the act or action. The distinction therefore needs to be borne in mind and sometimes to be explicitly noted, particularly when we are talking about moral agency and responsibility. Morality is not ultimately about behaviours, but about actions, that is, about our intentions, motives, and beliefs as much as our physical behaviour.

But let us now turn to some distinctions that do need to be observed. The first is between different kinds of good or value, specifically between moral values and values of other kinds. Not all values are moral, not all judgements are moral judgements, and it is an unfortunate but quite common mistake to see a question such as whether one should smoke, act politely, or keep one's house neat and tidy treated as a moral question. Among the many different kinds of value there is, for example, aesthetic value, which is distinct from, say, economic value; what is legally right is distinct from what is conventionally right (and continues to be distinct even if they happen to coincide; to say that something is legally right is different from saying that it is conventionally right); a broken knife is a poor knife in a quite different sense from that in which a poor sporting performance is poor. To repeat: not all values are moral values; there are other goods besides moral goods. So the focus here is not on goodness but on moral goodness; a lot of behaviour may be bad (or good) in quite non-moral ways as, for example, being drunk, being rude, or being conceited. Part of what a moral theory has to do is distinguish the moral from the non-moral domain and to explain what makes a moral issue specifically moral.

Lying, for example, is a moral issue, whether or not we think it morally acceptable in a given situation, whereas over-eating, on the face of it, though it may be deplorable, disgusting, or unwelcome, is not in itself a moral issue. Our interest is initially in the moral as distinguished from the non-moral, and only when we have defined the field of the moral in contrast to the non-moral does the distinction between the moral and the immoral (i.e. the morally good and the morally bad) come into play. In this connection attention should also be drawn to the difference between calling people 'immoral', meaning that they do wrong to some degree knowingly, and calling them 'amoral', meaning that they lack any sense of moral obligation.

Second, we need to distinguish between a specific code of practice (whether for a restricted group such as teachers, doctors, or lawyers, or for humanity at large as in the case of a Christian code) and a moral (or ethical) theory. What I refer to as moral codes are determinate lists of specific prescriptions and prohibitions such as the Ten Commandments. Moral philosophy and the theory it gives rise to are not necessarily (and I shall argue are in fact necessarily not) concerned with a specific list of this sort. Moral philosophy is concerned to uncover general principles that should govern our behaviour (actions), but these principles always need to be interpreted and, because contexts and situations change, the same principles can lead to a need for different conduct at different times and places. This, essentially, is the point that will help us to explain the issue of relativism: there is relativity or difference at the level of the particular, and often rightly so, but that does not imply that the governing principles are relative, let alone arbitrary.

A third distinction to note is between the (morally) good and the right. Certain states of affairs (e.g. a fair distribution of rewards), certain people (e.g.

honest people), and certain experiences (e.g. love) may be described as good, their opposites generally as bad. Certain actions, however, (e.g. keeping a promise) are generally described as right. It is unfortunately confusingly the case that we can also talk of actions as being good (e.g., 'it is good that he forgave her'), but the basic point remains: actions, rather than people, states of affairs, and experiences, are right or wrong. The latter are good or bad.

This may seem rather pedantic, but it is connected to the issue of the supposed conflict between teleological and deontological types of moral theory. A teleological theory (so-called from the Greek words *telos* meaning 'end' and *logos* meaning 'word', 'rationale', 'account', or 'reasoning') is one that subordinates duty, obligation, right conduct, and so forth to the good. It presumes that one ought to do what one ought to do because it is conducive to the greater good, and that an act can only be morally right if it produces a greater balance of good than alternative actions would do. A deontological theory (derived from the Greek word for what is necessary or incumbent on one) is one that sees one's duty as logically independent of the good and therefore something that is not to be justified or explained in that way: my duty is my duty regardless of the consequences in respect of contributing to the sum of goodness.

One cannot of course deny the possible distinction here: an action can be approved only because it is presumed to increase the goodness in the world, or it can be approved without reference to that consideration. But it is surely not the case that a moral theory has to rigidly incorporate one or other of these alternatives. Imagine a law officer who has in his custody a criminal whom the mob wish to lynch and who further knows that there will be widespread rioting, violence, and death if he doesn't hand over the prisoner to the mob. The superficial presumption is that those committed to a deontological moral theory will say that the officer should not hand over the criminal to be lynched because that would be a wrong thing to do regardless of consequences, while those committed to the teleological view would say that, given that the man is guilty and that the alternative will lead to the loss of other innocent lives, the greater good demands that in this instance the prisoner be handed over.

Usually, an example such as this is designed to expose the supposed flaw in teleological theories. But there are at least two very strong responses that can be made by those who see themselves as committed to a teleological position. First, they could argue that, notwithstanding the certainty of immediate rioting and death to some innocents, the officer should not hand over the prisoner because to do so would be to weaken respect for the law and to encourage other lynch mobs to form and make similar demands in the future, with the consequence that in the long term the greater good would not be served. Second, they could take the bull by the horns and argue that indeed they would and should choose the death of one bad man over the death of many innocents and therefore hand the criminal to the mob. Both responses are at any rate *prima facie* plausible defences of a teleological position.

But I want to suggest something more. Presumably, those (i.e. deontologists) who believe that duty is to be done for duty's sake and that therefore the officer should under no circumstances hand over the prisoner to a lynch mob ultimately do so because they believe that the world is a better place for such adherence to duty; they may not believe that it is better because it is happier, more reliable, or better in terms of any other specific and distinct good, but they must believe that it is a morally better place for the fact that people do their duty. It is, surely, more or less incomprehensible that somebody, whatever the grounds for his moral convictions, should at one and the same time see something as an absolute moral duty and as something that was of no material significance to the moral goodness of the world. Conversely, those who believe that whether the officer should act in this or that way is a matter of which is for the better (whether in terms of following a rule or making an exception to the rule) certainly acknowledge that their theoretical position gives rise to a number of specific rules and duties to be followed, generally speaking, once formulated, because they are right.

In short, not only is the presumption that teleological and deontological theories will necessarily lead to different judgements and prescriptions false, but, more than that, it seems difficult, if not impossible, to conceive of a theory that does not have at least some reference to both the idea of an ultimate good and particular rights and duties in determining the morally right thing to do. The question of whether actions are right because they contribute to the good or whether it is good to do what is right regardless of consequences, conceived of as an abstract question about all moral action (as opposed to a question asked about particular situations), thus seems a rather meaningless one.

A fourth and very important distinction is between a good act and a justified act, with a right act sometimes being equivalent to one, sometimes to the other. Think, for example, of the difference between saying, 'Kindness is good', 'I was justified in being unkind to her', and the ambiguous 'It is right that I should be kind to her'. The first makes a statement about kindness in itself (*per se* or intrinsically). Considered simply in and of itself it is a good thing. But there may be circumstances in which, given the available options, though unkindness is intrinsically bad, it is justified, perhaps, as we say, as the lesser of two evils. 'It is right that I should be kind to her' is ambiguous as between meaning 'It is in itself a good thing to be kind to her' and 'In the circumstances I ought to be kind to her'.

It is very important to emphasize that in life we often face dilemmas, by which I mean insoluble problems as opposed to problems which are presumed to be soluble. For example, I have promised not to reveal my friend's whereabouts to his wife (and I ought to keep my promise), but she is in evident distress (and I ought to help her). Faced with two obligations of equal force, what am I to do? Or, to make the point more strongly, perhaps I clearly ought to do something that is bad or wrong in itself. Thus, killing is wrong, but I kill the brutal psychopath to prevent him raping and murdering an innocent girl. And clearly we sometimes say of an example like this that 'he was right to do it' (even though it was an intrinsically wrong act). It seems to me that the distinction between this (an act that is intrinsically bad or wrong but justified by the context) and an act that is inherently right is so important that it should be marked by distinct language, so I shall refer to the former as a justified act and only the latter as a right or good act.

The importance of all this is that critics have been known to complain of a given theory that it doesn't solve all our moral problems and specifically that it may lead to condoning wrong acts. Both charges have been levelled against utilitarianism, for example. It has been argued countless times that we might face a situation in which killing ten people would save thousands more lives, and that a utilitarian might then say, 'All right, we should kill ten innocent people'; the conclusion is then drawn that there must be something wrong with a moral theory that says we 'ought to' do what is plainly wrong. But the answer to this is plainly that the utilitarian is not saying that what is wrong is right; he is saying that sometimes what is very far from right is nonetheless justified. And any moral theory, given the facts of life, has to face up to such problematic choices and, on occasion, unavoidable dilemmas. On what conceivable ground could one argue for the moral superiority of not taking ten innocent lives in the certain knowledge that it would involve thousands of innocent deaths? One could of course simply assert that taking the ten innocent lives was morally unacceptable regardless of consequences, and many people do hold such a position on certain matters. But to assert is not to argue and the question is not, in any case, whether such an act would be morally wrong in the sense of bad (which all are agreed it would be), but whether it might nonetheless be morally justified. On what conceivable grounds, then, could one argue that it must be morally preferable to act in such a way that thousands of innocent people die than to act in such a way that ten die? The problem here is in the human condition, not the theory of utilitarianism, and, on any theory, intrinsically wrong acts may sometimes be justified. Hence the importance of making the distinction between a right act and a justified act.

Similarly, the reverse side of the coin, the objection that a utilitarian often wouldn't know what to do because he could not know what effect his action will have, misses the point of a moral theory entirely. This objection can be raised against almost any consequentialist theory; it cannot be raised against a deontological theory, it is true, if that means a theory that asserts that certain acts must be performed without exception and come what may; but any such crude alternative runs into far worse problems. Is there anybody on earth who is seriously going to maintain that everybody should always under any circumstances keep a promise, prevent harm, tell the truth, and be kind? In the first place, sometimes these different principles (or those of any moral theory) clash, so that it is logically impossible to abide by them all. Thus, most of us, whatever our precise moral position, believe in a principle of freedom and a principle of equality. But it is impossible to live in this world without recognizing that sometimes these principles are in conflict, so that it is impossible consistently to uphold them both. Second, even when it is possible to uphold a particular principle, it is surely not hard to imagine circumstances which, despite our commitment to the principle, would make it seem wrong to do so. It is not only utilitarians who face dilemmas such as the one in the example. What is anybody supposed to do when told that ten innocent people will be shot if hundreds of others are not surrendered? What is anybody supposed to do when the burglar is about to murder his wife?

The truth of the matter is that people tend to ask too much of a moral theory: they think it can be legitimately criticized and shown to be faulty in so far as it fails to provide consistent prescriptions for life. But it cannot be expected to do this for all sorts of reason, logical and contingent. It is an important part of my argument that this is not what a moral theory is for. Indeed, I think one of the reasons why some people feel dissatisfied with moral philosophy is that they assume and are sometimes led to believe that they are going to get more than can be got – not because philosophy is like that, but because life is like that. There are of course instances of very specific rules for living or moral codes such as the Ten Commandments. The problem with a moral code such as this is that it is inflexible, and unsupported by justification. But the reason why this is inadequate is not that Christian thinkers haven't done their job well; it is that it can't be done.

If a fully justified moral code can't be provided, what can be provided? What can a moral theory do? It can provide understanding of how the domain of morality works; it can provide an argument for a set of principles that are the determinants of moral decision-making. That means inevitably that it will fail to prescribe specific conduct for every occasion. But it also means that it answers to the human condition and the nature of morality. For if we acknowledge that we are dealing with people who have freedom, then we must realize that there will be the unpredictable, the dilemma, and the difficult choice. One cannot criticize a moral theory for the fact that it does not solve all our problems or for the fact that it might on occasion justify an intrinsically bad action. One can only criticize it for failing to understand human nature or for some kind of logical incoherence. Just as good science may remain good science even when it fails to achieve any immediate practical benefit, so good moral philosophy may remain good moral philosophy even when it does not tie up every loose end.

Is morality, then, an objective or a subjective matter? The first thing that needs to be sorted out is what exactly this question means. Moral propositions such as 'Stealing is wrong' or 'Kindness is good' are certainly not scientifically demonstrable, so if anyone takes 'objective truth' to be co-extensive with what can be empirically demonstrated in the manner of the physical sciences, then there are no objective moral truths. But then there is no good reason to imagine that moral claims would or should be comparable to scientific claims, and no plausible reason for equating objectivity with what can be scientifically demonstrated. (There can obviously be claims about morality, such as that 'Many people believe that kindness is good', that are more or less objective in this restricted sense, but a claim about some aspect of morality such as this is not itself a moral claim.) Even if we equate 'objectivity' more broadly with 'demonstrable in some conclusive manner', we should concede that morality is not objective. Despite thousands of years of moral philosophy, we cannot claim that moral propositions are as conclusively established as, say, certain mathematical propositions. But why should this concern us? Moral propositions are not mathematical propositions any more than they are scientific ones. They are not going to be established in the same way or, very likely, to the same degree. Nor, while we are on the subject, are they going to be supported in the same way as psychological or sociological or historical claims. All of these fundamental disciplines work in different ways, which is why we recognize them as distinct and fundamental, and to equate objectivity with only the kind or degree of proof that we associate with any one of these particular disciplines would be absurd.

In the case of morality the question is whether there is enough dispassionate reasoning in support of certain truth claims to allow us to conclude that it would be unreasonable to deny them. In that sense, as I shall attempt to establish in Part II below, morality may be said to be objective; it is objective or the claims may be said to be objectively established in contradistinction to the view that it is subjective in the sense that it is ultimately a matter of varying taste or presumption. That is the sense that most people have in mind when they worry about the objective nature of morality: is a moral claim such as 'You ought to keep promises' objective in the sense of rationally defensible, or subjective in the sense of a matter of individual predilection?

But while I argue that morality is objective in this sense, I do not argue, and I do not think that we need to argue, that it is God-given in any sense, ranging from literally designed by God to the colloquial 'given in the nature of things' or there to be apprehended by us whether we do so or fail to do so. There is a tendency for people to think that if something is true it must in some way correspond to some actuality that is independent of human perception in any way. I confess to being unclear exactly what such a claim would mean; nonetheless, many people seem to feel a need to divide the world into truths that are given in nature and that would be true even if humans did not exist, such as that there are continents and seas, and 'truths' that, in so far as they are true at all, merely establish human preferences and hence would not exist if there were no humans.

All this seems to me very confused. It is true of course that if there were no humans there would be no morality. Just as if there were no humans there would be no human procreation, no relationships, no friendship, no enmity, and no purpose-built dwellings. Does this mean that procreation, friendship, and houses are not real? Of course not. Does this mean that whether this is an act of procreation, an instance of friendship, or a house is a matter simply of individual perception or preference? Of course not. The fact is that things (institutions, relationships, actions, even buildings) can be man-made but nonetheless objective. There can be truth and falsehood even in artificially created or man-made phenomena.

Given these considerations, I shall argue that what morality is, what is meant by the word 'morality', is less in doubt, less contentious, than is generally recognized. It is indeed, in a sense, a human construct or man-made thing, no more simply 'given in nature' than marriage, friendship, football, or art. But the questions that really need our attention are precisely what it means to say that such disparate things as football, marriage, and art are human constructs, whether they are all man-made in the same sense or in the same way, whether, to what extent, and in what way they might also be said to be given in nature or natural, and what the implications are of acknowledging in each case that they are to this or that extent variously either human constructs or given in nature. After all, man cannot make anything: he cannot make square circles, he cannot double the number of degrees in a triangle, he cannot make something black and white all over. Conversely, he can build theories that are coherent or incoherent, clear or obscure, complete or incomplete, and that do or do not conflict with facts about the world (including other well-grounded beliefs). The fact that we recognize that in some sense we create morality ourselves does not mean that what we designate as moral becomes arbitrary. At the very least, we should be looking for a clear, complete, consistent, and coherent theory of morality that is compatible with our other knowledge and beliefs.

Take, for example, a library that needs to classify its books. Now there are hundreds of ways that a library might classify its books, including by colour, by height, by weight, by size, by length, by type of jacket design, by librarians' preference, by subject matter, and so on. But only some of these approaches even begin to make sense in relation to the purpose of the library, which is to store books in a way that maximizes ease of retrieval or, more generally, use.

Given that people read books for their subject matter, we are immediately led to reject colour, size, and a librarian's personal preferences, for example. Some form of genre categorization is called for because it is a fact (not an opinion or a preference) that fiction, biography, poetry, history, and essays can be distinguished. This is not to say that it was written in heaven that they must be, but nonetheless the distinctions are not arbitrary; they are given in the sense that we cannot wish them away or deny them, despite the true observation that they wouldn't in some sense be there or have been formulated if there were no humans, and despite the fact that a particular group of humans might fail to make them. But the fact that some particular tribe does not distinguish between poetry and fiction (as in a sense the Homeric Greeks or Chaucerian England did not) doesn't stop the distinction being there to be made. It may be conceded that one can argue about where biography ends and fiction begins, about whether this particular library needs or does not need a particular distinction to be utilized (perhaps the clientele here simply don't mind what they are reading), about whether other categories are not equally or more important (sociology distinguished from history, perhaps; gay literature; ethnic literature). All this is true and takes a bit of time to say, so may look like a lot of objections. But there is no valid objection. The point is that given who we are and what a library is for, only a certain number (in fact relatively few) alternative systems make sense.

It's true that some parts of the system may be quite arbitrary and could in principle be changed at any time: thus, having established our genre, we generally proceed to shelve books alphabetically by author; apart from questionable arguments about relative ease, who could object if we proceeded instead by alphabetical order of title, or in reverse alphabetical order? But even here, not anything goes: to revert to stacking by colour would give the user no help at all and hence would be a bad feature of the system. I do not dispute, therefore, that some details of a classification system may legitimately change because of different circumstances (and I shall be saying exactly the same of morality: there are moral differences between cultures, and some of these differences are entirely legitimate in that they make sense and can be justified, but they do not thereby do anything to make the case for the relativity or subjectivity of morality as a whole). But that doesn't alter the fact that we can distinguish good from bad classification systems, quite regardless of individual tastes or preferences. A good system has to relate to what people's preferences are, but once it has done so in the appropriate manner (meaning coherently and reasonably) it is, *ipso facto*, a good system; those who for whatever reason do not like it, are incorrect to say that it is a bad system. If, of course, everybody or the clear majority say they do not favour it, then something has gone wrong and it is not a good system. But this should not be confused with saying that what is good is what the majority think is good; what is good has to, among other things, be based on a correct understanding of what the majority of people are like (e.g., in this case, whether they prefer to read the alphabet forwards or in reverse; whether they want to observe the distinction between poetry and fiction); but once it has done that it has to proceed in a rational manner based on the purpose of the system. *Mutatis mutandis*, the same may be said of marriage, friendship, or any other human institution; they have to take account of human needs and wishes, which may sometimes vary, but then they have to be devised in a coherent and rational way in the light of the purpose of the exercise as well as human preferences and inclinations.

In the same way, while of course any moral theory is and should be based on human inclinations (that is one reason why well-being already figures in this account: people care about their well-being – a moral system that ran counter to it or totally ignored it would be a non-starter), beyond that it has to sort and organize in a coherent and rational way that takes account of what morality is for. Once that is done it becomes a matter of objective truth whether the theory is more or less adequate. (It doesn't of course simply become either true or false in practice, because the matter is very complex; complexity and qualification, however, do not amount to subjectivity.)

Commentary

Some authors also use the term 'meta-ethics', generally to refer to philosophical inquiry into the meaning of moral terms. Here again I think the presumed distinction unreal, inasmuch as one cannot neatly distinguish between examining the meaning of moral terms and critically examining moral theories or, yet again, actual moral problems.

The extensive bibliographical references here are not really justified by concern for the distinction between 'ethics' and 'moral philosophy', which I anyway regard as a false distinction. But this is a convenient place for a number of references to works in ethics/moral philosophy to be added to those already given as introductory texts. (Of minor interest, at least to me, is that, if these references are taken as reasonably representative of the field, then 'ethics' seems more popular than my preferred 'moral philosophy'.)

Mary Warnock *Ethics Since 1900* deals with theories and theorists of the last century, while her *An Intelligent Person's Guide to Ethics* deals with moral issues surrounding, e.g., death; it also has chapters on rights and on 'where ethics comes from'. Her husband Geoffrey Warnock's *Contemporary Moral Philosophy* is an incisive account of developments during the first half of the last century, while Bernard Williams *Ethics and the Limits of Philosophy* is not dissimilar to his earlier *Morality*.

Many classic texts favoured the word 'ethics' in the title, for example Henry Sidgwick *The Methods of Ethics*, which offers a species of utilitarian grounding for ethical thought, and his *Outlines of the History of Ethics*; F.H. Bradley *Ethical Studies* explores such issues as why should I be moral, duty for duty's sake, and selfishness and self-sacrifice; G.E. Moore *Ethics* is a briefer, more introductory account than his *Principia Ethica*. See also W.D. Ross *Foundations of Ethics*; William Lillie *An Introduction to Ethics*, with an early twentieth-century focus; A.C. Ewing *Ethics*; and J.D. Mabbott *An Introduction to Ethics*.

For a while, during the latter half of the last century, 'moral' seemed to be the favoured term. R.M. Hare *The Language of Morals* had a major impact and was followed among others by his *Moral Thinking: Its Levels, Method and Point*; Alan Montefiore *A Modern Introduction to Moral Philosophy*; W.D. Hudson *Modern Moral Philosophy*; Stuart Hampshire *Two Theories of Morality* (being those of Aristotle and Spinoza, 1632–77, a strong determinist who nonetheless believed in a kind of freedom for humans and who sought to establish ethical conclusions on certain self-evident axioms); Joel J. Kupperman *The Foundations of Morality* includes a chapter on 'the need for an ethical theory' and discussion of what an ethical theory can and should do. More or less contemporaneously, we have John Hospers *Human Conduct: an Introduction to the Problems of Ethics*; Alasdair MacIntyre *A Short History of Ethics*, following the great names and schools of thought from the Greek Sophists to 'modern moral philosophy', with a distinctive slant that would later be forged into a somewhat relativistic take on morality; J.O. Urmson *The Emotivist Theory of Ethics* is more specialized, but serves to remind us that theories are generally called 'ethical' rather than 'moral'. J.L. Mackie *Ethics: Inventing Right and Wrong* has a chapter on the 'object of morality'.

Richard T. de George (ed.) *Ethics and Society* includes papers on 'love and justice', 'respect for persons', and 'the mental health ethic'; Jonathan Glover *Causing Death and Saving Lives* talks of 'moral problems' and 'the scope and limits of moral argument'. Peter Singer *Practical Ethics* deals with such things as animals, abortion, and euthanasia, also his *Rethinking Life and Death: the Collapse of our Traditional Ethics*; John Ladd (ed.) *Ethical Issues relating to Life and Death*; John Kleinig *Ethical Issues in Psychosurgery*; John Harris *The Value of Life: an Introduction to Medical Ethics*; Elke Henner W. Kluge *Biomedical Ethics in a Canadian Context*. Notwithstanding my comment in the body of the text that 'ethics' is the favoured word in the realm of applied philosophy, we do have: Stuart Hampshire (ed.) *Public and Private Morality*; Michael Lockwood *Moral Dilemmas in Modern Medicine*; and K.W.M. Fulford *Moral Theory and Medical Practice*. (Perhaps it is simply the alliteration of 'moral' and 'medicine' that explains the choice of words!)

But to my mind – though I am native here,
And to the manner born, – it is a custom
More honour'd in the breach than the observance.

The quotation is from Shakespeare's *Hamlet* (I. iv. 14–16). Hamlet himself is speaking and the subject is heavy drinking. Whether such ritualistic excess is a moral issue will be considered below. The distinction between behaviour and action has further significance in respect of the form of psychology known as 'behaviourism', a form of study that confines itself to behaviours in the strict sense, in some cases on the grounds that only the behaviour can be observed (as contrasted with, e.g., intentions), in others on the extreme view that there is nothing other than the observable behaviour, notions such as that of intention being either themselves reducible to behaviours or misleading fantasies. It would be argued by most who are not committed to some form of behaviourism that by its nature such a limited form of inquiry is misguided and misleading in the extreme. Humans are to be distinguished from most, if not all, other animals precisely in that they do not simply, or even generally, operate on a purely reflexive or stimulus-response model. They do have, and generally act in the light of, intentions. Therefore, to understand what humans are doing, it is necessary to go beyond the study of mere behaviours. (Two further comments: perhaps paradoxically some of the most famous behavioural psychologists, such as B.F. Skinner, while they may certainly be criticized along these lines, are nonetheless more complex than a summary of their position might suggest and certainly deserving of further study; it is more the general acceptance of a superficial behaviourism in society as a whole that is dangerous. Conversely, while 'behaviourism' as a term to describe a current school of thought is no longer fashionable, it would be a mistake to think that no psychologists any longer see the world in behaviourist terms, as many standard introductory textbooks of psychology reveal.)

The distinction between moral and non-moral values is one that the mass media are particularly prone to ignore, and not only the tabloid newspapers, that tend to turn everything they dislike into the object of a moralizing crusade, while quite often inconsistently parading some of the values they purport to condemn. Thus, 'fat cat' investors are derided and morally impugned while readers are lured into some new form of gambling for huge prizes; homosexuality is deplored alongside pictures of two naked women together in suggestive poses; or actual homosexuals are mercilessly hounded, though homosexuality is not formally condemned. But even the so-called quality press tends to see every important issue as a moral issue, as if there were no other kinds of value, nothing else of importance. One of *The Times*' more famous headlines (at the time of the 1963 Profumo affair, which involved prostitutes, spies, and telling lies in the House of Commons) thundered, 'It IS a moral issue'. Perhaps on that occasion there was some slight justification, and, by contrast, a July 2006 editorial in the Toronto *Globe and Mail* provides the exception to prove the rule in arguing that the political storm surrounding a decision by a newly elected Prime Minister to offer a cabinet post to an opposition party member who crossed the floor was not a moral issue.

But, out of a random list of items from today's newspaper, none of the following stories, all of which are treated to some extent in moral terms, is really a moral issue (as distinct from a political, a practical, a legal, a social, etc., issue). The leaking and publishing of Prince Charles's private diaries is, in my view, deplorable, but while it is possibly illegal it is not obvious that it is a moral issue. A teenager who uses the F word in a public park in private conversation with his friends, though it appears, rather remarkably, that he is breaking the law, is not behaving immorally. The fact that the majority of babies will soon be born out of wedlock may have religious significance or social significance, but it is not a moral issue. The fact that many of the most prestigious private schools have been in communication with each other in order to make sure that their fees are competitive is now defined legally as a 'restrictive practice', but it is not immoral. The fact that Kate Moss is, allegedly, a cocaine addict may be condemned for a number of reasons, but it does not make her immoral. It is not just that treating such stories with a moral slant is an error; it is also that it weakens our sense of real moral outrage if stories like these are not sharply distinguished from the story (on the same day) that the child torturer and murderer Ian Brady still refuses to divulge to the mother where he buried the body of one of his twelve-year-old victims; or the story of the hospital manager who defrauded the National Health Service of £600,000. While the man who hoaxed and misled the police looking for the Yorkshire Ripper, thereby it seems indirectly contributing to three more deaths, certainly acted in a way that had appalling consequences and should probably be morally (as well as legally, socially, etc.) condemned, it is strange to compare the moral tone of reports on him with the lack of moral fervour in reports of such stories (from another date) as the Great Train Robbery, in which one railway worker was brutally murdered and millions of pounds never recovered. One of the train robbers, who lived most of his life on his gains in Brazil, even enjoyed something of minor celebrity status among press and public alike. The man who hoaxed the police in the Yorkshire Ripper case, however, and who was an alcoholic and presumably did not intend to facilitate any more murders, is universally morally condemned.

The example concerning the lynch mob in relation to teleological and deontological approaches is adapted from one used by Robert G. Olson in his entry on teleological ethics in the *Encyclopedia of Philosophy*.

My reference to utilitarianism is, once again, only by way of example. Although I do regard myself as a utilitarian rather than anything else (if I must be labelled and if the traditional classifications of ethical theories are all we are allowed to use), and although I do draw something from the utilitarian tradition in the argument of this book, I draw equally from many others and I am not advocating utilitarianism as such here.

There was a time when concern about objectivity was for the most part confined to a few particular areas of knowledge such as the moral sphere. There was broad acceptance that there were objective truths abut the world and that, particularly through science, we could know some of them. Morality was thought of as being different from science and perhaps an area where knowledge was not possible, even where there might be no truth, the two – knowledge and truth – being different: something might be true but unknowable to us. (Interestingly, if we go back to the Ancient Greeks, the situation was rather different. They did not trust the senses particularly, had not developed much in the way of observational and experimental techniques, and, in the case of Plato and others, postulated a reality that lay in the mind rather than in the physical universe.) Today we live, we are constantly told, in a postmodern age. The term itself is very unhelpful, having no clear meaning and being applied to at least some pretty silly ideas. Arguing about postmodernism as such is therefore like jousting with shadows. (D.J. Enright *Injury Time: a Memoir*: 'postmodern: the very description of nullity, of the indisputably indescribable. All it suggests, if that isn't putting it too strongly, is that something comes after something else – as indeed most things do' (p. 155).) Some of the worst writing, such as Lyotard's extravagantly praised *The Postmodern Condition*, involves basic mistakes; in this case a simple confusion between sociological questions about conditions of belief and epistemological questions about grounds for knowledge. Some of the best, such as Stuart Sim (ed.) *The Routledge Companion to Postmodernism*, in a way gives the game away: it is good because it is fair, does not make exaggerated claims, and recognizes the polyglot nature of what is loosely classified together as postmodernism. The result, however, is a set of fairly commonplace and generally accepted truths that does not constitute any coherent theory in itself and lacks any real interest. It is also certainly not new, all of its insights having been anticipated, many from as early as Classical times. Fortunately, I do not need to go into this here. (Those who are interested may care to look at Robin Barrow 'The Need for Philosophical Analysis in a Postmodern Era' (*Interchange* 30(4)) or Chapter Nine, 'The Postmodern Challenge', in Barrow and Woods *An Introduction to Philosophy of Education*, 4th edition.)

The question of importance is in what sense of the terms we should conclude that moral discourse is either 'objective' or 'relative' and that is discussed in the body of the text.

4   Rights and procedures

Finally, by way of clearing the ground and laying foundations, something needs to be said about the nature of moral language, and two currently fashionable ways of approaching morality must be outlined and rejected.

One of the achievements of the intuitionists was to remind us that moral judgements are distinctive or *sui generis*. Just as not all values are moral values, so not all judgements are moral judgements. But, more than this, moral judgements such as 'That is wrong' do not work in exactly the same way as, for example, aesthetic judgements ('That is beautiful'), commands ('Go away'), judgements of taste ('I adore your hat'), or, of course, assertions of empirical fact ('That car was going at 75 m.p.h.'). Philosophers of the twentieth century made a particular contribution to our understanding of the nature of moral discourse – how moral utterances function or work – which tells us something about the nature of moral judgements.

First (in historical terms), it was suggested that moral utterances, though seeming by their form to make statements on a par with descriptive statements, in fact were literally meaningless in that they were no more than emotive outpourings, sometimes seen as designed to influence others, but sometimes seen merely as the verbal equivalent of emitting a sigh or a whoop of joy. Thus, 'Stealing is wrong' is not seen as making a remark about stealing, comparable to saying 'The car is brown'; it is seen as no more and no less than another way of going 'stealing – ugh!', with or without the hope of leading others to share or evince the same distaste.

This theory, as baldly stated, did not survive for long and did not deserve to do so. In the first place, it is not always the case that I am trying to influence others and it is arguable that it is not always even a form of self-expression. When I lie awake musing on the wrongdoing in the world, saying to myself, 'All this stealing is wrong, but I'm not sure whether speaking bluntly is wrong', I am certainly not seeking to influence anybody and I am not obviously giving vent to my disgust or enthusiasm. In the second place, this desire to influence or express oneself does not distinguish a moral utterance from many other kinds of utterance or activity such as advertising, political speeches, threats, and propaganda. But if one thing is clear it is that a moral utterance such as 'Kindness is good' cannot be equated with remarks of the type 'Do this or else', or with a shriek of joy celebrating Coca-Cola. It is true that it is part of the nature of (much?) moral discourse to evince our own attitudes and to attempt to influence those of others, and that is an important insight, but it is not by any means all that moral discourse does. If it were, then the criteria for a successful moral argument would be purely and simply the ability to get others to accept one's view or relative success in expressing one's passion. But this is not what constitutes a good moral argument. A moral debate is not to be compared with an Oscar night; it is not a popularity contest.

But there are other truths about moral utterances that derive not from contemplation of what we are trying to achieve by making them, but rather from what is involved in making them. Two of these truths are that moral language is prescriptive and universalizable. It is prescriptive inasmuch as moral utterances, whatever their grammatical form, may be seen as disguised imperatives. To understand and accept that 'I ought to pay back the money I borrowed' is to see the force of the command, 'Repay what you borrow'. One is logically committed not just to saying that one agrees that one should, but to the act of repayment. By your deeds shall ye be known. If you don't repay your debts, then (other things being equal, e.g. if you don't have a gun held to your head) you don't sincerely have that moral viewpoint; you don't truly recognize that you should repay debts, whatever you may say. But not only is moral language prescriptive, its implicit imperatives, unlike everyday imperatives such as 'Shut the door', carry with them implications for other similar occasions and for other people. The fact that I command you to shut the door implies nothing about whether I shall command or expect you to close it tomorrow or about whether I shall expect others to close it. There is nothing illogical about saying 'Shut the door' to one friend and not to another. But that is not true of a moral command, however it is phrased. Whether explicit ('You ought to be kind') or implicit ('Kindness is good'), it is logically implied both that we should all be kind and that we should always be kind (other things being equal). One way of summarizing this point is to say that moral utterances are, by their nature, universalizable. If I say or believe that my neighbour should not play his trumpet after midnight, then I should not play my trombone after midnight either; and if I say that consideration is a moral good, then I should be expected both to show consideration and to demand it from others.

In short, moral discourse is, among other things, emotive, prescriptive, and universalizable, and that gives us another fact about morality.

The two contemporary approaches to morality that are to be avoided are an emphasis on natural rights and an emphasis on procedural justice (the first of which, incidentally, besides being currently in vogue, has a long and venerable history). But I should emphasize at the outset that my objection is neither to the claim that we have rights nor to a concern that procedures should be just; my objection is to reducing morality to a matter of either rights or procedures; my concern is about the consequences of framing moral thinking and discussion in these terms.

An interest in grounding morality in certain natural rights goes back a long way in history. But to refer to 'natural rights' (rights given in or by nature) is inherently problematic. As we have seen, what is given in nature, what is natural, and how one determines what is natural are all highly questionable. Is co-operation natural or is competition? Is it natural for the strong to exploit the weak? Are love and caring more natural than envy and self-seeking? How are we to answer these questions, especially since at one level one might say that everything that is, is given in nature. In the second place, assuming that we agree that some attitude or behaviour is 'natural', how do we derive an imperative or obligation from this description of nature, how do we move from 'is' to 'ought'? Where is the reasoning that allows us to conclude from the descriptive statement that in nature the strong dominate the weak that it is right that they should do so? It sounds well enough in a time of slavery, for example, to talk of man's natural right to freedom. But, even if we believe in a principle of freedom, what does it mean to say that freedom is a natural right? As a matter of fact, it is not always given in or by nature, as witness the fact that people are being enslaved. And if it were argued that, though slavery exists, it is in some other sense unnatural, why would that lead to the conclusion that we shouldn't engage in it, any more than the fact that our marriage customs are unnatural leads to the conclusion that we shouldn't have them? Only if we take 'unnatural' to mean 'morally wrong' does the conclusion hold: slavery is unnatural in the sense of morally wrong, therefore it is morally wrong. But this is simply to beg the question: who says it is unnatural in this sense, and on what grounds?

All in all, while it is probably fair to say that the historical record of natural rights talk is on balance talk about moral goods that many of us would be inclined to accept, such as natural rights to freedom and happiness, it is difficult to avoid the conclusion that calling them 'natural rights' either begs the question or provides nothing in the way of argument to support the claim that they are morally important. In calling freedom a natural right, we are either merely asserting our view that it is morally important, or we are suggesting, without providing any supporting reason, that, because it is in some sense a feature of nature or the natural life (which very often isn't even true), it ought to be valued. Even the view that we are born free and lose our freedom through the encroachments of the dead hand of civilization is hard to sustain. In what way are we born free? Why should we maintain that the vulnerable and dependent new-born child is more free than the accomplished adult? Why is civilization to be seen as constricting rather than enhancing our freedom?

'Nature', then, and cognate terms such as 'natural' and 'unnatural' are not very helpful, as was argued in Chapter 2 above. Now we can add that the more specific appeal to natural rights is open to the same kinds of objection. We may regard some rights as being of universal significance and we may choose to emphasize their fundamental and universal status by calling them 'natural', as if given by God, by nature, or by life itself, but calling them 'natural' cannot serve as a substitute for reasoning to establish them as rights in the first place.

But it is not simply talk of 'natural' rights that is suspect. There are objections to talking in terms of rights at all, whether 'natural' rights, 'human' rights, 'universal' rights, 'the rights of man', or any other kind of right, as distinct from in terms of principles of morality. I must stress that my objection here is not, as some people's would be, to the idea of there being some universal moral truths, nor is it even to the idea that all humans may be said to have certain rights in virtue of being human (although I think that there are fewer such rights and that they are less specific than is commonly supposed). It would not actually misrepresent my position to say, for example, that I believe in human rights to freedom and well-being, for this can be taken to mean belief that the principles of freedom and well-being are applicable to all. My point is that there has to be independent reasoning and argument to lead us to recognize that these are important moral values, and then, if we wish, we can say that we have established that they are human rights. But we cannot treat the assertion that they are human rights as an argument in itself. It plainly isn't. However, there are several other objections to conducting moral debate in terms of rights besides this fact that to assert a right as human, natural, or anything else is not in itself to provide any reason for accepting the moral value in question. To these we now turn.

To talk in terms of rights, to depict morality as a set of rights, whether possessed by us all, or by some sub-group such as homosexuals, women, children, or blacks, brings with it a lot of dangerous and unnecessary confusion. For a variety of reasons it undermines the notion of responsibility and the outward-looking nature, one might almost say generosity of spirit, that are at the heart of morality. Morality is not just a matter of living by a code, still less by a code of rights: it involves recognizing responsibilities and duties too, and living by a code in a certain kind of spirit, most significantly out of concern for fundamental principles rather than adherence to specific rules.

One preliminary contingent problem with much rights talk is easy to pinpoint: the tendency to confuse legal and moral rights, which is of course just

BISHOP BURTON COLLEGE
LIBRARY

a variant of the general tendency to confuse moral and legal values referred to above. But, perhaps because legal rights are firmly encoded and are relatively easy to cite, the confusion between the two kinds of value is more tenacious and detrimental when we talk in terms of rights. It may also be that, since it is at least arguable that one has a moral obligation to obey the law, we tend to assume that any law that has been constitutionally enacted is a morally just law, which certainly need not be the case. Be that as it may, it is fairly uncontentiously the case that a lot of moral indignation and righteousness are inappropriately brought to bear on issues that are in fact matters of legal and not moral rights. We have all sorts of legal right that have nothing to do with morality and, conversely, many moral obligations that are not enshrined in law. For example, I have certain legal commitments, responsibilities, and expectations arising from my contract to write this book or, on an altogether different plane, there are many different legal rights to be considered by experts when the need to operate on Siamese twins joined at the head is at issue. Both of these examples may give rise to moral questions, but in themselves they present purely legal issues. To determine what I have to do, to determine what the surgeons may legitimately do, we go to lawyers, not moral philosophers. It is a question of interpreting the law and not of what the law ought to be. By contrast, I have various moral responsibilities to my friends that are not encoded in any law.

Countries with written constitutions may perhaps find this problem of disentangling the legal and the moral even more difficult, since legal experts are charged with interpreting the constitution, yet a constitution is often seen as a charter representing a nation's highest moral aspirations. The degree of moral sentiment that surrounds the issue of the right to bear arms in the United States, for example, is palpable. But, quite apart from the vexed legal question of how the constitution is to be interpreted on this issue (since both sides of the debate appeal to the constitution), one thing is certain: the fact, if it is a fact, that the right of every citizen to carry arms is guaranteed by the constitution has got nothing at all to do with the question of whether they have a moral right to do so. Furthermore, the question of whether they have a moral right to do so is subtly different from the question of whether it is morally desirable that they should do so. One might even argue that it is not a moral issue at all, so much as a prudential one: is it actually sensible, is it in our interests, to maintain the gun culture that is familiar to us? Were we to approach the issue by asking that question, the whole tone and nature of the discussion, and possibly even its outcome, would be very different. By couching the debate in terms of 'rights', however, besides confusing legal and moral issues, besides bypassing the fundamental question of what grounds our moral values, we set the debate up in terms of moral righteousness, implacable positions, and confrontational rhetoric. You can discuss whether it is sensible to treat guns in this way or that; you can't argue with a man who thinks you are challenging his inalienable right.

The prevalence of often fruitless and always costly litigation today is surely partly due, not simply to the rapacity of lawyers, and not only to the confusion between legal and moral issues, but to the tendency to talk in terms of rights rather than in terms of what ought to be done. Rights talk is always necessarily personalized. It is 'my right', 'your right', or 'our right'. Even when the ultimate reference is to a so-called human right (say, the right to freedom), in particular cases it becomes an argument about infringement of *somebody's* right to freedom. This leads directly to a confrontational style of debate. What, after all, can trump 'my right' in this inflated language game? Only 'your' right. Though there can be class-action suits, the language of rights is inherently individualistic rather than communal; it is agonistic, if not antagonistic. It is not conducive to conversation, genuine dialogue, or discussion, so much as to confrontation.

Another aspect of the language of rights is that it tends to underplay reference to duties and responsibilities. Formally, one may argue that if you have certain rights then I have corresponding duties to respect your rights. But the fact remains that thinking of morality as primarily a matter of rights seems to weaken our awareness of the need for moral people to exercise responsibility and to act in certain ways, such as kindly and considerately, because it is good to do so rather than because we are obliged to acknowledge somebody's rights. It would be difficult to dispute the claim that the litigious atmosphere of societies such as the United States, arising partly out of a stress on rights, has done a great deal to undermine the idea that morality is partly about giving, about respect, about acting in a principled manner, and about having duties and responsibilities, quite regardless of anyone else's rights. To emphasize the right to bear arms, and to confine argument to whether or not that right is guaranteed by the constitution, inevitably distracts us from thinking in a dispassionate way about whether there are moral reasons for opposing the gun lobby.

Using particular examples runs the risk of alienating readers. But my concern is not really with the good and bad sides of gun ownership in America. My point is the more general one that to couch moral debate in terms of rights is unproductive and distorting for these reasons: if the reference is to 'natural rights', it suggests that moral claims can be established straightforwardly by looking at nature or human nature (and sometimes, confusedly, by looking at the law or constitution). This is generally false in that what constitutes human nature and what is, more broadly, natural are not simple givens, and in that it erroneously assumes that if something is the case it is right that it should be. The language of rights takes emphasis off duties, and very often contingently leads to emphasis on 'my' or 'our' rights without corresponding concern for the rights of others, and thus tends to provide a lop-sided view of morality. It is framed in individualistic, inflexible, and demanding terms, which, not surprisingly, lead to confrontation, conflict, and litigation. Thus, on one side, people simply assert their 'right' to be free of second-hand smoke, without any consideration of the complex issue of whether, even assuming that second-hand smoke is a serious hazard, it follows that the non-smoker has a moral case for preventing the smoker from smoking any more than he has a right to stop the driver from driving (it being clear that the danger from car exhaust is at least as great). On the other hand, normally sane and reasonable adults demand to be compensated for illness caused by a habit that, notwithstanding the false advertising of tobacco companies, they have always known to be harmful and that they chose to adopt. For yet another indirect consequence of thinking in terms of rights is that it tends to weaken our sense of personal responsibility. In sum, it is counterproductive in terms of developing, nurturing, and spreading moral sensibility and responsibility and in terms of thinking reasonably about morality or specific moral issues, since its most notable effect is to reduce moral debate to the incompatible claims of two conflicting rights, whether simply yours and mine, or yours to do X and mine to do Y.

Reference to litigation brings me to the other notable tendency of the times that gets in the way of proper moral debate: a preoccupation with procedural justice, which is particularly prevalent in institutions. We can agree straight-away that we do want our procedures to be just, whether we are referring to a court of law, the rules for hiring, promoting, and firing in business or the professions, or the way in which we sort out informal disputes in the family or among friends. We want the courts to abide by the law and we want that law to be in accord with our sense of justice. (A phrase commonly used here would be 'natural justice', which is, however, open to the same objections as is talk of 'natural rights': what justice is natural and how do you know? In what sense is the justice of 'an eye for an eye' more or less natural than other kinds of justice? In what sense of 'natural'? Does the word actually serve to do any more than indicate that this is the type of justice the speaker believes in?) Similarly, we want employees to be treated justly and we want all procedures, ranging from the composition of a committee of inquiry through to the rules relating to conditions of work, reward, punishment, promotion, reprimand, and firing to be just. The objection, then, is not to the claim that there should be just procedures. As with rights, the objection is to the consequences of this way of talking, to framing our thinking about good and bad behaviour in an institutional or corporate setting in terms of procedural justice. For procedural justice is not enough. While our procedures should be just, they must also be capable of delivering substantive justice: we must be concerned that the end state of affairs is just. In the context of politics, it may be reasonable to say that a certain democratic system is to be admired in that it is fair, free, and in other respects genuinely democratic, even though the decisions made by this democratic body may often be regrettable. But in the context of morality, it is not all right to say that if the procedures for decision-making are morally defensible, it does not matter what the decisions are. Yet a quite common phenomenon in offices and universities today is for careful attention to be paid to such procedural matters as ensuring representative membership of a disciplinary panel, ensuring that charges are made formally and opportunity for reply afforded, ensuring protection of witnesses, etc., but little or no attention at all is paid to the questions of whether such a panel proceeding in such a way is likely to make a sound and just decision, and whether the practices that are variously accepted and condemned are so categorized on morally acceptable grounds. Did this woman actually deserve to be promoted? Is cheating of that sort acceptable in this university? Ought an individual to be penalized for flirting with a colleague? Questions such as these are all too often not being addressed in any serious way, while the focus is entirely on ensuring that the rules governing the decision-making process are clearly adhered to. That is plainly inadequate. A duly constituted jury or panel, representative proportionately of all members of the community, and deliberating according to clearly formulated rules, can still deliver outrageous judgements or substantive injustice.

In the case of universities, it can be fairly confidently stated that they have all too often offended against substantive justice as a result of their preoccupation with procedural justice. This itself stems from fear of litigation. The institution has seen that it is vulnerable to charges of neglect, irresponsibility, etc., and has responded by creating procedures that conform to contemporary prejudices which are wrongly assumed to be moral (e.g. the requirement of student representation on all committees, boards, etc.; the requirement of diversity; the requirement that the committee be quorate; the requirement that the accused have a right of reply). It has then further assumed, and been allowed by the wider community to assume, that procedural justice, i.e. following these rules, is sufficient. But it is clearly quite insufficient if the result is a flow of unjust, immoral, unfair, or simply silly and unwarranted decisions. This is not the place to establish that such has often been the result, but there is plenty of evidence available to show that it has. When a newly appointed president of a university appoints his partner to a highly paid advisory position, complete with free housing; when a president is hounded into recanting the observation that there may be many reasons why women are not well represented in science faculties besides culpability on the part of the universities; when a senior administrator is fired for no apparent reason and then paid $400,000 on condition that he remains silent; when a university allows a professor to continue in employment while aware that he is guilty of fraudulent research; when two students who both purchased the same essay from a third party are given pass grades and not penalized for cheating – when such practices are rife, it is not morally acceptable to observe that procedural justice has not been compromised in any of these cases. Whether due process has been observed or not, what has happened has proved to be substantively unjust – to be immoral, and that, at the end of the day, is what counts. Morality is better served by a just outcome, even following some procedural glitch, than by smoothly working procedures that deliver unjust conclusions.

The language of both rights and procedural justice are aspects, though not exclusively and not necessarily the outcome, of so-called political and moral correctness. This (for they can be conflated for present purposes) is a movement that has more to do with moralizing than genuine morality, and has on more than one occasion proved to be downright immoral, as for example in its baneful effect on free speech and its promotion of censorship in many forms. It is concerned with advocacy rather than the dispassionate pursuit of truth, with coercing people into a preferred pattern of behaviour and set of beliefs rather than with exploring the grounds for that behaviour and those beliefs. The driving force behind the political correctness movement is ideology. There is no serious philosophical debate about, for example, the role of gender, the relationship between the sexes, what is and what is not inherently offensive, or whether freedom may or may not be more important than conformity; instead there are merely prescriptions for conduct and belief imposed on others by force of will, political pressure, intimidation, and shaming. But the use of the language of rights and procedural justice are powerful weapons for the politically correct. It is difficult to withstand for long the insistent cry that somebody's rights are being denied or that procedures have been abused, whether they have or not and whether it much matters whether they have or not. As I have said, in themselves rights and procedural justice do matter; but the terms are very often being used as little more than slogans, and they are not the only things that matter.

It is worth remembering that wrongdoing is not the only enemy of the moral; we should also guard equally strongly against inappropriate 'moral' indignation, moralizing, proceduralism, misuse of moral language, ideology, indoctrination, dogmatism, and censorship, to name but a few. A self-righteous, literal, and inflexible adherence to a specific moral code is inherently antithetical to true morality, which necessarily involves, in practice, a flexible and generous adherence to fundamental principles: nothing less, but also nothing more. As we shall see in Chapter 7 below, one of the sources of confusion in the moral domain is the unwarranted presumption that there is always a clear right or wrong to be discerned and that we should judge people by what they do rather than by their reasons for doing what they do, and judge moral theories by how much clear practical guidance they give us rather than by how convincingly they explain morality. To approach morality by focusing on rights or on procedural justice is to miss the intricacy, subtlety, and complexity of morality, and it is to substitute dogmatism and mechanistic thinking for understanding.

The argument of Part I may be summarized as follows. We cannot turn to God or nature to find backing, legitimacy, or grounding for our moral views, for a variety of reasons ranging from our lack of clarity as to what is meant by God or nature and uncertainty as to what either of them in fact demands, to lack of obvious reason to regard whatever they 'demand' as necessarily moral. Similarly, it is confusing rather than helpful to think in terms of rights or procedural justice. It is not that we cannot arrive at a conclusion that certain rights should be respected or that we need not concern ourselves about having just procedures. It is that morality is about a great deal more than a list of inflexible rights or formally just procedures; sometimes just procedures and the upholding of rights combine to produce unjust situations, and, more broadly, emphasis on rights and procedures appears to be in various ways deleterious. More generally, we should avoid being intimidated by the idea that we have to choose between a number of historical schools of thought or systems of classification of moral theory. We need to give attention to what a moral theory is for, and to what we can and should expect from it.

On the other hand, positively, there are some basic facts about the nature of moral language (e.g., it is prescriptive and universalizable), and it is also the case that moral conduct is principled rather than rule-bound. There is reason to suppose that a moral sense, perhaps most conveniently represented as a sense of the importance of integrity, is as widespread and perhaps as reliable as the sense of physical sight. But, in order to arrive at a better understanding of what constitutes moral integrity or the nature of morality, one must first avoid expecting too much of moral philosophy, in particular expecting the wrong kind of thing. Moral codes are to be differentiated from moral theories. Moral philosophy is not going to lead to a *vade mecum* for life, because it is not supposed to. Nor should we judge the quality of a moral theory to any great extent by reference to its practical utility or its 'user-friendliness'. Rather, in order to ensure a clear and solid foundation on which to work, we should distinguish between moral and various kinds of non-moral value, between what is right in itself and what, though it may be bad or wrong in itself, can be justified. Problems that are in practice soluble need to be distinguished from those that are in practice insoluble, and dilemmas, which are by their nature insoluble, need to be distinguished from problems of any sort. Bearing these and similar basic distinctions in mind, recognizing that to a degree we have to rely on intuition and self-evidence in moral matters, but acknowledging also that the whole enterprise is predicated on some sense of people's well-being, we need now to build a positive theory by looking for the fundamental principles that define and hence govern the moral enterprise. Morality is certainly good for society or for people in general, even if it is admitted that there is no independent argument to dissuade an individual who wishes to and thinks he can get away with taking advantage of the system. A moral theory, like love or a library classification system, is partly given in nature in some sense, and partly man-made, but it is emphatically not arbitrary. Our objective is to lay out a moral theory by using dispassionate reason such that few, if any, will in sincerity be able to dissent from the conclusions.

Commentary

Emotivism is particularly associated with A.J. Ayer, whose *Language, Truth and Logic*, drawing to some extent on ideas derived from the Viennese school of logical positivism, had a major impact at the time, seeming to dismiss religious, moral, and aesthetic discourse as in a literal sense non-sense, and with C.L. Stevenson, who put more emphasis than Ayer on 'creating an influence'. The Vienna Circle is generally taken to have been founded by Moritz Schlick (1882–1936). The basic credo of the group was the so-called 'verification principle', according to which to be meaningful a statement must either be true by definition ('All bachelors are unmarried men') or be verifiable in principle by experience. They then argued that since a proposition such as 'God exists' is not amenable to any empirical test, it can be classified as 'meaningless', which does not of course necessarily mean that it is functionless or serves no purpose. Indeed, the point of Ayer's brand of emotivism was to say that both moral and religious discourse do have a function; it is just that they don't produce statements that are capable of being true or false. A common criticism of logical positivism has been that the status of the verification principle itself seems to contradict the theory, for it does not appear to be either tautologous (true by definition) or empirically testable.

'Prescriptivism' and 'universalizability' are terms taken from R.M. Hare's influential *The Language of Morals*. Working to some extent in the Kantian tradition here, Hare also wrote *Freedom and Reason*, which shows some clear affinities with utilitarianism, even as he critiques it. His *Moral Thinking: Its Levels, Methods and Point* refines and furthers his views on the nature of moral discourse.

In addition to the references to works on natural law given in the Commentary on Chapter 2 above, see L.W. Sumner *The Moral Foundation of Rights*. Both Mary Ann Glendon *Rights Talk* and Michael Ignatieff *The Rights Revolution* raise an interesting range of questions about the practical implications of the way we talk about and codify rights in contemporary society. D.J. Enright *Injury Time* comments in characteristically trenchant style: 'once we start to talk about human rights, there is no end to it. Often there ought to be, and promptly' (p. 49). Roger Scruton is similarly caustic in *Gentle Regrets*:

> But this world of rights and claims and litigation is a profoundly unhappy one, since it is a world in which no one accepts misfortune, and every reversal is a cause of bitterness, anger and blame. Misfortune becomes an injustice, and a ground for compensation. Hence our world is full of hatred – hatred for the other, who has got what is mine.
>
> (p. 238)

On the more strictly philosophical front, useful collections are: A.I. Melden (ed.) *Human Rights*; Joel Feinberg *Rights, Justice, and the Bounds of Liberty*; Maurice Cranston *What Are Human Rights?*; Jeremy Waldron (ed.) *Theories of Rights*; and Peter Jones *Rights*.

As I say in the body of this chapter, proceduralism appears to be a particularly institutional problem. I am not aware of a great deal of material relating to this issue, though some papers touching upon it are to be found in Robin Barrow and Patrick Keeney (eds) *Academic Ethics*. It is touched on, sometimes directly, sometimes obliquely, in a number of books concerned with higher education in the context of such things as political correctness and harassment procedures. See, for example, Page Smith *Killing the Spirit*; Dinesh D'Souza *Illiberal Education*; Nat Hentoff *Free Speech for Me – But Not for Thee*; and Keith Windschuttle *The Killing of History*. See also Neil Boyd *Big Sister* and Sarah Dunant (ed.) *The War of the Words*.

The incidents referred to as examples of questionable practice in universities regardless of 'whether due process has been observed or not' are all recent events that did actually take place. I have not bothered to provide details or sources as they are also all too commonplace.

Part II
Outline of a moral theory

5 Principles that define morality

Conventional wisdom has it that moral viewpoints differ widely from place to place, time to time, and person to person. It is certainly true that what are taken to be moral claims often differ. But this is not to say that morality does not have certain defining characteristics which would be recognized and acknowledged across cultural and historical periods. In this chapter I am going to argue that there are five such defining characteristics, and I suggest that, while philosophers as different as, say, Plato, Kant, Hume, Mill, Moore, Ewing, or Blackburn may subscribe to distinctive moral theories which involve a considerable degree of specific disagreement, they and most other philosophers throughout history would nonetheless agree that these five characteristics represent fundamental moral principles. The principles also seem to resonate or fit with what most ordinary people feel about morality, although most ordinary people don't articulate their reasoning in this way and other philosophers would perhaps not use the same language or express the argument in the way that I do. (I also believe that the principles presented here, although there is no denying that they are argued for and expressed in a manner that belongs to a Western tradition of philosophical thought, represent values that are shared by other major traditions such as Confucianism and Buddhism. But I will not pursue that line of thought here.)

The first principle is that of fairness. Who, whatever his or her specific moral values and general viewpoint, could deny that morality is by its very nature, among other things, about fairness? One cannot conceive of somebody arguing that being fair is not a moral consideration. There are of course people who are not fair or do not act fairly, and perhaps even some who claim that they see no good reason to be fair. Sometimes an individual may attempt to justify acting unfairly in a particular situation. But none of that makes any difference to the point at issue here. Certainly there can be situations in which it is justifiable to act in a way that is in some sense unfair: as we have seen, in life we sometimes face dilemmas and have no choice but to commit what we call 'the lesser of two evils'. As any parent knows, one sometimes has good reason to treat one's children in ways that are not strictly fair. More broadly, many would argue, for example, that while various features of our taxation system are to some degree unfair, they are nonetheless morally defensible. So most of us are familiar with and even ready to condone unfairness on occasion. But that does not mean that we cannot see that fairness is a moral consideration. Similarly, the fact that some people act unfairly or claim not be bothered about fairness in itself tells us only that some people are not very concerned about being moral. What nobody could coherently say and, as far I know, nobody has ever tried to say, is 'I care greatly about being moral, but I see no reason to try and be fair.'

Fairness, in other words, is built in to the very notion of morality, regardless of what particular moral views you hold or what particular moral code you adopt. If you say that morality requires that people receive the same reward for the same work or that older people deserve more than younger people do, in either case part of what you are saying is that the distribution you favour is a fair one. Does this perhaps merely mean that 'fair' is a synonym for 'moral'? No, it does not. One can proceed fairly but fail to act morally because, as we shall see, there is more to morality than fairness; but it is a necessary feature of morality on anybody's view.

There are various other terms, notably 'justice', 'impartiality', and 'equality', that need to be considered here. Unfortunately, we cannot reasonably pin any of these words to a categorical and distinctive meaning. The fact is that different people use them slightly differently and the same people sometimes use them differently on different occasions, with the result that sometimes the various words function as synonyms and at others they do not. So in what follows I am to a large extent stipulating how I would differentiate the terms: the important thing is that, however we choose to use the various words, the distinctions that I refer to are there to be made.

One might say that fairness implies equality and perhaps that fair treatment is equal treatment. But 'equal treatment' is itself notoriously ambiguous as between meaning 'treating people in the same way' and 'treating them with equal respect and concern'. In distributing food to a group of men, women, and children, for example, equal treatment could mean giving them all the same rations or giving them what is appropriate to their different appetites and needs. Likewise, there is a distinction to be made between equality in the sense of equality of outcome and in the sense of equality of opportunity. At the end of the day these well-known distinctions need to be thought about, but for the moment a distinction needs to be drawn between a concern for any of these things (equal opportunity, equal outcome, equal provision, and equal respect) and a more basic concern that people should be treated the same except where there are relevant reasons for treating them differently, which I call the principle of fairness. It can be expressed in other ways, but 'fairness' seems the commonest and simplest term, and fairness in this sense differs from equality in that the latter, whatever interpretation one gives to it, operates at a slightly more down-to-earth level. Fairness is a very general and abstract concept; once we have accepted the need to be fair, we begin to get involved in debate about what is fair in particular situations and this will involve paying attention to the lower-order question of what equal treatment implies, because equal treatment in some sense(s) or other is certainly a part of fairness. But it is not the whole of it.

This, of course, is part of the reason why there is no real dispute about fairness: it is because it is very general and abstract that we can all buy into it, in a way that, once we get more specific and down to earth and start thinking about food distribution, we cannot so easily do. It may also be pointed out, correctly, that of course 'fairness' will be generally acknowledged as a moral principle, since by definition it is a good thing and 'unfairness' a bad thing. Fairness could no more be regarded as bad than goodness could; they are both prime normative terms. This is true, and to claim to have an understanding of morality we shall need to do rather more than simply establish that fairness is good. Nonetheless, fairness – giving the same consideration to all in the sense of treating them similarly, except when there are good reasons for doing otherwise – is one undeniable defining principle of morality.

With regard to 'justice' and 'impartiality' not a great deal needs to be said here. 'Justice' is a word that, if only because of variations in its meaning over time and in different contexts and places, is perhaps best confined to a legal sense. Some have used 'justice' as more or less a synonym for 'morality', some as an equivalent to 'equality', and some indeed as an equivalent to 'fairness'. Clearly, I have nothing against justice, or any deep-rooted view about the word's meaning; for clarity's sake, however, I suggest that we do not use it. 'Impartiality', on the other hand, could be said to be synonymous with 'fairness'. Fairness and impartiality also both differ from equality in necessarily implying treating people according to certain rules or norms. One could treat a group of people equally, but unfairly, in that we ignore their claims equally. At a trivial level, it is unfair for an umpire to call a foul on players for no infringement of the rules, and it remains unfair even if he treats all players alike or equally.

This last consideration brings us to a second principle that is a necessary feature of anything that can count as a moral theory, another principle that, I maintain, any philosopher would accept: the principle of respect for persons as ends in themselves. This is distinct from the principle of fairness, although very closely related, in that the former simply maintains that all people should be treated the same except where there are relevant differences, whereas the principle of respect for persons (shorthand for 'recognizing and treating people as ends in themselves') maintains not that they should be treated the same in general, but that, more specifically, they are all equally to be recognized as autonomous beings who cannot be treated as if they were material objects or as a means to other people's ends.

Some readers, while sharing the sentiment that all human beings should be considered as ends in themselves rather than as a means to somebody else's purpose or gratification, may reasonably say that very obviously this principle is not universally recognized: from the explicit belief of the Nazis that various categories of person (e.g. Jews, gypsies, homosexuals) were not human and did not count as ends in themselves, to the less explicit but quite widespread view that various individuals or groups are beyond the pale (e.g. gypsies again, street people, drug addicts), there is surely evidence that this is not a principle that everybody accepts.

Generally speaking, the fact that a person or group denies a claim should not be taken as sufficient to establish its falsity, or even as directly relevant to the question of whether the claim is true. The fact that some people believe that the earth is flat has no bearing on that fact that it is not. It is true that it is part of my argument that there are certain basic claims about morality that nobody denies. But in this case, it is not clear that they would deny it, if they fully understood the issue. Second, the claim is not that every human being must share this view, but that historically all philosophers have either shared it explicitly or would have if pressed to consider the issue. Third, the real question is whether, on reflection, the reader shares this view. In other words, the key question is whether you, the reader, acknowledge that, on reflection, part of what you understand by a moral world is one in which no person or group of people can be assumed to be mere means for the use of others. Even slave owners attempted to justify their practice by some reasoning, not simply by asserting that some people are mere means. Even the Nazis went to the trouble of inventing claims about Jews, to justify their actions. They did not simply say: it is self-evident that we can use Jews as means to our ends if we want.

Nor should we allow the issue to be clouded by the fact that sometimes we do, whether we like it or not, whether we admit it or not, feel antipathy to people or argue that they have forfeited their right to certain kinds of consideration. Of course, if a man is a serial rapist, we can both abhor him and treat him differently from others; that is entirely in accord with fairness and with respect for persons as a principle. What the principle requires of us is that prior to discovering that somebody has offended in some way we assume his equal right to be treated as an end in himself, and that when we do recognize somebody as deserving of some kind of penalty or punishment, we nonetheless acknowledge that all the same he is not a mere means to our ends, a chattel for our use.

A principle of freedom is a third inevitable part of anything that is going to count as a moral theory. There are people who unreflectively assume that being moral consists simply in obeying certain precepts. But even they would surely recognize, if pressed, the distinction between following these precepts freely, by choice, and following them when threatened or forced to do so. This is a recognition of the fundamental point that part of what it means to act morally (regardless of the particular moral code you subscribe to) is to act freely, to act because you see it as your duty and not simply for hope of some reward or to avoid some pain. Even those who believe that there will be a necessary reward in Heaven, and who therefore to a degree may be said to be motivated by reward, know full well that even in terms of their own faith it is insufficient to act purely for the sake of that reward: one must also freely choose to act in this way because it is good.

At this stage we do not have to commit ourselves to any particular claims about freedom. Whether freedom of speech should be absolute, for example, whether one should be free to be abusive on occasion, whether there is such a thing as economic slavery and whether it can be justified, and how we are going to reconcile your freedom to act with mine are all crucial questions that moral philosophy ultimately has to come to grips with. We cannot at this stage define morality in terms of, say, absolute freedom of speech, for to do so would be to beg a contentious question. But to say that there must be freedom where there is morality does not beg any question. It makes an important point about the meaning of moral behaviour, which is, among other things, freely chosen behaviour, engaged in because the agent sees it as incumbent on him morally.

So a moral world is without question a world in which freedom is valued, but that does not necessarily mean freedom to do anything or freedom from everything. In point of fact, as already noted, in practice freedoms often clash, so it is inconceivable that we should all be free to do anything. An old saw has it that 'ought implies can'; if we cannot all in practice be free to do exactly what we want, because our free choices will clash sometimes, then it makes no sense to say that we ought to be. Morality, therefore, is not to be defined in terms of any particular freedoms (though we may later establish some by further argument), but it is to be defined partly in terms of recognizing a principle of freedom – the recognition that freedom is a moral consideration in a way that, for example, wealth and sex are not. There may ultimately be a case for various moral rules relating to both sex and wealth, but the idea of morality does not in itself self-evidently involve any reference to either. One would not say on encountering an island tribe who had no notion of or interest in wealth, that it obviously had no moral sense. But one would say exactly that of any society that allowed individuals absolutely no freedom. Freedom is a necessary moral consideration.

Truth is likewise universally acknowledged by philosophers of rival schools to be a moral good and an integral principle to any theory that is going to count as a moral theory. It could hardly be otherwise, since philosophers of whatever school are engaged in arguing for the truth of their viewpoint. So truth in the abstract, again as distinct from any particular truths, is seen to be another acknowledged value. It is perhaps conceivable that some would say that it is a value, but not a moral value. But it is surely impossible to make sense of the idea of a moral theory that does not involve caring (morally) that the moral claims made are true. It is not only of moral concern that we be kind, but also of moral concern that it be true to say that we should be kind.

To argue that any moral theory must value truth is quite distinct from saying that it is always morally right to tell the truth. In fact, it is distinct even from saying that it is generally right to tell the truth, although most moral theories would claim this, while allowing that we may nonetheless sometimes be justified in not doing so. Just as insisting that it is part of the nature of morality, on any view, that it should have a *prima facie* commitment to a principle of freedom does not imply anything specific about what particular freedoms are justified, necessary, or overriding, so insisting that truth is a moral value, or that there is a *prima facie* commitment to truth, does not imply anything specific about when or where it may be legitimate to ignore the truth.

Thought ultimately has to be given to the question of when it is morally legitimate to lie, suppress the truth, and so forth (questions which again may not have the definitive answers we would hope for), and to the distinction between valuing truth and valuing truth-telling. The latter two are obviously related and valuing truth presumably leads to valuing truth-telling to some extent. But there is a distinction between valuing truth in the sense of thinking it important that we get things right and approving of people telling the truth to one another. We might mark this distinction by referring to the former as the value of truth in inquiry, the latter as the value of truth in social intercourse. One might, for example, insist that scientists proceed honestly and arrive at true conclusions, without assuming that they should also give a true account of these conclusions to the world (if, for example, they are researching potentially lethal germs). But for the moment it is enough to say that a premium on truth is built into the very idea of morality.

The fifth principle to be introduced has already been mentioned: it is a principle relating to people's well-being. As I said in Chapter 2 above, it is not easy to find the most suitable name for this principle (happiness, benevolence, felicity, goodwill, non-malevolence, non-suffering), and to some extent these different labels may pick out subtly different concepts. A principle of 'benevolence' and a principle of 'goodwill' may just be two names for the same thing, or they may have slightly different connotations; and certainly there is a difference, however slight, between positive formulations such as 'benevolence' and the negative formulation 'non-malevolence', just as there is a difference between promoting happiness and diminishing suffering. As with the previous four principles, since the claim is that morality necessarily involves reference to them but at a very high level, such that it would be a mistake to understand them in terms of a set of specific rules, so here we need a general non-question-begging term, and that is a reason for opting for 'well-being'. Though it is not ideal, it seems more open and general than, say, happiness. And while some might want to argue that morality does not necessarily have anything to do with happiness, at least if that word implies conscious satisfaction and gratification of desires, I do not see how anyone could argue that a moral theory need not have any reference to people's well-being in any sense.

There is room for argument about what precisely the parameters of well-being may be, what induces it, both generally and in particular cases, and whether or when it should override other moral considerations. But the point here is to establish that a society that had a code of conduct that made no reference to people's well-being, even implicitly, would not have anything recognizable as a moral code. In the first place, it is hard to make sense of the notion that a claim such as that one ought to keep promises or ought not to steal could be made without presuming that to some extent in some way it was to the advantage of people to abide by these rules. 'One ought not to steal, I know; but it's a great shame, because we'd all be so much better off if we didn't have this rule' seems distinctly odd. Of course, as already conceded, there are complex and difficult questions to be answered about what does make people 'better off' or 'advantage' them, but that doesn't alter the fact that anything that is going to count as a moral code has to be presumed to be to the advantage of people, individually, collectively, or both, in some way or another. Part of the point of moral behaviour (and we should remember here that we are divorcing morality from religion and are therefore not thinking in terms of doing as we are told for the sake of salvation) is to regulate conduct according to certain standards or norms, but the regulation has to be to some purpose, and surely it is our well-being that is our ultimate concern, considering ourselves as social animals.

I am tempted to add a sixth principle of beauty or aesthetic quality, but I am not going to do so. I am tempted to do so because I personally identify with those philosophers who value beauty or aesthetic quality highly and think a world enhanced by beauty to be a better place morally as well as aesthetically. I would not identify the Beautiful with the Good, as some have done, and I would not argue that morality and aesthetics are indistinguishable (they are not); but I do incline to the view that a moral world would be as much concerned to combat ugliness as to combat falsehood, unhappiness, and so forth. I mention this view only to set it aside, in order to remind the reader that we have not merely been discussing values that I happen to hold; if we were, then a principle of beauty should certainly be included. But we have been discussing values that there is reason to think are undeniably part of the meaning of morality, part of what it is, regardless of one's particular situation or philosophical standpoint. I happen to value beauty as much as freedom, but I have to acknowledge both that many others do not and, more importantly, that it is not absurd to argue that, on the contrary, it is entirely distinct from and has nothing to do with morality. But that cannot be said of the other five principles: it *would* be absurd to argue that fairness, respect for persons, truth-telling, freedom, and well-being have nothing to do with morality. They are clearly, self-evidently, and undeniably (both logically and in historical fact) necessary features of what we understand morality (as distinct from any particular elaborated theory or moral code) to be. Morality is, by definition, about a *prima facie* premium being placed on being fair, recognizing all persons as ends in themselves, concern for truth, freedom, and well-being. These principles (and no others, I think) define the territory. (They do not of course tell us precisely what we ought to do on any given occasion.)

It might be thought that I am simply begging the question: I am defining morality in this way, but what is to stop somebody else defining it in a different way? But this question is misplaced. I am arguing and appealing to the reader to recognize the validity of the argument that if we think about what we understand by a moral as opposed to a non-moral theory we see that these principles are embedded in it. Only the reader can judge whether I have been successful.

Commentary

I have named seven philosophers by way of example (despite my avowed intent to avoid reference to particular individuals). They are supposed to represent a more or less random cross-section of philosophical opinion over time. Plato, the father of philosophy, has already been introduced. The German philosopher Immanuel Kant (1724–1804) has been extremely influential through works such as the *Critique of Pure Reason* and *Groundwork of the Metaphysic of Morals*. The Scotsman David Hume (1711–76) is often cited as one of the foremost thinkers in a distinctively British line of empirically minded philosophers. His most famous work is *A Treatise of Human Nature*, but note also *An Inquiry concerning the Principles of Morals* and his *Political Essays*.

John Stuart Mill, G.E. Moore , and A.C. Ewing have already been referred to. Simon Blackburn has the misfortune of being selected as a representative of contemporary moral philosophy. His books include the previously cited *Ethics* and *Truth*.

There is a mass of literature on each of the five principles that I suggest define morality. The approach that I take, trying to extract substantive

principles from an understanding of what 'morality' is or means, owes
something to the previously cited works of R.M. Hare and Geoffrey Warnock,
and to P.H. Nowell-Smith *Ethics*.

> Normative: a term or sentence, etc., is normative if its basic uses involve
> prescribing norms or standards, explicitly or implicitly; e.g., 'ought' is
> normative, and so is 'good', for anyone holding that, for example, 'Piety
> is good' either means or entails 'one ought to be pious'.
>
> (A.R. Lacey *A Dictionary of Philosophy*)

S.I. Benn and R.S. Peters *Social Principles and the Democratic State*,
though focused on political philosophy, is extremely useful in relation to most
of the concepts introduced here, particularly respect for persons and equality.
On the latter, see also John Wilson *Equality*. There are some interesting points
made about impartiality in Alan Montefiore (ed.) *Neutrality and Impartiality*.
H.L.A. Hart *Law, Liberty and Morality*, though beyond the immediate concerns of this chapter, remains a classic in its field. Of the many books and
papers relating to freedom, note Ted Honderich (ed.) *Essays on Freedom of
Action*. See also G. Pitcher (ed.) *Truth* and T.A. Roberts *The Concept
of Benevolence*. A comprehensive introduction to moral philosophy that
includes concern for these various concepts is John Hospers *Human Conduct*.
See also Wilfred Sellars and John Hospers (eds) *Readings in Ethical Theory*.

In commenting on the difficulty of choosing between 'happiness' and
other similar but not identical terms, I might have added that some opt for the
Greek word *eudaimonia*. The problem with that tactic is that some people use
it because they wish to refer to the specifically Greek concept of *eudaimonia*
(conventionally translated 'happiness' but in various respects quite distinct
from our everyday conception), while others revert to it precisely to avoid any
particular connotations, on the assumption that the reader will not be familiar
with the intricacies of the Greek concept.

The example of providing more food for an adult than a baby is first
recorded by Plato in the *Republic*. He also identified the Good and the
Beautiful, though there is room for argument as to how exactly to interpret
him, not least because the Greek word *kalon* ('beautiful', 'noble', 'good',
'right') covers a wide area, rather as the English words 'fine' or even
'good' do today. G.E. Moore more explicitly argued that beauty was a moral
good. On the question of freedom of speech, see below, Chapter 8.

6 Reasons for being moral

'Why should I be moral?' was a popular examination question for under-graduates at Oxford in the 1960s. In line with much of the analytic philosophy to the fore at that time and place, the general presumption was that one would respond by recognizing and unpacking the logic of the term 'moral' itself. More specifically, one would recognize the question as a strange one, since 'moral' referred to one's duty or what ought to be done. To ask for a reason to act morally suggests that one does not understand what morality is, just as to ask whether beauty is preferable to ugliness betrays a lack of understanding of the logic of the words in question: beauty is preferable to ugliness by definition; its intrinsic value is part of the meaning of 'beauty'.

Such an answer is all very well as far as it goes. Beauty is indeed by defi-nition preferable to ugliness, and morality is by definition a set of principles to guide conduct that is incumbent upon us. But in neither case does the answer get us very far; it certainly does not get us where we want to go. Once it is acknowledged, for example, that beauty is intrinsically good, we are faced with some rather more important and difficult questions: what is beauty or what are the defining characteristics of beauty? What things are beautiful? To what extent should the beautiful be pursued at the expense of other things?

Similarly, we may agree that to be moral is necessarily the right or a good thing to be, preferable by definition to being immoral, but this leaves open some rather more significant questions such as 'How do you determine what conduct is moral?' or 'What is it morally right to do?' And, if an answer to these questions is sketched out, for example in terms of the five principles introduced in the previous chapter, the question 'Why should I be moral?' returns but with the more specific sense of 'Why should I conduct my life in accordance with the principles of freedom, fairness, respect for others, truth, and well-being?' Then there is the further question of what commitment to these five abstract and general principles leads to in practical terms: when, for example, is it right or justifiable to tell a lie or desert a friend? Should I, for instance, risk torture and death to save a friend in time of war?

Let us focus here on the question of why I should accept, in the sense of determine to try and live by, these principles that define morality. It is true that some reasons have already been given for presenting these particular principles as defining morality, and one can therefore argue along these lines: morality refers to what ought to be done; reasons have been given for selecting certain principles rather than others to guide us in determining what ought to be done; therefore reasons have been given for behaving morally in this sense. This reasoning is coherent and has force; it is not, for example, merely circular. But psychologically it is doubtful how persuasive it will be. More needs to be said, if we are to convince sceptics and doubters that they should abide by these principles whether or not it is to their immediate advantage to do so.

Morality has been admitted to be, in some sense and to some degree, a human construct. That is to say, human beings have used their minds to evolve a view of a certain kind of conduct as ideally incumbent upon us. But this view of morally desirable conduct, if it is to be plausible and acceptable, must be based on facts and constraints of human nature, other facts of life, and points of logic. So, though evolved by humans, not anything that humans produce can count as a moral theory; a true moral theory must be constrained by logic and reality. It is conceded that it is hard to make sense of the rival idea that morality is somehow entirely given in nature as opposed to developed out of our understanding and ideals.

Why, then, should a particular individual play the moral game? Granted that if one chooses to play it one needs to understand its nature and rules, just as if one wants to be an artist one needs to understand what humans take art to involve and what they expect from it, the question remains: why should one play the game? After all, nobody supposes that we are all obliged to care about art or to become artists. Certainly, morality is distinctive in that it is about behaviour that ought to be engaged in, but why should I agree to be concerned about behaviour that ought or ought not to be engaged in in the first place?

One of the oldest answers to this question is that God requires it of us and that immorality will lead to damnation, fire, and brimstone in an eternal Hell; the moral life on earth will be rewarded in the after-life. There are those who still firmly believe this, but, for reasons already given, this line of argument cannot be accepted. It would provide a reason for acting morally, but it would be a prudential or selfish reason and not a moral reason; nor would it be a reason that would persuade those without faith or those who were willing to take a gamble on whether or not there is a God.

In addition to the unfortunate facts that there is not any plausible evidence for an after-life or indeed for God, that, if there were, there is no discernible way of distinguishing the true faith from false ones, and that, even if we were to accept that a certain religion has a claim to be the true one, we still have no way of knowing exactly what God wants of us, it being an open question whether the Bible, the Qur'an, or the evolved teaching of this or that Church accurately represents his views – in addition to all this, we are left with the problem that by 'acting morally' we do not mean 'doing what we are commanded to do for the sake of reward or fear of punishment', whether by God, the party, the state, or anyone else. By 'acting morally' we mean acting in ways that are in some sense good in themselves, because they *are* good, and not in response to command or for the sake of personal advantage either now or in the future.

The question is, even if I understand kindness to be an example of what we call a moral good, why should I be kind if I don't want to be or if I see some advantage to myself in not being so? What is there to persuade or convince me that I must try to be kind, once we have ruled out God, the after-life and any kind of reward, threat, or intimidation here on earth?

There is a variant on the religious argument that should be considered here. Granted that we have no conclusive reason to believe in the truth of any particular faith, and granted that there is no conclusive proof of God's existence, there might nonetheless be a God and there might be a Hell (to use Christian terminology). The arguments considered in relation to religion establish that its claims are not provable, not that they are false. That being the case, it might be wise, it might be prudent, to act kindly rather than unkindly on the grounds that, if God does exist, the penalty for having lived immorally will far outweigh the disadvantages of being kind. The best bet might be to put up with the inconvenience of being kind, which, if there turns out to be no eternal punishment, is only slight, and which, if there is eternal punishment, will prove to have been a very sound investment. There is also a non-religious version of this argument. Many believe that the basis of morality is to be found in a social contract of some sort. This might involve a historical claim to the effect that as a matter of fact people realized that in their own best interests they should contract with each other to tell the truth, keep promises, act impartially, and so forth. Alternatively, it may be argued that, while no such contract was ever formally made, morality should nonetheless be seen as a set of principles, rules, or behaviours that work to our mutual advantage and that we would contract into, were we to think about it. There are also various developments of this basic view, including, for instance, the suggestion that morality should be defined not simply in terms of principles that we recognize as generally beneficial, but specifically in terms of principles that we would subscribe to if we had no way of knowing in advance what our role, lot, or circumstances in life would be. For example, it might be argued that we would all see the justice in some degree of material equality, because none of us would want to risk setting up a system in which we might be a complete loser in a total free for all.

But all of these approaches have one common and fairly obvious drawback: they may present reasonable explanations of why people in general are well advised to formulate a moral viewpoint and act on it, but a prudential argument is not the same thing as a demonstration that something just is the right or proper thing to do. The religious wager does indeed provide a motive for acting morally. But it is unsatisfactory as an argument for convincing people that there is something compelling about moral conduct, and it obviously won't work at all with those who are convinced in their lack of faith. The various types of contract theory, whether seen as historical or more plausibly as logical, all provide a reasonable explanation for the origins or foundations of moral theory and a reasonable case for approving of morality overall in society. But they do nothing to persuade the individual who sees that he can gain positive advantage for himself by playing on the goodness of others. Why, other than for fear of God's wrath or the state's punishment, should *I* be moral? Why not take advantage of the moral goodness of others to cheat, lie, and generally pursue the immoral path? The tricky question is 'Why should *I* be moral?' rather than 'Why should I be *moral*?' To be sure, if we're all going to play cricket, we need to abide by the same rules. But why should I choose to play cricket? In the same way, if morality is merely a set of rules devised by humans for ease of life, why should I play? Why should I worry about being unkind any more than I worry about breaking the speed limit, provided that I can get away with it?

One possible response to this is as follows: there are good reasons for concluding that society as a whole should abide by the principles of freedom, fairness, respect, truth, and well-being. There is no difficulty, therefore, in establishing that these principles should govern our intercourse. But there is nothing that can be meaningfully said to the individual who proposes to take advantage of others by ignoring the principles, other than that, if detected, he will pay a price in terms of anything from disapproval, by way of ostracism, to punishment. At first blush, this response may seem to concede too much: it effectively says that there is no argument to establish that every individual should abide by moral principles beyond the fear of being found out and paying a price. But this is not quite so drastic an admission as may at first appear. The fact is that, if society as a whole recognizes the principles, people will be brought up to adhere to them and to appreciate the advantages of following them, and to some degree fear of shame or prison will keep people on the moral path even when tempted to stray. The few (and as a matter of fact, for whatever reason, it is generally a few) who nonetheless do proceed to break the moral rules flagrantly have simply to be guarded against. None of this would have any bearing on whether our depiction of morality in terms of certain principles and our belief that morality was both by definition and also in fact for the general good were well founded.

So much may be generally acknowledged. But one may argue further that there are certain considerations which, though when taken singly they do not establish what we are looking for, when taken together do, cumulatively and interdependently, add up to a case for saying that no individual could sincerely, in good faith, renounce morality, once they understood what they were renouncing. (That is to say, nobody could in good faith renounce the principled and flexible morality being discussed here. One might, of course, and with very good reason, reject any number of particular moral codes.) These considerations are to be found in our disposition or in human nature, in the fact that we cannot predict consequences routinely, in the logic of some of the principles themselves, and in our intuitive recognition of goodness. Each of these points has already been introduced and found insufficient in itself to establish a specific moral truth, but the argument here is that taken together they provide overwhelming reason for each and every one of us to abide by the five fundamental moral principles in question.

Moral sentiment and sense are not simply given in nature, as has been said. Humans are not without exception born with a disposition to be kind and generous or to tell the truth. On the other hand, humans as they have thus far evolved are generally disposed to proceed reasonably and morally, and they are predisposed to want and need certain things that are connected with morality. Humans, for example, do not like suffering, they are concerned with their well-being, they generally have some sense of others, they have an innate sense of fairness, and they do not want to be treated unfairly. The few may seek to take advantage, but all have some notion of doing as you would be done by. We all want to be treated as ends. We can see that some notion of truth-telling and promise-keeping is self-evidently necessary for any kind of predictable and reliable communication, and we are disposed to and can intuit the value of predictability and reliability. It requires no great intelligence to see that treating people differently for no good reason is arbitrary, and therefore unfair and offensive. And intuitionism is right to this extent: while we may condone or put up with this or that, we all see the beauty, the desirability, or, if you like, the goodness of the good. Those who torture, murder, steal, or otherwise act flagrantly immorally fall without exception into two groups: a very small group who genuinely see nothing wrong in their behaviour and who literally cannot understand the perspective of society as a whole, and the vast majority who will seek in one way or another to explain or justify their conduct. The latter show by their attempts to explain ('I was drunk and didn't know what I was doing') or justify ('I have been exploited all my life', 'It is necessary for some greater good') that they fully understand both the nature and force of morality; they merely, sincerely or insincerely, feel that they should be excused and forgiven. But, while they are guilty of acting immorally, they do not deny morality. As to the former, given their rarity and their singular vision, why should we not say that they are clearly morally blind, just as some are physically blind? We do not conclude that mountains and blue skies are not there, just because an unfortunate few cannot see them. Why should we conclude that the goodness of kindness and the wrongness of killing are illusory, just because a very small number of people cannot see them? And just as the philosophical difficulties surrounding knowledge, truth, and perception do not lead even philosophers to live their lives as if mountains and rivers were not there, so the difficulties of demonstrating fundamental moral truths beyond all doubt should not lead us to conclude that they must be false.

There are people who always put themselves first, there are people who are cruel by nature, and there are even those who never see what they do as wrong, but is it conceivable that anybody could think that causing pain gratuitously is intrinsically good or even morally neutral? Is there anybody who would justify telling lies on the grounds that it is immaterial?

Morality is bound up with behaviour that self-evidently suits and is to the advantage of human beings *qua* human beings, in respect of both overall social needs and individual satisfaction. The corollary is, of course, that all immoral conduct, when it is not the result of faulty reasoning, misinformation, or weakness of will, must be seen as aberrant in some way. People do wrong sometimes because they think incorrectly that what they are doing is right. This is an argument, however, within morality and not an argument about whether there is morality. Sometimes they do wrong because they give in to temptation, but again this does nothing to invalidate the idea of a universal moral truth. Sometimes they do wrong for reasons of self-protection or advantage, but know in themselves that they have done wrong. But occasionally people do seem quite unable to see the enormity of what they have done, and we should classify these people as psychopaths and recognize them as the exception that proves the rule. Most immoral conduct is not the work of sociopaths or psychopaths, but of ordinary people who at some level are fully aware that their conduct is not moral.

The line of reasoning I have adopted does not 'prove' that we ought to be moral, but it should be strong enough to show any reader (*ex hypothesi* somebody who is taking the question 'Why be moral?' seriously) why we should be moral: because we are who we are, because society is as it is, and because certain principles are what they are. You know if you decide to exploit others to your own advantage that you are doing wrong and you know that you should not behave in this manner (though you may well continue to do so); you know that while breaking this promise may be explicable and perhaps even justified, nonetheless it needs either explanation or justification, because in itself it is wrong; and you know that conduct that causes suffering for others stands in need of some kind of specifically moral justification, or else it is reprehensible.

In short, morality is a human construct in the sense that humans have made demands and set a pattern on behaviour, but the demands and pattern are bound by physical and logical laws. There are principles of conduct that make sense in terms of human intercourse and well-being and others that don't. This is something that the thoughtful can perceive. The ultimate answer to the question of why I should be moral is that, in addition to risking paying the price if I am not, in addition to it being absurd to imagine that I am somehow entitled to act differently from others, to fail to act morally is to turn one's back on a self-evidently advantageous and desirable human ideal.

Commentary

The question 'Why should I be moral?' lies behind the formal structure of Plato's *Republic*. In Book One Thrasymachus argues that no sensible person would behave morally if he could get away with not doing so; at the beginning of Book Two, Glaucon and Adeimantus less aggressively invite Socrates to establish that one should behave morally (be just) regardless of rewards on earth or in an after-life, and the remainder of the *Republic* sets out to do that. Chapters Two and Three of R.C. Cross and A.D. Woozley *Plato's Republic: a Philosophical Commentary* provide a good discussion of the relevant passages. For a contemporary argument see papers by Hospers and Nielsen in Chapter Five, section C, of Sellars and Hospers *Readings in Ethical Theory*.

The argument that on balance it is wise to presume the existence of God is often referred to as 'Pascal's wager'. The French philosopher Blaise Pascal (1632–62) was particularly interested in mathematics, physics, and religion. The *Pensées*, unpublished and indeed unfinished at the time of his death, is now his best-known work. It is here that he argues that, given that eternal happiness will be the result of belief in God and following the dictates of religion, if there is a God, and given that nothing is lost by believing in him if he does not exist, the reasonable gamble is to believe. Jamie Whyte *Bad Thoughts: a Guide to Clear Thinking* adds another objection to Pascal's argument:

> once you see that Pascal's wager supports equally not only Christianity, nor even all established religions, but all possible Heaven and Hell religions, the game is up. For infinitely many such religions are possible. Which will you choose? Choose any one of them and the chance that you have made the best bet is not 50:50 . . . it's one in infinity.

> (p. 29)

(The *Pensées* also contains the celebrated line 'the heart has its reasons of which the reason knows nothing'.)

Plato discusses contract theory obliquely. As noted in the Commentary on the Introduction above, Thomas Hobbes (1588–1679) in *Leviathan* advances the notion of a social contract, remarking that without one life would be 'solitary, poor, nasty, brutish and short'. Jean-Jacques Rousseau (1712–78) wrote *The Social Contract*. One of the most influential contemporary works in political (and moral) philosophy has been John Rawls *A Theory of Justice*, which has a strong contractual element.

References in respect of intuitionism have already been provided above in the Commentaries on the Introduction and Chapter 2, but, given the explicit reference to the Western tradition at the beginning of Chapter 5 above and the premise that reasoning is relevant to establishing moral truth, I should add here reference to some works on the broad theme of reason. See Richard Tarnas *The Passion of the Western Mind*, Robert Nozick *The Nature of Rationality*, and Roger Trigg *Reason and Commitment*.

It should be evident that this book is predicated on Francisco Goya's (1746–1828) precept that 'the sleep of reason brings forth monsters' (unfortunately misquoted as 'the dream of reason' in Ian Crofton *A Dictionary of Art Quotations*). I attempt in the text to do justice to sociological factors without accepting the extreme view that reality is simply a human construct. On this issue, see John Searle *The Construction of Social Reality*.

7 Relativism

There are certain moral principles that define morality. A system or code of conduct, if truly moral, must be based upon these principles of fairness, freedom, respect for persons, truth, and well-being. There is a self-evident value and desirability about these principles, since to posit unfairness or lack of well-being as goals seems to make no sense; truth and freedom, besides being intuitively preferable to falsehood and enslavement, are built into the very idea of moral conduct, and to treat others as mere means appears to be a flat contradiction of the spirit of morality. In addition, it is plainly to the advantage of all to abide by these principles whether we think in terms of the common good or in terms of the majority.

These first-order principles give rise to a number of second-order principles, so-called not because they are less important or less to be valued, but because they are less abstract and more specific. Thus, the first-order principle of truth leads to second-order principles such as sincerity and honesty, while kindness and friendship may be seen as second-order principles dependent on the principle of well-being. Several second-order principles derive from more than a single first-order principle, as tolerance may be seen as derivative from the three principles of freedom, truth, and well-being. More will be said about second-order principles in Chapter 8 below, but for the moment we need to note that they in turn may give rise to even more specific values such as fidelity and promise-keeping.

The real problem in relation to morality lies not with the question of whether there are first-order moral principles and, if so, whether the five that have been introduced are the true ones, but in interpreting them, or in trying to establish what we should actually do in the name of the principle of truth, well-being, or whatever. And the same problem arises with the second-order principles, even though they are more specific: granted that friendship is a good and that sincerity is to be valued, what am I actually supposed to do in the name of either? Surely friendship does not imply some determinate list of actions to be engaged in at all costs and in all situations; and surely 'sincerity' cannot be interpreted to demand that, for instance, we always, under any conditions, blurt out our true opinion. What, then, is morally required of a sincere person? What are the demands of friendship?

The need to interpret, and the problems and difficulties thus raised, are unavoidable. In the first place, even at the first-order and most general level of abstraction, the claims of the principles may clash. My freedom to play my trumpet loudly at night is in conflict with your freedom to enjoy a good night's sleep. The principle that I should be concerned for truth may sometimes be at odds with the principle of concern for people's well-being, as, for example, when I am threatened by a murderous lunatic and asked to reveal where his would-be victims are hiding. Sometimes, it is true, the various principles lend support to each other and help each other out; for example, in trying to determine a fair distribution of food we can look to the principle of well-being and argue that the full-grown adult needs more than the baby. But in general terms the principles do not provide an unambiguous and secure guide to appropriate action in particular cases.

It is important to remember here that moral theories are not designed to provide a sure and unambiguous guide to specific actions, and it is a mistake, though a common one, to judge them on this criterion. In the same way, one theory of aesthetics is not superior to another by virtue of its greater definitiveness or its more direct utility as a guide to evaluating the worth of works of art. The extent to which a moral or an aesthetic theory should give precise and unequivocal direction is a function of the nature of a particular case, not of some *a priori* presumption about a generally requisite degree of certainty. While those who say that morality is just a matter of arbitrary preferences are very wrong indeed, nonetheless morality is not an area where we can expect or are going to find specific incontrovertible rules for conduct in all situations. Recognizing that fact is one small part of grasping the true nature of morality. Nor is there anything remarkable or worrying about this: all sorts of different fields of human endeavour and inquiry allow of differing degrees of certainty, as the truths of mathematics are obviously more secure and particular than the truths of judgements in art. All that those who wish to have true understanding of morality need to worry about is being aware of and appreciating the degree and nature of certainty that is possible.

Even when principles do not clash, there are questions about what action a particular principle enjoins or demands of us. Regardless of the claims of other principles, what is required, for instance, in the name of a concern for well-being? Does it mean we should never harm another, and, if it does, what counts as harming? Is saying 'no' harming the child who wants a surfeit of cream and, if it is, does this make the parent who says 'no' immoral? Does the principle of well-being imply that we ought to go out of our way to help the less fortunate and the needy? If so, to what extent? Until we ourselves have become the poor and needy? Does the principle of truth demand only that I do not lie to you, or that I should also point out your unfortunate lack of charm and your ugliness? What is involved in treating a person as an end rather than as a means? Which am I doing when I invite you to accompany me on a weekend fishing trip? How do we tell? And, of course, exactly the same kinds of question can be asked about second-order principles such as kindness and friendship. What does kindness require of me in this particular situation, and is there never ever a moral justification for refraining from a kind act, if not actually being unkind? (Is it, indeed, possible to refrain from being kind, without actually being unkind?)

In order to deal adequately with such questions, one important task is to go beyond arguing about the status of moral principles and to attempt to analyse key moral concepts. A central concern of moral philosophy should be to consider the possible dimensions, the defining characteristics, the criteria that have to be met, in the case of concepts such as friendship, sincerity, tolerance, fidelity, cheating, treachery, meanness, and closed-mindedness, as well as explaining the contours of the first-order concepts. Analysis will not settle all disputes or solve all problems, because an analysis of the concept of friendship, for example, is not like a mathematical proof. One can demonstrate a truth in mathematics, but one cannot similarly demonstrate that friendship unequivocally means this and that. Rather one has to consider hints, suggestions, and possibilities and exercise judgement in the light of other things we know and believe. But, certainly, by spending time teasing out the implications of an idea like friendship, one can arrive at a clearer and more detailed understanding of it, and that is a necessary and helpful step towards making decisions as to what we should and should not do in the name of friendship. What constitutes true friendship may to a certain extent be debatable or negotiable, but it is not entirely open to choice: there are severe limits on what can be reasonably, truthfully, and meaningfully said about it.

Nonetheless, it is unlikely that analysis of this or any other moral concept will alone settle all moral problems in a definitive manner. And it is at this juncture that relativism appropriately comes in to the picture. Relativism, and associated notions such as subjectivism and postmodernism on some interpretations, have generally referred to some variant of the view that any set of moral values or principles is simply the product of preference, whether cultural (relativism), individual (subjectivism), or, more broadly, because the very idea of objective truth in any field is dismissed (postmodernism). This, as I hope I have already shown, is confused, mistaken, and wrong. Morality is not just any set of values a society chooses to adopt; they have to be principles of a certain kind, so that, for example, anyone who opted for a principle of walking downstairs backwards with closed eyes on the first of every month as a *moral* principle would simply be missing the point. More seriously and more realistically, one who adopted the guiding principle of pure and naked material self-interest might conceivably be smart, happy, and a number of other things, but he can no more claim that this is a moral principle than a person who 'writes' a book by doing no more than copying down verbatim the conversations he hears can claim to be following a literary or aesthetic principle.

A person who thinks that torturing, telling lies, betraying trust, and being intolerant are in themselves morally good (as distinct from occasionally possibly justified) is simply wrong. There are of course societies that have systematically done things that I am claiming are indisputably morally bad. But it may be doubted whether even such societies are really denying the moral principles in question. For instance, societies have been known to tear the hearts out of living people and to presume that they are justified in so doing; but if the justification lies in the priestly caste maintaining that this is the wish of the Gods or the necessary way to appease them, then there is not even a pretence of a moral justification. Nazis, Stalinists, Maoists, and many other horrific regimes have certainly seemed at first blush to have a different view of morality from the one that I am presenting. But in fact they do not. Closer examination shows them trying, by bad science, by bad argument, and unsuccessfully, but nonetheless trying, to justify their stance in familiar 'moral' terms. Thus they do not simply ignore or deny the principle that people are deserving of respect; they attempt to argue that for various reasons this or that group are not fully human or have forfeited their right to be considered as such; or perhaps they invoke some other recognizable principle such as that of the general good or well-being. The arguments are in these cases preposterous but they still revolve, however fallaciously, around a moral sense and one that is recognizable as such.

It is a grave error to see these political monsters as simply being amoral. Alas, they are generally all too human and their catastrophically immoral regimes owe more to false and pernicious moral reasoning than to a denial of morality. Immoral societies exist because they get away with implausible justifications, but the justifications, though based on crazy premises, misinformation, etc., are still cast in a form that bears witness to familiar and genuine moral values such as truth, well-being, and fairness. It is mistaken to assume that Hitler or anybody else didn't recognize these as fundamental moral values. The problem, to repeat this important point, is that they interpreted the principles differently.

But, while I have referred to examples of interpretations of the principles that are absurd and have led to horrendous wrong, it is nonetheless to be expected that there should be some differing interpretations of the principles, for there are variations in circumstance, including both material conditions and some legitimate differences in belief systems, from place to place and

BISHOP BURTON COLLEGE
LIBRARY

time to time. Of course, if you believe in a God who commands you not to covet your neighbour's ass and who will cast you into Hell if you do, you are going to see reason not to do so and to say that it should not be done. Your mistake is not due to a different conception of morality; your mistake is a failure to see that obeying a jealous God is something different from acting morally, and, very possibly, your thinking that there is a convincing reason to believe in such a God. Of course, if you have come to believe that some individual or group does not count as persons you will not respect them or treat them as such. But your mistake here is that you believe a lot of pseudo-scientific mumbo-jumbo about race, not that you have abandoned the principle of respect for persons. And beyond these glaring failures in rational thought may lie entirely legitimate differences at the level of particular practice: what counts as a kind or friendly act, what particular form kindliness and friendliness should take, is bound to differ in radically different cultures and societies; even whether it is justifiable to go back on a promise may differ according to circumstance.

The fact of cultural and temporal variations in particular moral practices, then, is neither a proof nor necessarily a sign of relative views of morality at the level of first-order moral principles or moral theory. It is a confirmation of what we all know and have no need to deny: different circumstances or situations make different demands on us, even though we continue to subscribe to the same basic principles. It may be said that we should all honour the dead. But some cultures, we know, bury the dead, some cremate them, and at least one is on record as eating them. Such differences speak to different climates or different sets of non-moral beliefs, not to a conflict of moral judgement. Friendship is always a good, but whether friendship should be between members of the same sex or opposite sexes, whether it should involve a sexual element, whether it should be proved, celebrated, or practised in this or that way are further essentially non-moral questions. To anticipate a point to be taken up later, reflection on friendship and human relationships generally may lead one to feel uneasy about the widespread tendency to see sexual relations as a moral issue at all, let alone a pivotal one. There is a notable difference between Classical Greek attitudes to sex, friendship, and love, for example, and contemporary Christian (or even post-Christian) attitudes, but it is far from clear that there is any moral, as opposed to religious, justification for our puritan attitudes. Of course treating people decently in sexual, or any other, relationships is a moral requirement and equally obviously rape, for example, is morally repugnant. But the extension of rape to so-called 'date rape', the idea that marriage is the morally right form of relationship, or the view that homosexuality is wrong, to take but three examples, seem on the face of it very problematic and probably quite unwarranted as moral positions. At any rate, the immediate point is that it is more or less inevitable that customs and attitudes surrounding relationships should differ from culture to culture, but that is a function of non-moral differences between cultures rather than a function of differing views of the fundamental nature of morality; where there are genuinely contrary moral positions, they, it is suggested, will be the outcome of faulty non-moral reasoning on the part of one society or another (or both).

The truth of the matter is, then, that many specific acts or practices may reasonably be regarded as morally appropriate or incumbent in one society and not in another, and that this in no way necessarily implies that the values in question are arbitrary matters of preference. But there is also another most important fact to be faced in relation to conflicting moral judgements; namely, that some moral problems are actually dilemmas rather than problems, meaning that it has to be conceded that there is no indisputably right way to solve them, not because in a specific case it is difficult to get the evidence or we in some way fail to mount an argument (although that obviously happens too), but because there is in the nature of things no straightforward solution. But the fact that there are such occurrences no more makes morality as a whole a subjective matter or a matter of taste than the fact that one is sometimes justified in breaking a promise invalidates the principle that promise-keeping is good.

The existence of admitted moral dilemmas no more threatens the objectivity of moral judgement in general than the fact that it is sometimes difficult to establish whether a work of art is good, bad, or indifferent means that there is no such thing as better and worse art. The mere fact that, as we have acknowledged, sometimes even our first-order principles may clash means that it is inevitable that we should be faced by some moral dilemmas. A common example is provided by the principles of fairness and freedom. Though I have distinguished between fairness and equality, we have seen that there is nonetheless a moral presumption in favour of equality deriving from the principle of fairness; fairness demands that people should get equal treatment, though there is room for debate about whether, when, and to what extent we should focus on equal opportunity or end result and whether or not certain further qualifications should be included. But, leaving such qualifications aside, it is clear that every specific rule that is established to ensure some aspect of equality is an infringement on people's freedom. The mechanisms devised to ensure that we can all receive an education, receive a certain minimum wage, have similar access to transport and so on are all constraints on our freedom. In short, first-order principles are universal and absolute in the sense that they must be part of any theory that is to be recognizable as moral, whatever the time and place, and in the sense that they are good without qualification. But they are not absolute in the quite different sense of admitting of no qualification or curtailment under any circumstances. Yet they nonetheless provide substantive guidance of practical import in that we must give consideration to first-order principles if we are to be moral, and, where there is no clash with another first-order principle or other practical impediment, following them ensures that our conduct is moral.

With the exception of clashes between first-order principles, both moral problems and moral dilemmas (i.e. moral problems, whether soluble or not) are complex matters involving both philosophical and empirical issues. For example, whether expressing sympathy to someone when one doesn't actually think that they deserve sympathy counts as an act of friendship is a philosophical, more specifically conceptual issue, while the question of whether such sympathy actually achieves anything is empirical. Whether abortion is morally acceptable, sometimes morally justifiable, or morally wrong depends not only on interpreting first-order principles such as those of respect for persons, freedom, and well-being, but also on further philosophical questions such as what constitutes a person, and on empirical questions such as what the state of the mother or the embryo may be. But an important conclusion needs to be drawn here that is commonly overlooked. If we are agreed that on an issue such as abortion the difficulty of establishing answers to so many different kinds of question and of weighing very unlike considerations against each other in the light of principles that make competing demands on us leaves us with a genuine dilemma, we are in fact confronted with a fairly clear moral imperative, and that is that the issue should be a matter of individual choice. This is not on the false grounds that freedom is the most important moral principle and that therefore free choice is always morally desirable, but on the grounds that where there is no convincing argument to settle the matter, it is wrong to treat either viewpoint as correct. There should therefore be no state ruling on the issue.

In a subsequent chapter we will consider some actions that are more specific than second-order, let alone first-order principles, such as gambling, smoking, and tax evasion. I shall argue that many commonly perceived moral issues are not moral issues at all and that it is a distressing tendency of our times to seek to legislate on too many particular practices on pseudo-moral grounds. Just as second-order principles pay a price for being more specific or particular than first-order principles, and that is that they are even more prone to qualification by circumstance, so the notion that very particular acts such as committing adultery or being drunk are in themselves immoral (as distinct from sometimes morally culpable, and as distinct from something other than immoral such as rude or boorish) is hard to sustain. And that should alert us to the possibility that the morality of our society should be gauged less by the number of demands and prohibitions we make on behaviour, and more on how much freedom we allow and how much tolerance we exhibit.

One must face up every so often in philosophy, given its abstract nature, to the question of how useful it is. How useful, for example, is it to come to the conclusion that there are a number of moral dilemmas where we literally do not and cannot know what it is right to do, or to recognize that even first-order principles, though fundamental, can clash and that they invariably need further interpretation? Well, if one is simply looking for dogmatic rules of conduct, it is not at all useful. But if we are looking for true understanding, it is very useful. It warns us that those who would sell us some particular moral code are false prophets; it enables us to see that being moral is something rather different from subscribing to a list of unyielding commandments and prohibitions. It gives us one moral judgement of great significance: beware those, such as religious zealots, ideological fanatics (whether hidebound *Telegraph* readers, embittered Marxists, or hopeless hippies), and other species who insist that they and their kind have privileged access to a revealed truth. Those who claim to know too much do not understand morality at all. On the other hand, those who maintain that there is nothing to understand, because it is all a matter of taste, of chance, or of self-interested choice are wrong too. Taste is indeed subjective, in the sense that its source is in the make-up of the individual, and it is arbitrary inasmuch as it might have been otherwise, as you like strawberry flavour and I do not. Morality is not a matter of taste in that sense. Generally speaking, if you take your neighbour's property, rape his wife, torture your dog, or lie and cheat your way through life, you do wrong, as surely as someone who drives over the speed limit breaks the law. Then again, those who maintain that it is moral for the strong to take advantage of the weak are obviously wrong too, although their position is slightly more interesting. There is no purchase for this view of morality, because the only sense of morality that we understand, whoever we are, is one that is intimately tied up with such fundamental values as freedom, respect, truth, well-being, and fairness. It may make sense to reject morality – to say I understand what it involves, that it has a self-evident value, and that it is, generally speaking, advantageous for us all, but I am going to ignore moral considerations – but it doesn't make sense to attempt to define morality in terms of exploiting, using, and maltreating others. It would be like arguing that love was about causing maximum pain. Such an argument betrays a basic inability to comprehend.

What has been said so far is useful, indeed it is essential, because it tells us what principles we have to be guided by; it tells us how to set about dealing with and responding to moral questions; it tells us very importantly that some are unanswerable, and thus tells us that often the morally appropriate thing to do is to avoid laying down a specific rule, and rather to value freedom and tolerance. Sometimes misconception is worse than ignorance. Understanding what has so far been revealed about morality should not only help us to proceed to examine further questions, but also warn us off dogmatic and unjustified commitment to rules that are not in fact warranted, commitment that has arguably proved more damaging throughout history than mere ignorance.

Commentary

'There is nothing either good or bad, but thinking makes it so.' Shakespeare's Hamlet (II. ii. 256–7) does not here endorse relativism, although the quotation is often taken to do so. Hamlet is not enunciating the view that whatever you think is good is good. He is politely disengaging from Rosencrantz; it is his way of saying 'if you think so . . .', rather than getting into an argument. Jamie Whyte *Bad Thoughts* maintains forthrightly:

> Cultural relativism is so absurd that it is hard to believe anyone can be so fevered as to assert it. If it were true, gods, planets, bacteria . . . would come into and go out of existence according to what people generally believe to exist. Which they obviously do not . . . Iranians believe there is only one god, not only in Iran, but everywhere. The belief cannot be true in Iran but false in Papua New Guinea. If it is false anywhere, it is false everywhere.
>
> (p. 149)

As mentioned in the Commentary on the Introduction above, Aristotle first drew attention to the need to expect different degrees of certainty in different subjects. On friendship, besides Aristotle's views in the *Nicomachean Ethics* referred to above, see Lawrence A. Blum *Friendship, Altruism and Morality*. On postmodernism, see Lyotard and Sim cited above in the Commentary on Chapter 3, and Christopher Butler *Postmodernism: a Very Short Introduction*. On rationality, see the brief discussion and references in the Commentary on Chapter 6 above, and on the view that might is right, see the Commentary on Chapter 2 above.

Somewhere, I feel, I must make a comment that goes beyond general reference to malignant regimes and refers to the particular scourge of our times: the terrorist. What does one say of the suicide bomber and other fanatics committed to killing in the name of a cause? One says that the argument shows unequivocally that there is no cause so securely founded and important that it could under any circumstance justify the deliberate, random slaughter of innocents. The terrorist may be sincerely committed to a creed or ideology but he cannot rationally justify either the foundational tenets of that ideology or the presumption of entitlement to destroy others in its name.

Herodotus (b. *c.* 484 BC) *Histories* is one of the earliest texts to exhibit a sociological interest in cultural variation. Herodotus travelled widely and was struck by differences between peoples, and he records that those 'Indians who are called Callatiae . . . eat their dead parents' (3.38) in the course of arguing that every nation regards its own customs as the best.

On abortion, which will be considered again in the next chapter, euthanasia and related issues in the field of what is sometimes called 'bio-ethics', there have been a number of publications in the last twenty-five years. See Robert Campbell *Ending Lives*, Ronald Dworkin *Life's Dominion*, Rosalind Hursthouse *Beginning Lives*, Jonathan Glover *Causing Death and Saving Lives*, Peter Singer *Rethinking Life and Death*, Joel Feinberg (ed.) *The Problem of Abortion*, and John Ladd (ed.) *Ethical Issues relating to Life and Death*. See also on ethical questions relating to genetic engineering, Michael J. Reiss and Roger Straughan *Improving Nature?*.

I should make it clear that I do not deny that rape may take place on a date or within marriage or that other sexual advances that, though short of rape, are unacceptable may take place. My point is that it is not helpful to use general terms or to extend the scope of familiar terms to include a variety of acts that are in a number of possibly significant ways quite distinct. W.S. Gilbert put it neatly in *The Gondoliers*: 'When everyone is somebody, then no one's anybody'. Call it what you will, plying somebody with drink, for example, with no particular intent initially in mind, and subsequently seducing her with her 'agreement', whether defensible, deplorable, unforgivable, or whatever, is quite obviously not to be equated with a paradigm case of rape, even if to some it is (rather strangely, perhaps) equally obnoxious. (Jamie Whyte again: 'I have even seen undergraduates, who I was fairly certain were virgins, marching with placards declaring "I am a rapist".' p. 150.) My further point is that sexual preferences, when pursued in private, do not have any moral dimension one way or the other. If, for example, the practice of one person urinating on a partner strikes one as disgusting, as it well may strike many readers, that is not to say that it is morally disgusting. See further the comments on rape in the next chapter.

Perhaps I do not emphasize quite enough in the text that tolerance is a key moral virtue and one which, alas, does not seem particularly to the fore today. It is a key virtue because of the limited nature of our legitimate moral certainty. There is moral truth. We have some moral knowledge. Nonetheless, there is unavoidably, for reasons that I try to explain, a fair amount of moral uncertainty, and that demands that we exercise open-mindedness and tolerance. (And, it must be stressed, it is a degree of moral uncertainty that we have to recognize, which is quite different from the erroneous supposition that moral judgements are subjective, relative – except in the specific sense outlined – or arbitrary.)

In this chapter, not for the first or the last time, I have referred to aesthetics as an illustrative device, sometimes in contrast to morality, sometimes as a parallel. Those who are interested in pursuing aesthetics or the philosophy of art might try: Ian Ground *Art or Bunk?*; John Hospers *Meaning and Truth in the Arts*; Roger Scruton *The Aesthetic Understanding*; B.R. Tilghman *But is it Art?*; Richard Wollheim *Art and its Objects*. R.W. Beardsmore has a book specifically titled *Art and Morality*, while Harold Osborne (ed.) *Aesthetics* is a collection of standard papers.

8   Second-order principles

First-order principles do not always provide clear and unambiguous direction. But sometimes they do, and sometimes they give rise to more specific second-order principles (so-called because they are at a lower level of generality and abstraction, rather than because they are of secondary importance).

Commitment to the principle of truth, for example, gives rise to further, more particular values such as sincerity, open-mindedness, and honesty, since these concepts are ineluctably tied up with the value of truth. They are good primarily because and in so far as truth matters, though they may also serve and hence be seen as derivative on other first-level principles: sincerity and honesty, for instance, are also characteristics that, broadly speaking, oil the wheels of social intercourse and contribute to well-being. Thus, we can say, in more concrete and specific terms than we could when focusing on first-order principles, that a moral person should be honest, sincere, and open-minded. The caveats still have to be acknowledged. Sincerity alone is not always enough. A sincere fanatic may do bad things. Sincerity, therefore, can be misplaced. And there may be occasions when one is justified even in being dishonest. Likewise, open-mindedness can sometimes be criticized on moral grounds. But honesty, sincerity, and open-mindedness are always in themselves good, which means that, other things being equal or in the absence of competing moral considerations, one should always aspire to be honest, sincere, and open-minded.

The value of a system of promising and other aspects of truth-telling are likewise derived from our commitment to the first-order principle of truth. That one should keep a promise is entailed by the notion of promising; it is self-evident that the purpose of a system of promising is defeated if one presumes that there is no obligation to keep a promise. But the commitment to the idea of promising in the first place is based on the moral value of truth. It may on occasion be morally justifiable to break a promise or tell a lie. But we recognize that in themselves (i.e. when there are no conflicting moral demands or practical restraints) promising and truth-telling are moral goods.

In recognizing these and other goods similarly derivative from one or more of the first-order principles we begin to build a more specific picture of moral conduct.

From the principle of well-being may be derived such further values as compassion, kindness, tolerance, friendship, trust, and perhaps beauty. The basic insight that a defining characteristic of morality is to enhance well-being leads directly to placing a value on these secondary moral characteristics. (Here too other first-order principles may endorse some of the same values, as trust is partly a value derivative from truth and tolerance partly derivative from freedom.)

One might say that intolerance is bad by definition; it is a word with negative connotations. But now we begin to see why it is bad: it offends against our fundamental commitment to freedom, as well as to truth and respect for others, and it is presumed to be detrimental to the overall well-being of the community. (There are, incidentally, issues here about the differences between individual, collective, and aggregate well-being, which I shall not pursue, since they do not affect the thrust of my argument.) Tolerance is a virtue because truth matters (and one truth is that we do not have a hold on all truth), because people's freedom to do and act as they choose matters, because it is reasonable to suppose that in the long run people's well-being is best served by tolerance, and because it is an aspect of treating people with respect. (I surely no longer need to add that this is not to deny that sometimes we may not be willing to tolerate something, sometimes we should not tolerate something, and sometimes it is debatable whether we should or not. Nonetheless, in principle, in itself, if there isn't a moral counter-consideration or a practical restraint, we ought to be tolerant.)

To say that friendship is a good because it is a relationship that embodies and contributes to respect and well-being does not of course do away with the problem of defining friendship or testing its limits. Perhaps the precise form it takes doesn't matter: there may be good reasons for friendship to be practised and expressed in different ways in different places, while the defining characteristics remain the same. But, though that is quite likely, we still need to determine what those defining characteristics are, for not anything can count as friendship; not anything that is a relationship between persons is in itself morally good. So there do remain complex and intriguing questions about friendship. But we can now at least draw the conclusion that the fact that someone is your friend is a relevant moral factor in conducting your life – it is something positive about your life, it is something to be valued, and it may lay specific obligations on you – in a way that the fact that someone is your neighbour, your kin, or of the same race has not been shown to be. Some might wish to argue that the latter also have moral significance, but they would need to produce an argument, whereas the assertion that friendship is a moral good is already vindicated. Similarly, compassion and kindness can be categorically listed as moral virtues, whereas patience and stoicism, for example, cannot be: the latter may be moral qualities, but further argument would be needed to establish the fact.

Forgiveness, which is often cited as a virtue, provides an interesting example to illustrate the overall argument at this point. I do not have a ready answer as to whether it should be considered inherently morally good, but I can say that it is not immediately obvious that it is. We are generally inclined to think that, given human frailty, we should forgive others as we would wish to be forgiven, and there may be something to be said in empirical terms for the value of forgiveness as a contribution to well-being. But it is nonetheless not clear that it is an inevitable aid to social well-being, and it is still not clear that I am morally the better for forgiving those who have, for instance, gratuitously tortured me half to death. To deny that friendship is in itself a morally good thing seems to betray a failure to understand the nature of morality in a way that denying that forgiveness is in itself morally good does not. I do not wish to attempt to settle this issue (as I say, I cannot); my concern here is to distinguish, on the one hand, between an example of a second-order principle that is indisputable and a claim that would need further argument, and also to draw attention to the fact that my argument does not simply endorse convention. Most, if not all, of the further values I am now introducing are conventionally accepted as moral ones (which is reassuring, incidentally, but not in any way a proof or confirmation of the argument); but some conventionally accepted moral goods are not endorsed by my argument. The argument agrees with the conventional view that kindness is morally good; it disagrees with the conventional view that forgiveness is necessarily morally good.

Throwing in beauty as another example is perhaps not particularly helpful. I do it, as I did in Chapter 5 above, to highlight the nature of the argument. While beauty may not be a fundamental or first-order moral principle, it seems *prima facie* plausible to argue that it is morally desirable to promote or enhance beauty rather than ugliness in the world. It is certainly better in some sense: those who say that, if two worlds are identical in all respects except that one is beautiful and the other ugly, it makes no sense to deny the superiority of the former, are surely correct. But it is not clear that this is a moral 'better'. It might, for instance, be said that one world is better in the more general sense that while being equally moral, it also has aesthetic value. On the other hand, it might be argued that a concern for beauty and the provision of beauty in place of ugliness are conducive to our well-being and for that reason, other things being equal, beauty should be seen as morally desirable. I leave this question open and admit that, even if we do take beauty to be a moral value, much work is needed to distinguish different kinds of beauty and to establish how one determines what is beautiful and what is not.

In the light of our commitment to tolerance and the first-order principle of freedom, two more specific second-order principles can be discerned. The first is that freedom of speech should be absolute. The second is that in the sphere of actions as distinct from speech people should be free to do anything that does not impinge on anyone else. These are more particular, more explicit, and more demanding in form than any second-order principles so far considered, and it must be acknowledged that there are some well-worn arguments on both these topics and a great deal of contrary opinion. Nonetheless, I still believe that the principles should be upheld and that the following arguments hold.

If freedom of speech matters at all (and the premise, which most, if not all, parties to the debate support, is that it does), then it must be absolute. That is to say, you are free to say absolutely anything that you choose. We can say straightaway that freedom to say anything is to be distinguished from freedom to speak on any occasion or in any situation. So, without going into detail or trying to oversimplify and resolve extremely complex issues, the defence of absolute freedom of speech is not a defence of anybody's right to say anything at any time or in any place. One might, to take some of the more familiar examples, quite reasonably argue that people should not be allowed to reveal state secrets in time of war, to engage in propaganda for the enemy, to deliberately cause panic by shouting 'Fire' in a crowded cinema, or to incite people to violence. Difficult as it may sometimes be to settle what is acceptable in such situations and to distinguish unequivocally between incitement to violence and expressing an opinion, there remains a clear and often discernible difference between use of language to induce action and the expression of opinions. It is the latter that is the concern of advocates of free speech: freedom to state one's views with no other purpose than to be understood and in the hope that others may recognize the truth or wisdom of those views. Even when the view is judged to be pernicious, there remains a clear difference between, say, stating one's low opinion of some group and giving reasons, good or bad, for that opinion, and, on the other hand, seeking to instigate action against that group. This difference remains even when, in the first case, the hope is to give others reason to share one's views, which may indirectly lead to action. Whatever may be said to the contrary, there is a very clear and very important difference between getting people to agree that a discernible group is objectionable and getting people to act against the group. Nor should the fact that in practice it is sometimes difficult to tell what effect the utterance of an opinion will have deter us from upholding the principle. Just as the fact that it is sometimes difficult to determine whether a person is or is not to be classified as bald is no reason to deny the distinction between baldness and a full head of hair, so the fact that sometimes expression of opinion leads to trouble is no excuse for pretending that there is therefore no difference between the utterance of an opinion and an attempt to instigate action.

The point of valuing freedom of speech is precisely to assert that people have a right to hold and in a limited sense to voice their opinions even when other people don't like those opinions or don't agree with them. To say that one values freedom of speech provided that it does not harm or cause offence is, if not absurd, at any rate not worth saying, since nobody objects to what they don't object to. It might be asked why, given that I accept that the claims of one principle may clash with those of another, in this case I refuse to countenance the rival claims of other principles. Surely, it may be said, the interests of well-being may suffer in the name of absolute freedom of speech. That is quite true, but there are two overwhelming counter-considerations. First, there is the argument, by its nature unprovable but nonetheless persuasive, that, on balance, despite all the problems and pain that absolute free speech can cause, we gain more than we lose by respecting this principle. Second is the point we started with: free speech is only free speech if it is absolute. It is the assumption that we should never be so dogmatic as to dictate what is true or acceptable, combined with the belief that in the long run such freedom is to the benefit of all that undergirds the defence of free speech; it is contemplation of the actual misery brought about by every regime in history that ignored this principle that confirms its wisdom. To accept any limitation on freedom of expression on the grounds that the claims of other fundamental principles may clash with it is in itself to abandon the principle of free speech, in favour of the quite different view that there are some things that people ought to be free to say and others they should not. This, besides abandoning the principle in question, would necessitate then establishing precisely what counter-claims do and do not serve to trump freedom of expression. This is where such forces as political correctness gain their footing, for political correctness attempts to impose the value judgements of some on others. It is the antithesis of a moral movement precisely because it ignores the claims of freedom, open-mindedness, and tolerance, which, according to the argument, are fundamental to anything that can count as a moral theory.

If freedom of speech necessarily implies absolute freedom, why doesn't freedom of action? Because actions, generally speaking, clearly impinge on others in a way that the holding or expressing of opinions doesn't. Your opinions may delight, irritate, provoke, or inspire me, but they do not in themselves prevent me doing anything, force me to do anything, or otherwise materially affect me. But actions can impinge on me in these ways and, when they do, sometimes there will be moral reasons for objecting. I may not like you complaining that my garden is an eyesore, but it is a quite different order of event from your coming into my garden and clearing it. There are notorious problems concerning how one determines that an act is entirely self-regarding, i.e. does not impinge on anyone else, but that is no reason to deny the second-order principle that in so far as an action does not impinge on others it should be free. Needless to say, when it comes to actions that do impinge on others the question of whether they should be permitted or prohibited should be determined by reference to the various established moral principles. Not everything that impinges on others, nor even everything that upsets others, is to be regarded as morally unacceptable. Your walking down the street may irritate me, but we can hardly say that you therefore ought not to be free to do it. But if you poison my cat, the situation is rather different. However, my purpose here is limited to establishing that in principle people should be free to hold and express any opinion they choose and to perform any action that does not impinge on others. Those who believe, for example, that masturbation is immoral can categorically be said to be mistaken. They are mistaken because there is nothing in the activity itself that has any connection with the defining characteristics of morality. It is not, it cannot be, a moral issue. It might, for all I know, be a religious issue, a medical issue, or an issue of convention, but it is not a moral issue. And this is not because I have argued that it is not morally reprehensible; it is because it is not an activity that can be assessed in moral terms.

If freedom of expression and of self-regarding activity should be absolute, this is clearly not the case with most principles, where the distinction between what is wrong and what is not morally good but may be justified is of crucial importance,

Rape provides a powerful illustrative example here. Rape is always wrong and never justifiable, for reasons that derive from the very nature of morality and should now be familiar. The argument has become confused because some foolishly want to extend the scope of 'rape' to include such things as 'date rape' and 'conjugal rape'. This is foolish, because to widen the meaning of a term inevitably gives it less force. 'Fabulous' is a less telling word than 'beautiful' because, being even more general, it is less precise. 'Person' is less specific than 'female' and therefore provides less precision. To converse in broad terms is to say less, to provide less clarity, to discriminate less exactly, than to converse in terms of fine and meticulous distinctions. Recognizing fine distinctions is an essential part of understanding and making sense of our world. Hence, in moral matters as well, it is advisable to operate with concepts that are as specific as possible. Obviously there can be rape both within marriage and on a date. But we would be well advised to recognize the distinction between forcing oneself sexually on a stranger against his or her will and being party to a drunken or drug-induced seduction. We need to recognize the difference between various kinds of force and methods of forcing: holding a knife to someone's throat is different from taking advantage of drunkenness, different again from making false promises or threatening to blacken a reputation; and these kinds of difference may be (though are not necessarily) material. Likewise, the nature of a relationship and other features of the circumstances in which intercourse takes place may all be relevant to assessing the degree of acceptability/unacceptability of the behaviour. It is not that a spouse or a date cannot be accused of reprehensible behaviour, but it does not help to put a husband forcing himself on his wife, even when the circumstances are more or less repugnant, on a par with assaulting a stranger. But rape as such (i.e. forcing sexual intercourse on an unwilling person who has no reason to anticipate any kind of sexual exchange) clearly offends the principles of respect, well-being, and freedom in a dramatic and traumatic way. It is morally wrong. By contrast, torture, while always bad in itself or wrong, might be justifiable. Torture is clearly inherently repugnant and I am certainly not advocating it. But one recognizes that there can be situations in which at least some degree of torture is felt to be morally justified: the familiar sort of example posits that thousands of innocent people will suffer hideously, unless one very unpleasant individual can be 'persuaded' to talk. But that line of argument will not serve to justify rape ever. Consider the assault on Nanking by the Japanese, in which brutal and nearly unspeakable atrocities, often including rape as a minimal part, were perpetrated on Chinese civilians. One can perhaps imagine someone fired with moral indignation at such atrocity, in line with the philosophy of an eye for an eye, suggesting that those who did these things should themselves be raped as a form of punishment. I can imagine that being suggested, but I cannot see it as morally justifiable. The blatant and inevitable offence to some of the defining principles of morality, combined with the fact that it is impossible to see it as in any way contributing to any other foundational moral principles, means that it is always unjustified, always morally inexcusable. Suppose someone were to argue that it has been conceded that torture might be justifiable on occasion, and that rape might merely be the chosen form of torture. I cannot explore this contention in detail here, but I would respond that rape cannot ever be a morally acceptable form of torture, because it is intrinsically and always unjustifiable and wrong. Causing pain, however, is (alas) not always and necessarily unjustifiable; thus some forms of torture may be justifiable in certain circumstances, but never rape.

I am not suggesting that torture is less serious than rape, or that we should be sanguine about the fact that cruelty, telling lies, and breaking promises may be justifiable. I am merely facing up to the fact that according to the argument (and, in fact, on any truly moral theory as distinct from a moral code that consists of dogmatic injunctions) while such things are plainly wrong they might, in exceptional circumstances, be justifiable by reference to fundamental principles of morality, whereas it can never be justifiable to commit rape.

Rape is a particularly brutal and vivid example of the morally unjustifiable and for that reason is widely recognized as such. But some behaviour that does not appear to be directly threatening in the same kind of way, and is therefore less readily condemned so universally and resoundingly, is nonetheless equally unacceptable. I refer to fraud and various types of hypocrisy. These are of course generally formally condemned, but it seems fairly clear that people tend to get far more morally indignant about various kinds of sexual offence than they do about major corporate corruption. So senior Enron executives who, on the face of it, have acted in an outrageously immoral manner do not seem to excite the ire of the public in the way that some relatively harmless sexual offender might. Perhaps not surprisingly we also find that thousands of people who regard themselves as moral nonetheless cheat a little on their income tax.

It may seem strange to some to link such an obviously brutal and widely condemned act as rape with such peaceable and in fact widely condoned activities as tax evasion and other familiar forms of fraud and hypocrisy which, though routinely condemned, are routinely accepted as a necessary evil. But part of what I hope to achieve is to establish that some of the time we are looking for morality in all the wrong places. Morality is indeed partly concerned with things like avoiding brutality, but I suggest that we mistakenly tend to associate it far too much with areas such as sexuality and far too little with quieter kinds of conduct that involve taking advantage of others and transgressing the principles of fairness, truth, and respect, and that occur on a daily basis.

The statement that fraud and hypocrisy can never be justified obviously depends partly on what exactly we mean by 'fraud' and 'hypocrisy'. They need in particular to be distinguished from deceit and dissembling respectively, both of which, though unattractive qualities, may on occasion be morally justified despite being inherently bad. By the same argument deployed in the case of torture, we can see that it may be justifiable to employ deceit: the interrogation of a would-be suicide bomber might legitimately benefit from a little misdirection. But deceit is something that one consciously employs for a purpose (which may be good or bad). Hypocrisy is a state of mind; if it isn't, if the argument is that a person is just being hypocritical in this situation for some particular reason, I should call that deceit. A hypocrite is one who routinely adopts a false *persona* to advance his interests. A hypocritical person is one who routinely and characteristically presents a false face to the world. One cannot be unconsciously hypocritical. While it is sometimes possible to justify misleading someone in a particular situation, there is no justification possible for consistently and deliberately presenting a false image of oneself to the world. Similarly, a starving individual might be justified in stealing a loaf of bread in certain circumstances, but the deliberate and conscious circumventing of rules as part of planned activity for personal gain, as in fraud and corruption, can never be justified. Fraud is not the same as a one-off act of deceit, which might in exceptional circumstances be justified. It is systematic deceit in one's own interests. The difference is between a particular and desperate breaking of the rules and a cynical, self-serving disregard of them. As I say, part of my point here is that a lot of what we commonly treat with moral indignation is not truly immoral, and a lot of what we rather sheepishly condone is downright immoral. We show more moral indignation about the tramp whom we suspect of a little bit of pilfering than we do about corporate or indeed personal tax evasion. But there can never be moral justification for sustained and systematic cheating and deceit for the purposes of self-advantage on the part of those who do not even lack basic necessities. It is true that what count as 'basic necessities' is debatable – true, therefore, that sometimes it may be contentious whether someone is guilty of an act of justifiable (or at least forgivable) wrongdoing or unjustifiable fraud. But the occasional difficulty of knowing how to classify an act does not alter the fact that nothing that is clearly fraud can be justified.

Indoctrination is always and necessarily morally wrong. It strikes at the heart of the values of truth and respect for persons, being the attempt to close the minds of individuals on contentious because unprovable matters. Taking innocent hostages is always an unjustifiable way of promoting a cause. Producing and selling useless counterfeit drugs and medicines that inevitably lead to deaths is categorically and blatantly wrong. The arms dealing that our governments are heavily engaged in, without, it seems, much troubling the conscience of the populace, is yet another obvious and undeniable act of immorality that cannot possibly be justified. But enough has perhaps been said to make it clear that the defining principles of morality certainly have teeth; there are a variety of acts that are quite clearly morally wrong and unjustifiable in any circumstances. But they are not always the acts that most excite the daily press. It is also clear that while some acts are always wrong there are other bad behaviours that may nonetheless be justified in certain circumstances. What circumstances do justify what actions is a matter that has to be considered on a case-by-case basis, but here again it is important to recognize that cases can often be decided by a judicious attention to the facts and the fundamental moral principles.

These have been examples of acts that can be categorically condemned as immoral, but some issues that are indubitably moral ones nonetheless cannot be resolved, particularly those concerning life and death. I am not thinking here of the problem of determining whether, for example, a particular killing is morally justifiable. Killing is clearly wrong in itself but can, on most views, be justified in exceptional circumstances such as war or, sometimes, self-defence. By contrast abortion and euthanasia present us with dilemmas or insoluble problems, as noted in the previous chapter. This is not so much because different moral principles make conflicting demands as because there are other philosophical questions that do not have any clear and uncontentious answer, most notably what constitutes personhood, and empirical questions to which we do not have the answer, most notably what the state of mind of a comatose patient may be.

The argument surrounding abortion is popularly summarized as a clash between pro-life and pro-choice groups, but the issue is much more complex than that simple dichotomy suggests. As just noted, some of the difficulty arises in relation to empirical questions, such as how one knows what is going on in the mind of the so-called brain-dead, what a foetus at a given age can actually experience, or what the consequences of giving birth, terminating a pregnancy, or ending a life will be. Even if one ignores that sort of question and focuses on, say, choice, there are the questions of whose choice and whether a given 'person' is capable of making a choice. In the case of abortion the intent is obviously to focus on the right of the mother to choose what to do with her body, but a case can be made for saying that the father, albeit on different grounds, should also have some choice in the matter, and perhaps others too; there is the question of whether it makes sense to consider the choice of the foetus or, in the case of euthanasia, the 'patient', who may of course be more or less capable of articulating a choice. In the case of the foetus it has sometimes been argued that we must consider what it would choose, if able to articulate a choice, and while many will find that unpersuasive it seems less obviously absurd when the same kind of argument is applied to the brain-dead (who may even have expressed a choice at an earlier time). Certainly many other people besides those immediately involved may be said to have a legitimate interest in what happens.

On the other side, even the presumption that a human life is sacrosanct would not in practice always settle the issue: what if giving birth may cause the death of the mother, for example? Then there are many other morally relevant questions: what if the pregnancy is the result of rape? What if it is known that the child will be handicapped in some extreme way? What will the consequences be in terms of the general good of pursuing this or that policy either in a particular case or in general? In the case of euthanasia there is a particular question here: what effects (good or bad) will it have on people to be aware that they may be the subject of euthanasia? On the other hand, what of those who are forbidden to end a life which, for whatever reason, they no longer wish to continue? Beyond these and other questions about the acts of abortion and euthanasia themselves there are related questions such as what tactics are morally acceptable in pursuit of one's position. (There is *prima facie* something odd about those who seem willing to kill abortionists in the name of life, as there is about those who are willing to kill or maim human animals in the name of animal welfare.) There is also a set of questions to be asked about the morality of performing abortions, assisting suicide, and practising euthanasia.

There is no shortage, then, of questions to be asked about such issues. But the reason why they are to be classified as dilemmas rather than problems is not primarily that they are so complex and subject to so many different considerations that it is impossible to weigh them all up dispassionately and coherently (although that may be true); it is that in both these examples the crucial issue is what counts as a human life. It is important to remember the distinction between morality and religion at this point, for clearly a great deal of the actual objection to both abortion and euthanasia is religious. As we have seen, a religious objection is not a moral objection and there are no rational grounds for accepting the claims of any particular religion and therefore no rational grounds for enforcing its demands on those who do not share the faith. The basis of the argument for religious tolerance is itself the fact that no faith can establish its claims to truth in a rational and publicly acceptable manner, and, by the same argument, we cannot accept the view of a given faith as providing the solution to the question of the moral acceptability of these or any other practices. From a philosophical point of view, the concern is that there does not seem to be any way of resolving the problem of what constitutes personhood (any more than there is of resolving the question of the nature of God). Needless to say, there have been many erudite contributions to the debate and attempts to pin down the concept, but there has been no consensus on, let alone resolution of, the question of what exactly constitutes personhood, and, therefore, whether a foetus of a given age, a brain-dead child, or a comatose adult should or should not be regarded as persons or as experiencing human life in the appropriate sense (the question being, of course, what is the appropriate sense). It is perhaps worth commenting briefly on the argument that there is a slippery slope between a seed, an embryo, a foetus, and a human being, just as there is between a speed limit of 1 m.p.h. and 100 m.p.h. But in neither case does it follow that you cannot set a reasonable limit. While 30 m.p.h. is certainly not the 'correct' speed limit within a town in any inherent or demonstrable sense, it is sensible and reasonable in a way that neither 10 m.p.h. nor 50 m.p.h. would be. In the same way, while there is nothing sacrosanct about, say, three months as the legal age of a foetus after which abortion is not permitted, it may be argued that it is reasonable. Be that as it may, we will never arrive at universal agreement on the point at which the embryo or foetus becomes a person. Personhood is a prime example of what has been called 'an essentially contested concept'; that is, what is taken to count as a person will inevitably and always vary in accordance with a culture's other beliefs and understandings, including particularly its values.

What counts as a human life is not ultimately to be determined by science, biology, or philosophy; it is a matter for our judgement.

That being the case, while there are all sorts of good reason for being concerned about, discussing, and perhaps even regulating in some way the practices of abortion and euthanasia, there are no legitimate grounds for dictating a view of what is and what is not morally acceptable. Unlike systematic fraud, rape, hypocrisy, betrayal, indoctrination, and intolerance, which are always inherently wrong and seldom if ever morally justified, abortion and euthanasia cannot be said to have been shown to be inherently wrong. The fundamental principles of freedom and truth (and arguably well-being and respect as well) lead us to accept that where reasoning cannot conclusively show a practice to be wrong or right, it is for the individual to do as he sees fit. This is not because 'the right to choose' trumps 'the right to life', but because it is morally wrong to impose a course of action on others without warrant.

I hope that by now a map of the moral terrain is beginning to emerge, in the light of which we can distinguish true moral issues from other kinds of value judgement, outline the principles that constitute the essence of morality, differentiate between acts that are never justifiable and those that while wrong may sometimes be morally justified, and between situations where we do have reasonable certainty, where we don't, and where we cannot expect to have, and recognize that some of our problems are dilemmas such that we must leave the choice of action to the conscience of the individual. Now it may be added that, paradoxical though it sounds, one of the consequences of getting a better understanding of morality is that it enables us to make some firm negative points. It is as important not to treat issues that are not moral as moral, as it is to be moral. To treat 're-gifting' (the business of passing on unwanted presents) as a moral issue, for example, is as mistaken as to believe that it is morally neutral to cheat on one's tax returns. Similarly, it seems to be widely assumed that offending or upsetting people is morally deplorable, that differentiating or discriminating between people is wrong, that various sexual practices are immoral, that ecological issues are moral issues, and that one has a moral obligation to honour one's father and mother. All this seems to me incorrect, as I shall argue in the next chapter. I am not of course advocating that we *should* offend people or that we *shouldn't* honour our parents. I am suggesting that these are not moral issues in themselves, in the way in which most of the examples we have so far considered are, even when they do not admit of a clear resolution. I throw in the injunction to honour one's father and mother as a reminder that many people have some very specific moral commands to offer. But, generally, it is hard to find a moral warrant for such dogmatic and specific claims. In so far as 'honouring' people is a good thing (and as far as that goes it is generally but not always preferable to honour than to dishonour them, but problematic as to in what precisely honouring consists), one should honour one's father and mother. In most cases we have particular reason and a wish to do so. But some people don't, and that has no necessary bearing on their moral standing.

What I have tried to show in this chapter is that, despite the high-level abstract nature of the first-order principles, they give us a purchase; they do serve as a practical guide and they do lead to some fairly clear second-order principles, values, virtues, and even, occasionally, specific injunctions. But it should be remembered that part of the argument is that theories that are too specific are liable to be mistaken.

Commentary

The notion that the value of promise-keeping is entailed by the notion of a promise derives ultimately from Kant. His argument in skeletal form is that none could wish as a universal law the maxim that 'when in difficulties I will extricate myself by making a false promise'. He writes:

> I can by no means will a universal law of lying; for by such a law there could properly be no promises at all, since it would be futile to profess a will for future action to others who would not believe my profession . . . and consequently my maxim, as soon as it was made a universal law, would be bound to annul itself.
>
> (*Groundwork of the Metaphysic of Morals*, p. 403)

On the difference between individual, collective and aggregate well-being, which I do not discuss in the text, see Geoffrey Scarre *Utilitarianism*.

G.E. Moore specifically used the argument that if there were two worlds identical in all respects save that one contained beauty and the other not, the former would be morally preferable. In fact he goes further. He asks us to imagine a beautiful world and 'the ugliest world you can possibly conceive'. Then, even supposing neither world will ever be seen by any human being,

> well, even so, supposing them quite apart from any possible contemplation by human beings, still, is it irrational to hold that it is better that the beautiful world should exist than the one which is ugly? Would it not be well, in any case, to do what we could to produce it rather than the other? Certainly I cannot help thinking that it would.
>
> (*Principia Ethica*, p. 84)

The classic text on freedom generally and freedom of speech in particular remains John Stuart Mill *On Liberty*. I believe, though others wouldn't, that what I say in the text is more or less in accord with Mill's view. See John Gray *Mill on Liberty: a Defence* and Frederick Schauer *Free Speech: a Philosophical Enquiry*. In my view, Mill's essay provides a good example of an argument that has been irrelevantly criticized on the grounds that it does not provide clear and certain guidance in all cases. That much is true, but it does not follow that it is either unclear or false, and in fact, I suggest, it is neither.

A few points of detail. 'Essentially contested concept' is a phrase first coined by W.B. Gallie 'Essentially Contested Concepts' in *Proceedings of the Aristotelian Society 1955–6*. The liberal Canadian scholar, journalist and Member of Parliament, Michael Ignatieff, has recently aroused some controversy by suggesting that torture might sometimes be morally justified. The full horror of the rape of Nanking is exposed in Iris Chang's book of that title. For further reading relating to aesthetics, see the Commentary on Chapter 7 above. Discussions of indoctrination are to be found in I.A. Snook (ed.) *Concepts of Indoctrination*.

In *At Mrs Lippincote's* Elizabeth Taylor has a character remark:

> 'You think me a ridiculous figure, stiff with my own dignity, acting a melancholy but undistinguished role, falsely romantic. All right. But if I am a poseur, I am not at the same time a hypocrite. I have never deluded you, nor myself, nor anyone who is real.'
>
> (p. 111)

Jamie Whyte's *Bad Thoughts* has a section on tolerance. He specifically asserts that 'tolerance is irrelevant in the abortion debate. If the abortion isn't murder, toleration isn't required; if it is murder tolerating it would be a vice' (p. 108). But he is combating (correctly) the view that we should simply tolerate what we think is wrong. My point is that in this particular case we cannot reasonably claim to know what is right or wrong, and for that reason we should exercise tolerance.

The example of the bald-headed person is sometimes referred to as the 'slippery slope argument'. There are in fact two related but distinct types of so-called slippery slope argument. One is a form of argument that suggests that some act is not bad in itself but might lead to other acts which culminate in something that is bad. It is seen as the thin end of the wedge. Thus, people should not be banned from washing car windows at traffic lights because it is bad in itself but because if it is allowed it will lead to other types of activity that will eventually bring traffic to a standstill. The bald-headed man example is an instance of a more general type of what is sometimes called a 'sorites' argument, wherein the admission that one hair doesn't make a man hairy is taken to mean that adding another hair to make it two still doesn't make him hairy, and so on until we reach the paradoxical and false conclusion that a man with thousands of hairs on his head is nonetheless bald.

China's official policy limiting the number of children couples may have raises political or social rather than moral issues. According to my argument, it would be wrong for the government to enforce this policy on moral grounds, but it might be acceptable on other grounds. (Whether it is or not, I am not really in a position to say, but I am inclined to think that it is.) On the distinction between morality and politics, see further Chapter 9 below.

Part III

Some implications of the moral theory

9 Moral vs. social, ecological, and sexual values

I have argued that morality is defined in terms of certain first-order principles and that some more specific second-order principles can be derived from them. In this chapter, I want to suggest that some of what are widely classified as moral issues, though they may be serious issues, are not in fact specifically moral ones. In doing this, I hope to substantiate my argument that the principles outlined in Chapter 5 above are the foundations for determining what is right or wrong, and that morality has to be seen in terms of these principles rather than in terms of a set of prescribed and proscribed acts. Attempts to list examples of good and bad behaviour and to treat them as the essence of morality, as in the case of the Ten Commandments or the seven deadly sins, are inappropriate. We should think instead in terms of the general principles that need to be adhered to and the related characteristics of the moral person, such as the virtues of tolerance and open-mindedness referred to in the previous chapter.

Does it matter whether we save the white whale, slow down global warming, and preserve the rain forests? Very probably. But are these moral issues? It may well be true that we should abide by the Kyoto agreement, cut back on greenhouse emissions, and protect endangered species, but it does not follow that this is a moral 'should'. Perhaps we should do such things in order to improve the climate or in order to protect and preserve nature. It may be sensible or in our interests to do so, it may even be vital if the planet is to survive, but that doesn't make it a moral issue. (Arguments about different ecological issues naturally vary in quality and strength. If greenhouse emissions really are going to bring life on this planet to an end within, say, five hundred years, that may be of more concern than if a particular species of fish is going to disappear from a pond in Vancouver within five years. But in neither case is it clear that this is a moral issue.) Sometimes the argument is made to look moral by referring to our duty to unborn generations or to nature itself. But we have no moral duty to nature, and it is unclear why or whether we should acknowledge a duty to future generations. This does not imply that future generations are of no concern, or that we need not care about them. Indeed, I have not even said that we shouldn't save the fish in Vancouver, let alone the future of the planet. All that has been suggested is that these questions, important as they may be, are not in themselves moral questions. They are questions of survival, perhaps, and quite explicitly they are eco-logical questions, and as such have their obvious importance. But whereas a moral person necessarily strives to be honest, there is no comparable impli-cation that he strives to protect the environment. (Ecological issues may raise moral questions: for example, a factory that does not honour its undertaking to deal appropriately with toxic waste and that lies about the matter is acting immorally; and it seems reasonable to suggest that in this sort of way cor-porations, businesses, and governments quite often act immorally. But that is a different matter.)

It may be asked why this distinction between a moral and an ecological argument matters, if it is conceded that both may lead to the conclusion that we ought to do something to protect the environment. The first reason why it matters is simply that it is a matter of truth or getting it right. Even if it can be successfully argued that in order to ensure the survival of future gen-erations it is necessary to act in certain ways now, it remains a mistake to confuse the argument that we need to do *X* in order to ensure the survival of future generations with the argument that we have a moral obligation to ensure that survival. Second, as already noted, all distinctions matter in that the finer or the better our ability to discriminate, the more precise our understanding, the better our grasp on reality. Discussion and thought become more vague and inchoate in direct proportion to their generality. Critical understanding depends upon fine distinctions. Third, recognizing the difference should help us to keep inappropriate 'moral' indignation out of the debate. An argument with someone who thinks that whaling should be banned should not auto-matically be imbued with the same kind of outrage that an argument about the slaughter of innocent children might properly have. (The 'should not' in that sentence is a logical rather than a moral one: it 'should not' be imbued with moral indignation because such indignation is not relevant, rather than because it is not right.)

There is, it must be admitted, a further problem when it comes to arguments involving animals (as distinct from other aspects of nature) in that there are competing views on the relationship between morality and non-human animals. I can only outline the position and assumptions that I would argue for here. I do not believe that any animals other than humans are themselves capable of moral or immoral behaviour, essentially because I do not see that it makes sense to attribute moral responsibility to beings without charac-teristically human minds. (By the same token, I would not ascribe moral responsibility to young children or those suffering from, e.g., an advanced state of Alzheimer's disease); however, that does not mean that there is no moral issue about how we treat animals (or the young, the sick, and the elderly). On the contrary, we should have moral concern about all animals that are capable of suffering and should, other things being equal, avoid causing them suffering, since suffering and an assault on well-being are self-evidently bad in themselves. This certainly raises moral questions about vivisection and other animal experimentation, and, for example, battery farming and the manner in which we slaughter cattle. Perhaps seemingly paradoxically, however, it does not follow that eating animals or using their skin to make, e.g., leather handbags, or even killing them are in themselves morally wrong. We are, for the most part, disgusted and shocked by the idea of eating dead humans, but there is no obvious reason why we should be morally shocked, and the same applies to other animals. A dead being is no longer part of the moral universe. It is more difficult to be sure about the moral dimensions of the act of killing. Here, much more tentatively, I would observe that while killing another being is certainly treating it as a means, it is not clear that one could or why one should treat a non-human animal as an end in itself. It is also the case that animals, lacking human minds, cannot suffer through anticipation of fear of death as humans can. (I am not referring here to a sense of death such as, it has been plausibly said, some animals do have. I am referring to the fact that humans are conscious of the idea of death, and their state of mind can be dramatically affected by such things as the awareness that they have cancer, that they are living in a dangerous neighbourhood, or that they are at the mercy of the secret police.) Thus an animal can be killed, in principle, without suffering. But why should and why would we kill them? The answer is surely as a necessary means to our survival, referring not only to our diet but also to the need to cull some species. There is a moral obligation on us not to cause animals unnecessary suffering, and there is a variety of prudential reasons for showing concern for them, but we are under no moral obligation to protect them come what may or to refrain from making use of them in certain ways. On this view, then, ecological arguments to do with the preservation of species should not be confused with a moral argument. It is not in itself immoral to kill animals or to make use of them when dead, though we have a moral duty to treat them humanely, even in the manner of their death.

We move from ecological issues to the broad realm of social values. Some social values may be moral values, but some are not, and some moral values are not social values. This is close to, but not identical with, the distinction already made between legal and moral values. Offering one's seat to a lady in a crowded train is an example of a social value. Such behaviour used to be the convention, but is hardly so today, not because we have become less considerate (though we may have become so), but because the social context in terms of such things as working conditions and gender roles has changed. What used to be regarded as polite and considerate is now commonly viewed as patronizing and even offensive. Personally, I see no harm in the old custom, even today, but that is neither here nor there. The point is that a given social custom, a societal value, may change; what matters is to know the current code in order to avoid embarrassment and for life to run smoothly. But there is no hint of morality in any of this. It may be considered rude, taken exception to, even in some way costly to get the convention wrong, but it is not immoral to fail to offer your seat when convention says you should, or to offer it when convention says you shouldn't.

It may perhaps be argued of any convention that ultimately it becomes a moral matter, because it is in the interests of general well-being that we should all observe the same conventions, and because in behaving in a way that defies the convention we may upset people. But this line of reasoning is to be resisted. Any rule or act can be said to have a moral dimension inasmuch as any rule or act might cause upset. But moral behaviour is principled behaviour that goes beyond time and place. We must remember again that the claim is not that it doesn't matter whether we abide by or flout convention; it may matter a great deal in all sorts of way. All that is being said here is that morality is neither about obeying all laws and rules, no matter what they are, nor about such things as conventional rituals between men and women in crowded trains or elsewhere. The claim is that this is not a moral issue. Just as it is not contradictory to say, 'I try to be a moral person, but I am not concerned about whether the planet will be habitable in five hundred years' (while it *is* contradictory to say, 'I try to be a moral person but I am not concerned about other people's welfare'), so it is not contradictory to say, 'I try to be a moral person, but I still like/refuse to offer my seat to a lady'. While it is true that the point of social rules is to ease the wheels, morality is not about easing wheels as such, even though it contributes to that end. It is about abiding by principles. I do not, in an appropriate or significant sense, strike at your welfare simply by being rude or otherwise upsetting you. In this case, it is not even clear why anyone should take offence at an old-fashioned courtesy; but even when behaviour is widely condemned as offensive, as when the same railway carriage is invaded by swearing, drunken, abusive individuals, it does not necessarily follow that the behaviour is immoral.

It may be said that upsetting people is clearly a moral issue, on the terms of my own argument, since to upset people is certainly to diminish their well-being and might involve showing little or no respect for them. The first point may be true and would be sufficient to explain why in general we shouldn't go around upsetting people. But giving offence can equally certainly be justified on occasion (by reference to one or more of the other defining principles of morality or circumstance), and sometimes the problem arises with the person offended rather than with the one who gives offence. For example, my talking to my neighbour, who happens to be black, may cause offence to my other neighbour, who is a white racist. But in a case like this we surely don't need to appeal to some calculation relating to the claims of different principles to see whether I'm justified in talking to my black neighbour. We just say that this clearly has nothing to do with morality, that I can talk to anyone I want, and that the problem which is a moral one is my white neighbour's (and his problem is that he is a racist, not that he is offended or offensive). Moral exception should only be taken to the fact that offence is given, if the offence is moral offence, in which case it is the morality of the situation that needs to be examined rather than the offensiveness. As to the argument from respect for persons, it too only works within the broader moral context. Respect for persons is a fundamental principle; if one's offensiveness is offensive in that it ignores that principle, that is morally sufficient; but offensiveness that does not involve any disrespect for persons is not morally relevant. Here, one needs to beware of interpreting respect for persons in too populist a manner. The moral principle involves recognizing others as persons and ends in themselves; it does not involve feeling warm towards them, making them feel good, etc. To use somebody as slave labour, to rape them, or to mug them shows no respect. To tell a joke that they don't approve of, to act in ways they don't like, or to otherwise irritate them does not involve failure to respect them in the relevant sense.

The point that not all offence is moral offence is important in an era when 'taking offence' is becoming quite common and is often associated with litigation and moral condemnation. There is something very wrong with the contemporary tendency to think that the mere fact that one is upset or objects to something in the behaviour of another is an adequate reason to lay a formal charge of some kind; and something even more wrong when such allegedly objectionable behaviour is overlaid with implications of moral turpitude. This is why it is disturbing that, increasingly, work-places adopt formal harassment policies and treat them as moral issues. If people really think that on balance it is desirable to have rules of conduct to govern collegial life, so be it, but they should not imagine that they are moral rules or rules demanded by morality as distinct from expediency, somebody's private agenda, or political correctness. The rules of any such policy are only moral if they pertain to truly moral issues. To rape a colleague is immoral, because it is wrong to rape anyone (but since it is also a criminal offence, we hardly need an institutional rule on the matter). To make a pass at a colleague is clearly not immoral, although it may be frowned upon or even formally outlawed in some institutions. Whether and to what extent pursuing somebody, in the sense of what used to be called anything from 'flirting' to 'making advances', is a moral issue is a debatable matter, which makes it disappointing that many institutions have clumsily classified practically anything that anybody chooses to regard as unwelcome to them as harassment. Certainly, any kind of approach can be vexatious or irritating, but it is not for that reason immoral. The principles of well-being and respect for persons do not imply doing only what suits the company around one. They are much less prescriptive than that, and this is one of the aspects of true morality that needs to be stressed: in the interests of morality, we need in general to start being a little more open and tolerant, a little less demanding and officious. What many see as a problem with the state of moral knowledge – that it is not certain, and that it does not always tell us exactly what to do – may equally well be seen as one of its virtues: moral people ought to be very tolerant, because there is so much that we do not and cannot know.

The context needs always to be borne in mind. Free speech, it will be recalled, should be absolute in the sense that one should be free to voice any opinion, however stupid or offensive, otherwise there is no point or truth in claiming that speech is free. But to say that you can express any opinions in the context of moral discussion (whether in the classroom or the pub, the home or city hall) does not mean that you can say it in any circumstances. You cannot say something in order to incite violence, or to create panic and chaos; you cannot publish your opinion of somebody in such a way as to wreck his life by false and malicious innuendo; you cannot betray state secrets in time of war; you cannot publish a fraudulent prospectus. But in such examples you are doing more than stating an opinion; you are using language to achieve particular effects, and in so doing you are being, variously, fraudulent, malignant, malicious, and treacherous, and serving morally objectionable ends. That is why you are not free to engage in these activities. In the same way, there may be circumstances in which making an advance to a colleague, offending people, or destroying a species of animal becomes morally wrong. But it remains true that in and of themselves ecological and social issues are not moral issues.

It may be maintained, however, that one always has a moral duty to obey the law of the land, so that while social, institutional, and legal rules are all distinct from moral rules, the distinction doesn't matter, because at the end of the day, since we are morally obliged to abide by society's laws, all its laws become effectively moral imperatives. This, too, is unconvincing. Even if we focus on society's laws, while it may be legally incumbent on one, prudent, socially commendable, or a good rule of thumb to abide by them and even in some sense something one owes to society or has in principle contracted to by remaining a member of society, it does not follow that it is morally required of one. It is in fact absurd to suggest that every law, historical, current, or conceivable, ought to be obeyed by a moral person: one has only to think of the appalling immorality of the laws under the Nazis, Khmer Rouge, Stalin, or the Cultural Revolution to see that, from whatever precise moral standpoint, a moral person must sometimes take a stand against the law, even if that means, as it generally will, that a price has to be paid for so doing. Indeed, one could argue that one of the serious moral problems of our day, far from being resistance to the law, is an unwillingness to stand up and be counted in opposition to unjust and improper laws and rules. In general terms, assuming we have the good fortune to live in moderately fair societies, we should obey the laws, and the only laws we have moral justification for breaking are those which make immoral demands; furthermore, in opposing even them, we must expect to pay the legal penalty. Nonetheless, from a moral point of view, we should speak out against unjust laws. (We do have a moral obligation to abide by moral and duly constituted laws, even if they irritate us, because it is fair and in the general interest that we should.)

Both political correctness and Christianity tend to see sex as an area of great moral concern. But the notion that homosexuality, polygamy, sex with multiple partners, serial attachments, promiscuity, and prostitution in and of itself have any moral significance is hard to fathom, unless it is seen as a hang-over from, or a confusion with, a religious viewpoint. For, fairly clearly, so-called pagan societies do not have the attitudes that religious communities do, and it is hard to link specific sexual practices with moral principles. In what way is it self-evident or arguable that our institution of marriage is morally superior to that of other cultures? From what moral principles could one possibly derive a moral attitude to homosexuality? Of course, in sexual as in all other relationships there is plenty of scope for a range of moral and immoral behaviour, but that will raise moral questions about trust, honesty, betrayal, promise-keeping, and so on, rather than about the nature of the sexual relations. There may be a quite separate non-moral case for maintaining marriage as an institution, regardless of the affections and feelings of those involved; there are moral considerations about such things as divorce settlements and children, of course. But any idea that the institution of marriage is somehow the morally right form of relationship is a non-starter. Recognizing this is important, since the muddled but widespread feeling that sexual relations are a moral issue adds unwarranted guilt to an already fraught situation for many couples. If any reader is tempted to assume that I am advocating free love, supporting the sex trade, or preaching licence, I can only say that I am not actually arguing for or against any particular form of sexual activity, and I fully accept that there are moral questions to be raised concerning such things as fidelity, caring, telling lies, and deceiving in sexual as in any other human relations. My point is simply that it is mistaken to see homosexuality, casual sex, marriage, or any other sexual practice between consenting adults as in itself moral or immoral.

Adultery is the name we give to the act of being sexually unfaithful while married. This, it may be said, perhaps correctly, involves breaking promises and treating others as means rather than ends in themselves. Certainly people who deliberately and without concern for others deceive and make use of people are, other things being equal, doing wrong. But we should be careful: some married people who do not actually commit adultery may nonetheless act wrongly or immorally in the context of marriage, and some adulterers might be argued to have acted justifiably, even morally correctly, and certainly not immorally. As in so many other cases, the *ceteris paribus* or 'other things being equal' clause reminds us that how one commits adultery in the sense of both what the full circumstances are and how one actually proceeds, in particular how one treats all the other parties concerned, is a crucial factor in considering its moral tone. If a severely physically handicapped spouse actually wants the partner to take a lover, for example, that is surely a morally relevant factor. It is true that, generally speaking, married people make vows or promises to love each other for ever but it is arguable that it may not be within their power to keep such promises since we are not entirely masters of our desires and emotions. In reply, it may be pointed out that it is possible to promise to be faithful, possible to keep that promise, and possible to overcome or withstand our emotions even if we cannot stop ourselves experiencing them. But, whichever way we argue, it is apparent that the issue only arises in the context of treating marriage as a sacred thing. There is no a priori reason to assume that deserting one lover for another is a moral issue. It may still be considered offensive in the eyes of God, and it may be argued that there are (non-moral) advantages in a traditional approach to such relationships. But there is really no warrant for saying that morality demands that a person who committed herself to another many years ago must under any circumstances remain in that relationship. This is not to say that adultery, changing partners, or having lovers is a good thing; it is merely to say that it is not in itself a moral issue, although of course there may be important moral implications, depending on the precise situation and how exactly one conducts oneself. Playing fast and loose in a way that simply makes use of others without consideration for them is a moral failing; uncritically and systematically deceiving someone who has reason to trust you is a moral failing. But, for example, falling in love with one person while committed to another is not a moral failing, and, at least in some circumstances, embarking on an affair in such a situation is not in itself morally unjustified. Thus conduct of this sort is not in itself a moral issue.

My argument that truly moral questions are rather rare and more circumscribed than ubiquitous references to 'morality', 'moral issues', 'the moral dimension', etc. seem to imply, raises the question of the relationship between morality and politics. It seems to me that it is rather important to distinguish between them. Politics has been called 'the art of the possible', and rightly so, for it is a pragmatic business. Of course politicians can and should behave morally in their professional life no less than their private life, but the notion that we can reasonably assess politicians *qua* politicians or political acts entirely in moral terms is, I would argue, quite mistaken. Failure to recognize this perhaps explains why political arguments often get heated: we approach them from a moral viewpoint, assuming that somebody did morally wrong or right, when we cannot coherently judge in these terms alone. The 2003 invasion of Iraq, to take an obvious and useful example, may well have incidentally involved immoral conduct on the part of various politicians (e.g. they may have lied, fabricated evidence, and made innocent people scapegoats), but whether Iraq should have been invaded or not cannot reasonably be seen solely as a moral question. It is a political question, which essentially means a question of what is in the interests of the parties or states in question. A state can of course adopt a more or less moral concern in its policy, but dealing with other states, for any purpose ranging from trade to war, is ultimately a matter of national self-interest. In saying this, I do not endorse or celebrate the fact; I merely observe that it is so. The question about Neville Chamberlain, for example, is not whether he was morally right or wrong to strive for 'peace in our time' and to accept Hitler's increasing demands, and I for one am quite prepared to believe that he was on balance a decent man who tried to do what he thought was right. The question is whether he was politically right or wrong, which is clearly different: did he do what was in the best interests of his constituents in the widest sense? Did he do what, given the realities of the world, it was most appropriate that he should do? The answer here is not necessarily clear – one is tempted to say that he encouraged Hitler to think he could get away with anything; but it is arguable that he bought urgently needed time for Britain – but it is clear that whether he did or did not do the right thing politically is not the same thing as whether his policy was moral or not.

Those of us who deplore US political actions in relation to the ongoing war on terror should not and do not need to accuse the United States of acting immorally: US policy is, we believe, to be condemned because it is dangerous, counterproductive and ultimately not in the interests of either America or its allies. This does not mean that there is no moral issue involved in, say, killing innocent people in war or invading other states, but it does mean that the political decision to go to war (any war) is not purely, if at all significantly, a moral one. Is this, then, to say that leaders such as Stalin and Hitler (or for that matter George Bush or Neville Chamberlain) cannot be assessed in moral terms? No, of course not, and of course Stalin and Hitler are to be morally condemned for forwarding various immoral policies. But it is not viable to conduct, or therefore to assess, politics in purely moral terms. The reason for this is straightforward: morality is defined in terms of five fundamental principles, but in certain circumstances, particularly when their claims clash, they cannot tell us precisely what to do. The political reality is such (not, I think, inevitably but certainly in practice) that many, if not most, issues are, so far as the moral dimension goes, true dilemmas; but in politics one cannot, as one can as an individual moral agent, say, 'Well, since this is a dilemma, one may choose either option'; the politician has to make a decision on how to act and he will do so by recourse to something other than morality. Faced with a problem that seems to involve right and wrong on either side, as in the decision whether to declare war, the politician will inevitably and properly take non-moral factors into consideration and, not surprisingly and again not wrongly, these will generally centre on the interest he represents. Able politicians will, however, be aware of the need to take the long-term view and to get the facts right. It is failure to read either the present or the future accurately that is the most obvious characteristic of the poor politician.

In this chapter I have tried to establish that, given the nature of morality, given what we may reasonably claim to know about it, and given what we must acknowledge is in one way or another for a variety of different reasons uncertain, there are a great many issues which are commonly regarded as moral issues but are not in fact so. A major implication of the recognition that fundamentally morality is to be defined in terms of five particular principles is that a great number of value claims should be recognized variously as social, ecological, or sexual values rather than moral values, and as such do not make the imperative demands on us that the latter do. To uphold a social value such as a certain form of politeness, an ecological value such as the need to recycle, or a sexual value such as the inappropriateness of certain forms of liaison, requires in each case some distinct non-moral form of argument, except in cases where the conduct in question can be shown to be directly related to one of the basic moral principles.

Animals, it has been suggested, though not capable of moral or immoral conduct, are nonetheless deserving of moral respect from humans in those cases where they are capable of experiencing suffering and being treated as ends rather than means, as is also the case with very young children or severely mentally handicapped individuals. Though in the opinion of a number of people not a moral issue at all, our treatment of animals is therefore sometimes, as in the examples of vivisection, battery farming and other kinds of unpleasant treatment for purposes of research or food production, a true and significant moral issue, in contrast to many fashionable social concerns that are not moral issues at all. Whether the polar bear becomes extinct, thanks to the melting of the ice-cap brought about by global warming, may be a matter for concern of some kind, but it is not a moral issue in the way that the cruelty of battery farming is.

A further and very important implication of the line of reasoning deployed here is that morality demands more of us in the way of open-mindedness and tolerance and less in the tendency to revert to legal and social restraints on conduct. We do not have good moral reason to make some of the demands that contemporary advocacy and other pressure groups, not to say governments, want to make, and it is in any case antithetical to a truly moral society to have too many rules and too little freedom. It is antithetical partly because in truth we do not have sufficient grounds to insist on some of the rules, and partly because true moral conduct requires freely chosen rather than mandated action.

Commentary

I argue that some ecological concerns are more important than others and I do so notwithstanding the so-called 'butterfly effect'. It may be true that, if a butterfly flaps its wings in the Amazon rain forest, this has some indirect and far-distant effect on the totality of the ecological system. (This reminds me of Benjamin Franklin's (1706–90) maxim, prefaced to *Poor Richard's Almanac*: 'for want of a nail, the shoe was lost; for want of a shoe, the horse was lost; and for want of a horse, the rider was lost'.) But it is surely not true that, for example, preserving every individual specimen of every rare species is important, or even that preserving every single species is. Certainly neither is as important as cutting down on the level of greenhouse gas emissions. Species have died out in the past without the world disintegrating, and no doubt some will do so in the future to no ill effect. There is a difference between arguing that a particular species should not be allowed to die out and arguing either that no species should die out or that every specimen of a given species is sacrosanct at any time and place. Neither Patrick Curry *Ecological Ethics: an Introduction* nor Wilfred Beckerman and Joanna Pasek *Justice, Posterity and the Environment* take precisely this line, but they provide useful surveys of the issues.

The point that we need to discriminate more than we do has come up in the text before. It is worth stressing it. Some people shy away from the very word 'discrimination', presumably because they associate it with wrongful discrimination or erroneously think that it carries pejorative connotations. But such things as racial and sexual discrimination are not bad because they involve discrimination. They are bad because they involve differentiating between people on grounds of race or sex (gender) when it is inappropriate to do so, as, let us suppose, when we are looking for the most suitable person to take on the position of CEO. Thus the phrases 'racial discrimination' and 'sexual discrimination' are, by usage, pejorative or condemnatory in a way that the word 'discrimination' itself is not. But to say that it is often wrong to differentiate on grounds of race or gender is not to say that it always is. It is not hard to imagine particular situations in which there are very good reasons for preferring a black candidate to a white one or a woman to a man. 'Racial discrimination', then, is shorthand for 'discrimination on grounds of race alone, when it is inappropriate'. But 'discrimination' itself, meaning 'the art of perceiving distinctions', is one of our most valuable assets and the word itself does not and should not be allowed to carry negative connotations. It is thanks to our ability to discriminate, i.e. note distinctions, that we can impose order on our world. A discriminating person has judgement, refinement, and taste. To fail to discriminate is to fail to note differences that are there – it is to fail to see. Those who lack discrimination are those who cannot distinguish between diamonds and paste. The greater an individual's discriminatory capacity, the greater that person's acuity, subtlety, and precision of understanding. Thus, the person who can distinguish between an ecological and a moral argument has a more perceptive and accurate understanding of the world than one who cannot. I have attempted to argue this point at slightly more length in Chapter One of Robin Barrow *Injustice, Inequality and Ethics*.

It would be a mistake to presume from my relatively unsentimental comment in the text about eating and using animals that I have little or no concern for them. I am in fact something of an animal liberationist (philosophically rather than politically, and I deplore the immoral actions of the more extreme activists such as those who threaten and intimidate others). But my points are: first, following Jeremy Bentham, the significant consideration in moral terms is whether a creature can experience suffering. (One implication of this is that our moral duty to apes is real, whereas to shrimps it is probably not.) Second, we can owe moral concern to non-humans without it being erroneously supposed that they are capable of being moral agents; and, third, most, if not all, non-human animals lack 'mind' in the sense that humans have minds.

The claim that other animals do not have minds obviously depends on a theory of mind, essentially that only humans can theorize, anticipate, hope, regret, dream – in short, exhibit self-awareness and consciousness and move beyond stimulus-response activity, no matter how sophisticated. This is very possibly because, in terms that Chomsky, *Syntactic Structures*, argued, humans and humans alone are genetically programmed to employ a type of language that uniquely enables such mental activity. John Searle *Minds, Brains and Science* and *Mind* provide eloquent and erudite presentations of the kind of non-materialist view to which I subscribe. A very different view is provided by Antonio Damasio *Looking for Spinoza*. Stephen Pinker *The Blank Slate* tries, without success I think, to have it both ways. Gilbert Ryle *The Concept of Mind* remains a classic, while V.C. Chappell (ed.) *The Philosophy of Mind* contains some substantive papers. Sadly, Richard L.

Gregory (ed.) *The Oxford Companion to the Mind* does not in its cumulative effect do any justice to the basic issue of whether and in what way a non-material mind is to be distinguished from the physical brain.

Regardless of Chomsky's particular thesis, I do not accept that any research on animals has established that any species has a recognizably human mind. If and when it is established that some species does have such a capacity, the important conclusion will be not that we are more animal-like than we had supposed, but that the species in question is more human. Such an admission will have no bearing on our understanding of the human mind or on something specific such as our moral theory, but only on what can and should in future be expected of animals of that species. If, for example, an ape turns out to have a human mind, we should be inclined to send the ape to school, rather than to release human children into the forests. At the time of writing (June 2006), there is a report in *The Weekly Telegraph* headed 'The Monkeys Who Can Speak Sentences'. It maintains that 'the first evidence that monkeys string "words" together to say more complicated things, as humans do, was published last week.' Referring to research conducted by Drs Arnold and Zuberbuhler of St Andrews University, it claims that a series of calls of 'pyow' means one thing, a series of calls of 'hack' another, and a combination of 'pyows' and 'hacks' something else again. This, even if true, hardly seems to affect the argument that no monkey has been shown to be able to formulate such utterances as 'I am extremely bored with being studied by these researchers; I wonder if they will go away, if I deliberately mix up my hacks and pyows.'

A doyen of those concerned with animal nature and rights is Peter Singer *Animal Liberation*. See also Paolo Cavalieri and Peter Singer *The Great Ape Project* and Tom Regan and Peter Singer *Animal Rights and Human Obligations*. Stephen R.L. Clark *The Moral Status of Animals* and Michael Bavidge and Ian Ground *Can We Understand Animal Minds?* are directly relevant, while Jeffrey Masson and Susan McGarthy *When Elephants Weep* explores the related topic of animal emotions. Mary Midgley *Beast and Man* explores the concept of human nature with direct reference to biological study of other animals. Taking a broadly contrary stance to all the preceding is Michael P.T. Leahy *Against Liberation*. My own statement of commitment came in Robin Barrow *Injustice, Inequality and Ethics*.

A word should be added about hunting. It is not a moral issue (except in those cases where a form of hunting that is clearly unnecessarily cruel is adopted). The arguments that foxes need to be culled and that hunting is not a peculiarly cruel method of doing so seem to me to stand up and to justify the practice in the context of my overall argument. The behaviour of some anti-hunt saboteurs, by contrast, does raise moral questions, while the question of why a government should think it has any business interfering in such

BISHOP BURTON COLLEGE
LIBRARY

a matter, though not a moral question, would be well worth pursuing. Contrast the issue of hunting with that of, say, obesity, which, while also not a moral issue, might at least be argued to be a proper concern of government and schools.

According to the argument presented, rudeness is not immoral. I hope I also make it clear that this is not to say that it is not objectionable. It may be objectionable in all sorts of way, but the question at issue is whether it is morally objectionable. The issue that needs further examination at this juncture, I concede, is whether, inasmuch as rudeness upsets people, it can be said to militate against their well-being. I have nothing to add to what I say in the text here, but I am not fully satisfied with my attempt to distinguish between behaviour that upsets a person and behaviour that is in some much stricter sense antithetical to their well-being. I have an uneasy feeling that it may be a matter of degree and that there is therefore danger of a slippery slope kind of argument (see the Commentary on Chapter 8 above). But at any rate my intention and attempt was to argue that behaviour that upsets me is of a different order from behaviour that materially impinges on or affects me – in some way this is along the lines of the playground chant 'sticks and stones may break my bones, but words can never harm me'. We may also note Jamie Whyte's contention that 'we mustn't confuse being sensitive with being right, nor rudeness with error' (p. 43). (I have quoted Whyte a number of times in the Commentaries, partly because I have only recently come across his work, partly because he writes with a refreshing lucidity, and partly because he reasons better than most.) The next step is to do the conceptual work on happiness, well-being, and respect for persons. See Elizabeth Telfer *Happiness* and Robin Barrow *Happiness*. See Geoffrey Warnock *The Object of Morality*, with reference to well-being, and R.S. Downie and Elizabeth Telfer *Respect for Persons*. In regard to the latter concept, see also S.I. Benn and R.S. Peters *Social Principles and the Democratic State* and R.S. Peters *Ethics and Education*.

To return to the matter of why such distinctions as that between moral and social values should be of concern, my claim that drunken louts may be offensive without being immoral has at least this important practical consequence: if we are concerned to combat drunks and loutish behaviour, we should look elsewhere than to moral education. Not only is the development of civility different from moral education, it may be that divorcing the issue of socially offensive behaviour from its moral overtones will make people more rather than less inclined to be concerned about it.

I also return to the theme of tolerance. In terms of virtue ethics, I would argue that courage, in the specific sense of the courage to stand up and be counted in relation to what is morally right, open-mindedness, truth-speaking (as contrasted with the rhetoric and 'spin' that are prevalent everywhere these days, in journalism, commerce, sport, and academia, no less than politics), and tolerance are key, though I have not chosen to approach the issue in these terms. These are crucial virtues because of the nature of morality, which is why I have approached moral philosophy in the way I have: one comes to see that there are virtues, and what they are, through appreciating what we do and do not know about morality. In relation to virtue ethics, see also Philippa Foot *Virtues and Vices* and G.E.M. Anscombe 'Modern Moral Philosophy', *Philosophy* 33.

On free speech, see Chapter 8 above. It should be remembered that 'to voice' an opinion in my terms means to 'hold and admit to' a certain belief and, other things being equal, to express it publicly, it being recognized that other things are not always equal.

That we have a moral obligation to obey the law of the land was a clear conviction of Plato's Socrates who explains in the *Phaedo* why he rejects the option of fleeing the country to escape the death penalty (which was a common and accepted practice at the time). Here I cannot follow Plato. As I say in the text, it seems transparent to me that there may be situations in which the path of virtue demands that we resist the law.

The distinction between politics and morality that I attempt to sketch is, I think, fundamentally correct and important, but I am very aware that what I have written is inadequate in various ways and merely scratches the surface of the subject. Obviously related to the topic is Niccolò Machiavelli (1469–1527) *The Prince*, although I wouldn't want anyone unfamiliar with the complexities and subtleties of that work to think that I am advocating being 'machiavellian' in the popular pejorative sense of that term. Once again, I find that Jamie Whyte *Bad Thoughts* has something pertinent to say on the matter:

> Ironically, it is the desire to present his actions as conforming to pure principle, rather than being the best compromise available, that makes Mr. Blair's positions so often seem arbitrary and unprincipled. His invasion of Iraq is a case in point. Had Mr. Blair admitted the many forces of *realpolitik* involved in making the decision to invade, rather than claiming a simple moral imperative to liberate oppressed peoples, his lack of action in the world's many other dictatorships would have exposed him to fewer accusations of inconsistency.
>
> (p. 90)

Further, even those of us who thought his calculations wrong would not be morally indignant, and indeed might accept that it is not in fact realistic to maintain that one must invade either every or no such state. But if we (or Mr Blair) confuse the moral and the political, then we must demand the sort of consistency that is built into the former in the case of the latter too.

10 Moral vs. health and safety values

In the previous chapter, I argued that various social, ecological, and sexual issues, though widely regarded as inherently moral issues, are not in fact so. This is an important point in the context of trying to gain a greater understanding of morality: morality does not cover everything; not every dispute is a moral dispute, regardless of how important or emotionally charged it may be for us. Recognition of this point may also encourage us to be more tolerant, open-minded, and respectful of others, and these *are* moral virtues.

In this chapter, I want to comment briefly on a number of examples which, though they may be genuine moral issues, we tend to consider in terms that are too black and white. These are areas where little is neat and tidy and where we are forced to face up to the fact that moral theory by its nature is unable to yield hard and fast, straightforward prescriptions and proscriptions. Sometimes the problem resides in a clash of moral principles, sometimes in the difficulty of establishing empirical facts, sometimes in conceptual uncertainty, and sometimes in a combination of two or more of these. The main purpose of reviewing these examples is to suggest that typically we look for too much certainty and are too dogmatic in moral matters, and to emphasize that it is not a deficiency in a moral theory that it cannot answer all our questions. There are grey areas in morality; it is the nature of the beast and there is something wrong with any theory that denies, overlooks, or sidesteps this. But again it must be stressed that this is quite distinct from the untenable doctrine that there are no moral truths and that all moral judgements are relative.

Those who traffic in drugs, besides being engaged in criminal activity, are very likely acting in an immoral way: they are, generally speaking, taking advantage of people and causing suffering, and often offending against second-order principles by engaging in extortion, blackmail, and threatening behaviour, if not worse. But smoking cannabis in a private house is a different situation. To be sure, where the smoking of cannabis is criminalized, to smoke it is illegal. But, as we constantly have to remind ourselves, an activity can be illegal and not immoral and, in addition, it is not always immoral to break a law: the private cannabis smoker is not on that account an immoral person. Once again, this is not necessarily to support the taking of this or any other drug; there may be good reason to make even the taking of soft drugs illegal, perhaps on the grounds that it tends to lead to taking harder drugs, which in turn may tend to lead to more serious criminal and even genuinely immoral behaviour. But to argue that there is good reason to make it illegal does not amount to saying that it is immoral. However, the situation becomes more complex when we ask whether getting into substance abuse and addiction at the heavy end of the spectrum is in itself to be acting wrongly; it may seem a little awkward to characterize such a person as wholly moral, and yet it seems strange to claim that the cocaine addict is for that reason alone to be judged a less than fully moral person. Such addiction, no doubt, is to be avoided, should perhaps be criminalized, and very likely will lead directly or indirectly to immoral acts such as mugging, stealing, and cheating. But in itself it is hard to classify drug-taking or addiction as either moral or immoral, not in this case because it is not a moral issue, but because it is difficult to know what to make of arguments either way. Thus, this would seem to be an instance of behaviour that should not in itself be assessed and evaluated in moral terms, although, as already conceded, there is a danger that getting involved with drugs will lead to activity that is immoral. That danger may provide a reason for being concerned about drugs and might conceivably justify certain social and legal restraints. But it does not make drug-taking a morally suspect activity.

Drinking, particularly to excess, despite the fact that in many societies at many times it has been a norm, is currently – rather surprisingly – often regarded as morally repugnant. In the eyes of some, the taking of any alcohol is morally wrong, but we may charitably assume that for the most part those who hold this view are confusing religion with morality, or even social manners with morality. At any rate, there is no conceivable reason to think of imbibing alcohol as in itself a moral issue. But what about drunkenness? Isn't doing anything to excess by definition going beyond a tolerable limit or norm and therefore wrong? It is by definition wrong in some sense, but not necessarily in a moral sense. Drunkenness may very reasonably be classified as boring, disgusting, self-destructive, leading to violence, abuse, and trouble for others, depending on the occasion and the form it takes. There is no need to glorify or even be particularly tolerant towards drunkenness, but that is different from saying that being drunk or drinking to excess is immoral. Even though it may lead to morally bad consequences, such as abuse and violence, it is not in itself immoral: whether one drinks too much or not may be a very serious and important issue for all sorts of reason, but it is not a moral issue.

To question whether drunk-driving is a moral issue might seem more contentious. Surely it is appropriate to experience moral indignation in the face of a drunk driver who, whether he actually harms anyone or not, puts others at risk. Surely the person who wakes the following morning and knows that he can remember nothing of his five-mile drive home should feel specifically moral shame? This is much more difficult, but still I incline to the view that we are wrong to classify drunk-driving as an immoral act, despite the fact that it is a serious matter to be discouraged by various means. It would incidentally help to keep this argument well grounded if the legal limits on alcohol consumption for drivers were not so ridiculously low, even in some cases zero. And it would be helpful to distinguish between those who drive when they are not in a state to remember doing so and the matron driving home over-carefully after two Christmas sherries. But, regardless of these points, while the consequences of heavy drinking, like those of being addicted to hard drugs, can undoubtedly be morally bad, there is still no reason to see the act of drinking more than is good for one as a moral issue. The weakness of will or character that it possibly betrays is not in itself a moral failing. And it is not clear that drunk-driving is in itself a moral issue, especially since, by the nature of the case, the agent is presumed not to be in charge of himself.

At this point, I think of cell-phones or mobiles. Most people, if thinking in moral terms, would probably regard drunk-driving rather than driving while using a mobile as the moral issue. This, I think, is a consequence of our puritan heritage, which still affects our moral attitudes and makes us associate the pleasures of sex and drink, and other forms of relatively uninhibited enjoyment, with lack of restraint and abandoned behaviour. So drunk-driving is worse than driving while using a cell-phone, not because of any facts about the dangers of either, but because being drunk is Dionysian while using a phone is all in a day's work. But the evidence and the reasoning suggest that driving while using a hand-held phone, dialling and talking, is at least as dangerous as driving while just over the legal alcohol limit. For this reason, I argue that driving while phoning is on a par with some illegal driving and drinking and that the use of phones while driving should be made illegal (as it already is in the UK but not in, e.g., Canada and the US), but that this is an issue of safety and not morality. But what are we to say of the person who, in a confined space (a restaurant, an otherwise quiet railway carriage, a bus stop, a bookshop), bellows into a mobile, disturbing the peace and privacy of all around, usually with a torrent of self-absorbed trivia? (I confess to being perplexed as to how anybody, given the multiplicity of cutting jokes, sneers, and adverse comment on the subject, can continue these days to bray loudly into a mobile in a public place. But let that pass.) This is certainly inconsiderate. It certainly causes irritation. It certainly intrudes on others. It certainly, generally speaking, has no obvious extrinsic justification. Is it therefore immoral behaviour? Alas, I am forced to conclude, in line with the general argument, that it is not. Unwanted intrusion is just that – it is not immoral. And, although talking on the phone while driving may be as dangerous as driving while slightly over the limit, and the driver on a mobile may be more thoughtless than the drunk driver inasmuch as he is acting soberly, such considerations do not make either of them guilty of immoral conduct, still less immoral people.

Context is all, as we keep seeing, and this is surely true in the case of pornography too. In so far as the business of pornography involves exploitation, manipulation, cheating, bullying, beating up, deceiving, blackmailing, brutality, and even death, we are of course straightforwardly dealing with immorality. But there is no obvious reason to accept the view that all sex-trade workers are exploited, still less the argument that they are by definition, on the grounds that to freely choose to engage in the business is impossible and therefore inevitably a self-delusion. I am not referring here to such things as the use of minors, enforced sexual activity, or so-called snuff movies. But, when it comes, for example, to sexually explicit movies made by people, including the participants, who choose to do so, and to the people who find sexual stimulation in watching such movies, again there seems no reason to regard this as a moral issue. If, as some would argue, those who freely choose to engage in the making of such films in reality have no alternative because of their economic or social servitude, the immorality would reside in the social system that created the situation. The point here is simply that if some people choose to be filmed performing sexual acts for the gratification of an audience, there is no reason to regard that as immoral. It is not a moral issue, because it is not connected to any of the five defining principles of morality or their derivatives. We think there is a moral issue, though there isn't, because we have been brought up to confuse moral with social, religious, legal, and other such taboos. Personally I think pornography of the type I am referring to is harmless and, indeed, welcome, but it should be remembered that my argument here is nonetheless not that it is necessarily a good thing in any way – merely that it is morally neutral.

Gambling is now becoming big business for governments and municipalities as well as corporations. There is not much doubt that it can lead to an individual's ruin, either in the sense that he may lose all he has or, worse, in that he becomes an addict and repeatedly squanders his livelihood and often that of his family. Not much doubt either that it is alien to the puritanical and probably not a good thing to become involved in. But on this issue there is a fairly clear degree of hypocrisy on the part of legislators, who, while recognizing and often deploring the dangers, nonetheless turn to and encourage gambling as a source of revenue. Ever since British Prime Minister Harold Wilson instituted the premium bond scheme, which he had previously damned as 'a squalid lottery', governments have fallen over themselves, not simply to liberalize gambling laws and license casinos, but to create lotteries on a daily basis. All of this is pretty distasteful, and the hypocrisy of such governments is certainly immoral, but gambling itself is nonetheless not immoral. It is yet another activity which may be unwise and in some sense unhealthy, despite being in this case, unlike that of smoking, encouraged by the powers that be, but which is in itself morally neutral.

Traffic laws, such as those governing speed, driving on one side of the road or another, and parking, are quite often used as examples to illustrate the difference between a normative rule (a social rule, a legal rule, etc.) and, specifically, a moral rule. Clearly, we need a rule about which side of the road we should drive on and it is important that the rule be followed; so it is desirable that people be fined, banned from driving, or whatever, if they break the law. But it is not immoral to drive on the wrong side of the road – not because it is all right, desirable, or forgivable to do so, still less because it is morally justifiable to do so. It is not immoral because it is not the kind of activity, despite being illegal and dangerous, that comes into the moral reckoning. It is true that driving on the wrong side might in fact be the consequence of the driver having a very imperfect moral character, the kind of person who thought nothing of others or the suffering he might cause; but even in such a case we would not conclude that the act of driving on the wrong side of the road is morally bad in the way that mugging someone is. Mugging, even if one's imagination can produce a situation in which it was morally justified, is always in itself morally bad. Driving on one side of the road or another simply isn't in itself either morally good or bad. It is a convention – and it is necessary to have and abide by conventions – but it is not a demand made on all humans by the nature of morality, as tolerance and kindness are.

But what about one of the most common infringements of the law, namely breaking the speed limit? To judge from the fact that virtually every driver has sometimes done it, and will probably continue to do it from time to time, we do not think it a very terrible thing to do, if we think it wrong at all. And this common view is correct, if for the wrong reasons. It is correct to think that it is not in itself an immoral act, but it is wrong to think that it necessarily doesn't matter. It may be thought that there is an important difference between careering down a crowded high street at 60 m.p.h. and proceeding down a deserted street at 3 or 4 m.p.h. over the speed limit. And so there is, but it is not immoral in itself to be breaking the law, as one would be in both cases. Although those guilty of the former may properly be criticized and penalized more strongly because they are more reckless and dangerous, it cannot be said that they are more immoral than the latter.

Smoking, which paradoxically is widely regarded as a moral failing, is no more a moral issue than gluttony or drinking. To do something disliked or frowned upon by others is not immoral, and the mere fact of causing upset to others cannot be construed as making an act other- rather than self-regarding. Morality does not come into the picture here because people ought to be free to do whatever does not impinge on others. Even if the smoker is contributing to his own death, he is not acting immorally. When it comes to smoking in front of others and the issue of second-hand smoke, the argument is partly unclear because of lack of certainty on an empirical issue. If it were the case, which I do not believe it is, that second-hand smoke directly kills other people in the way that shooting them does, rather than being, at worst, something that, like driving cars, creating fossil fuel-based energy, using pesticides, and maintaining industrial plants is contributing to a less than healthy climate, then of course there would be a case for saying that it is immoral. But in that case consistency demands that we recognize that it is not obviously any more immoral than driving our car or spraying our garden with certain insecticides. The 'moral' indignation to which smokers are subjected does not seem justified, whatever good reasons there may be for not smoking.

Gambling, smoking, drinking, dangerous driving, drugs: these are examples of social problems that are very much to the fore today and that do raise interesting and important questions. Some of the empirical claims made in relation to them are dubious, and some of the argument is equally so and often selective to a depressing degree. Nonetheless, there are problems and issues of concern here. But they are not in themselves moral issues. They should therefore be discussed in terms of the empirical claims about the consequences rather than in moral terms. Were that to happen, it is possible that the focus on the empirical claims would lead to a more critical evaluation of them and, ultimately, to less emotional, more rational conclusions.

Let us look now at some acts that are not generally speaking particularly frowned upon, certainly not regarded as immoral, but that are in fact more plausibly seen as moral issues than some of those we have considered so far in this chapter. While teenage children are downloading pop songs, their parents may be practising various small expense fiddles or tax evasions. The way in which such practices seem to be reconciled with our conscience is by saying that it is only a small amount, everybody does it, and the tax laws are quite outrageous anyway. But though all of this may be true, it is quite clear that such practices are dishonest and immoral, involving the telling of lies, the defrauding of others, and regarding oneself as somehow entitled to differential treatment (this last is probably why we try to convince ourselves that 'everybody is doing it'). Fiddling one's expenses and tax evasion, unlike driving over the speed limit, are in themselves wrong because in themselves they contravene the defining principles of morality. By acting in such ways one offends against truth, fairness (because, despite what we say, it is not true that everybody does it), and well-being. Such practices may not be as damaging as, say, dangerous driving (though they certainly can be, and are when practised at a corporate level), but to make that point is to confuse the issue. Morality is not intrinsically about health and safety or damage control, and it is no more about physical harm than any other kind of harm. It is about what principles of conduct we ought to observe, whoever we are and wherever we are. The fundamental principles being what they are, to cheat and defraud are paradigm instances of immoral conduct, while driving too fast, gambling too much or drinking to excess are not.

Betraying a friend, though it might in extreme circumstances be justified, is inherently wrong in a way that committing adultery and smoking are not. First, you have free choice and are not incapacitated by chemistry, as you may be said to be in the other two cases. (If you are overcome by, say, terror into betrayal, that might be some kind of exculpation.) Second, it offends directly against the second-order value of loyalty. Loyalty is owed to a friend out of respect for persons and for truth, as well as out of consideration for people's well-being. In general, friends, figuratively speaking, vow to stand by one another. To betray that trust for self-advantage, profit, or convenience, or for lack of courage, is like breaking a promise for such reasons. It is the kind of thing that one simply shouldn't do, in a way that smoking and driving too fast are not. As with promise-keeping, nobody could intelligibly subscribe to the view that it wouldn't matter if people generally let their friends down, for that would defeat the object of friendship.

Equally wrong, although often socially endorsed or tolerated, are: any form of mental or physical cruelty to any sentient being, partial hiring practices (which is nowadays often actually institutionalized, so far do we fail to see that hiring someone because they are of a certain ethnic background or the spouse of someone else we want to hire is unfair discrimination against properly qualified candidates), and the kind of spin or deception so prevalent among politicians and not uncommon in other walks of life. Selling arms is surely one of the most immoral acts in the world, and yet, as already mentioned, it is practised on a daily basis, without stigma, not just by individuals and corporations, but by governments as well.

My point throughout this chapter has been partly that the specifically moral indignation that is aroused by sexual peccadilloes and unusual practices, by the breaking of social conventions and legal rules, is very often misdirected and should be brought to bear instead on certain things that we either tend to laugh off, such as tax evasion, or that we fail to focus on because they are not apparent in everyday life, such as the major evil of selling arms.

The traditional 'sins' of lust, gluttony, sloth, greed, anger, and pride are not necessarily moral failings. They can of course lead to moral failings, but they do not inevitably do so and they can sometimes be morally justified. Some of them are characteristics over which we do not have full control: one can deny or tame lust, but even the saintly cannot altogether prevent themselves from feeling lust. None of these characteristics are perhaps attractive, most of them sooner or later lead to trouble, and they may be inextricably tied up with seeming vices such as selfishness. The fact remains that it is not in itself morally wrong to feel or even on occasion to display anger or pride. Certain kinds of greed and lust are arguably even desirable (greed for honour and praise, and lust for life), but even the more commonplace gluttonous greed is not morally reprehensible; once again, it is difficult to see that it has anything to do with morality. (To stuff oneself with food at the expense of the starving would be quite a different matter, of course.) The bias against sloth is surely a social or civic matter; we do not want people to be slothful and we do not admire it, but it is not therefore immoral.

Finally, there are four concepts that are intriguing in themselves, that would benefit from further consideration in respect of their moral status, and that deserve to be introduced here because, among other things, they take us into conceptually grey areas: forgiveness, selfishness, vanity, and caring. Forgiveness has already been mentioned briefly in Chapter 8 above. But some of the key questions can be repeated and a few more added. Is forgiveness a moral virtue? Should I forgive the murderer of my child, or even the 'innocent' driver who ran her over? Is there not something morally improper about forgiving immoral people? This is another concept where the historical fact that religion has been confused with and played a part in shaping our moral views has made a difference. Forgiveness is certainly a Christian virtue. But is it in fact a moral concept? Is it in itself morally good, bad, or indifferent to forgive? This may be a morally grey area, but I incline to the view, without attempting to justify it here, that it is morally indifferent.

We urgently need a thoroughgoing analysis of selfishness in all its various forms. Is self-centredness the same as selfishness? Is egotism? Is *amour-propre* the same as either? Is it selfish to put one's family before others? Fairly clearly, a crude selfishness that simply says 'me, me, me' and pursues its own gratification without thought for others, or indeed without moral restraint, is immoral. But the selfishness (self-absorption?) which is rather an honest self-preoccupation, a concern with trying to understand who one is and, further, trying to live within the bounds of morality, in a way that is honest and true to oneself, does not seem so obviously a moral failing.

Vanity seems to me particularly obnoxious, but I am not sure that I can see it is as a moral deficiency, as distinct from something that is unattractive and uncongenial to many of us. Caring, which I mention because it is very much in vogue as a value, particularly among teachers, while obviously not something that one can be against or disapprove of, at any rate in the abstract, is perhaps nonetheless not the central value that many take it to be, and, more particularly, not a specifically moral value. I would in the first place distinguish caring from compassion. The latter does seem to be morally incumbent on us, demanded by our commitment to people's well-being and to respect for persons, but I remain unconvinced that we have a moral obligation to care about others in general, if that implies some active emotional attachment to them. Some people used to attempt to distinguish between empathy and sympathy, the former implying getting inside and sharing the experiences of others, rather as I am interpreting caring, the latter implying a more dispassionate but compassionate concern for their experiences. In this terminology, then, I think sympathy a moral virtue, while empathy is more than morality calls for.

I have argued for the importance of seeing morality in terms of principles rather than in terms of specific rules and particular acts. But it is also helpful (and necessary) to understand morality by reference to the characteristics or dispositions of the agent. What makes a person moral as opposed to immoral, besides adherence to the fundamental principles? A moral person is, generally speaking, disposed to be truthful, kind, generous, considerate, thoughtful, open-minded, courageous, tolerant, and compassionate, all of which are entirely compatible with being a smoker, an adulterer, a homosexual, or a drinker, but not with being a tax evader, a dishonest businessman, or a person who routinely ignores others in distress. One particular thing that the moral person is not is hypocritical, because his commitment to truth, honesty, and sincerity is incompatible with hypocrisy.

It may be felt that the previous paragraph involves trickery or sleight of hand (and not in a very subtle form), since by definition honesty, courage, and kindness are good and their opposites bad. But that, though true, misses the point, which is that we have given more specification than we would by simply saying that the good is the good; most importantly, we have shown that some approaches to morality and some common claims about morality won't stand up. We are trying to understand morality, not to provide a key to determining what choices are moral on each and every occasion. Part of the argument has been that we have in the past looked for too much certainty and too much practical guidance. But the dogma that certain sexual acts or inclinations are morally wrong, that it is always necessarily wrong to break a promise or tell a lie, that social taboos such as those on smoking and drinking are moral taboos, has been shown to be misplaced. We cannot do more than say that the moral person should have such qualities as kindness and tolerance and should try to act in accordance with the five first-order principles of truth, well-being, respect, fairness, and freedom, and second-order principles such as promise-keeping that follow from them.

That being the nature of morality, much will necessarily remain uncertain. Principles will clash, there will be competing claims on one's kindness and one's truthfulness, empirical situations will change, making it morally wrong to do here today what it was clearly right to do yesterday or somewhere else, and most of the moral concepts introduced, such as friendship, need to be further considered and interpreted. It cannot be too strongly stated that this openness, this lack of resolution, is not an argument against the validity of the moral theory outlined. We judge a moral theory not by its usefulness as a guide to action, but by its plausibility.

The theme of Part III has been that we are far too ready to classify a multiplicity of issues as moral that are not in fact so. In the previous chapter, social, ecological, and sexual issues in particular were distinguished from moral ones. In this chapter the focus has been on what might be regarded as a subset of social issues – activities that are widely stigmatized as immoral or morally wrong (the connotations of the latter phrase being perhaps slightly less dramatic), but which are in fact at best health and safety issues, in some cases not even matters for much concern on those terms.

Morality, according to the overall argument of this book, is defined by the five principles of fairness, freedom, respect, truth, and well-being. That much is as objectively true as it is that the world is round. Any society that has no interest in conducting itself according to these principles is not interested in morality. Understanding that this is the essence of morality does in many cases give one clear and solid guidance as to how to conduct oneself morally: keep promises, tell the truth, be kind, be loyal to friends, and so forth. But circumstances must be taken into account in determining exactly what one should do and therefore there will sometimes be legitimate differences between what it is right to do in different places and at different times. In addition, there will be times when it is morally justifiable to do something that is intrinsically wrong and there will be dilemmas: situations where it cannot be determined what ought to be done (although usually a number of options that ought not to be adopted can still be discerned).

These limits do not show that we do not fully understand morality. On the contrary, they are the product of our understanding. It is part of moral knowledge or wisdom to recognize that much of what passes for moral behaviour, moral argument, and moral praise and blame has actually little or nothing to do with morality. Given all this, the moral person ought to be truthful, compassionate, kind, tolerant, and open-minded. These are the cardinal virtues. And, in a word, the moral person is one who acts with integrity at all times, that is, out of commitment to the basic moral principles, and not one who subscribes to any set of particular unyielding rules, most especially not rules that are in fact social, legal, ecological, sexual, or health and safety rules rather than moral ones.

Commentary

The most important point to stress at this juncture is that the recognition that some particular moral judgements are relative (in the sense and for the reasons fully outlined in the course of this book) is to be sharply distinguished from any claim to the effect that they are arbitrary. A great deal of so-called post-modern thought is based upon a simple confusion between the truth that some statements are true in one context but not in another (which applies as much to empirical claims as to moral ones) and the quite false idea that all statements or claims are equally acceptable. The latter does not follow from the former and, to anybody who reflects on the matter rather than accepts the fashionable ideology, is very obviously not true. To say that moral (or any other) claims are inevitably arbitrary is to say that they are merely the product of whim, prejudice, or taste. Nobody disputes that they may sometimes be so or that very often there is a degree of prejudice or personal preference that comes into and thus contaminates our judgements. What is being strenuously denied is that this commonplace observation is all there is to be said. No developed form of human inquiry, be it science, history, or morality, can be dismissed as arbitrary. To imagine that they are is to misunderstand them. The quite different observation that differences of moral judgement sometimes legit-imately arise because the basic moral principles are being applied in radically different circumstances is nothing to be worried about. Far from discrediting rationality, its truth is discerned by reason.

At first sight, it may seem that the argument that becoming involved with soft drugs may lead to hard drugs and ultimately to various kinds of immoral conduct is an example of the slippery slope argument (see the Commentary on Chapter 9 above). But it is not. To say that we cannot tolerate the taking of soft drugs because it will lead to the taking of hard drugs and immorality would be an example of the slippery slope. But I am not saying that. I am raising the empirical question of whether addiction to one kind of drug does lead to another, but my conclusion is that we do not have conclusive evidence on this subject and, in any case, my argument is that there are no grounds for classifying drug-taking of any type as in itself immoral. Perhaps some readers will feel that both drug-taking and drinking are grey areas where it is unclear whether or when behaviour becomes morally reprehensible. But that is not my position, which is that in itself neither should be classified as a moral issue, though obviously they can both be social and legal issues.

The mention of cell-phones later in this chapter might also raise the ques-tion of the slippery slope. Granted that driving while using a cell-phone is not a moral issue but that it may nonetheless be dangerous, some might reason that if using a hand-held phone is dangerous because distracting, then so is using a non-hand-held phone, in which case so in turn is talking to passengers, and then again even carrying passengers. Consequently, it might be said, we should not make using cell-phones while driving illegal. This line of argument seems to me to be unconvincing (and is a species of the slippery slope). Some things are more dangerous than others, and there is nothing irrational (though it may be incorrect) about arguing that driving while using a cell-phone is more dangerous than talking to passengers, and that the former should be made illegal but the latter not.

A Canadian branch of MADD (Mothers Against Drunk Driving) recently aired a curious advertisement on the radio. A 'doctor' was heard to say that even after six drinks a 200-pound man who also ate something and who waited for two hours, would not register as over the limit if breathalysed. On the face of it, this would seem to lead to the conclusion that, if you are going to drink six glasses, you should also eat, weigh 200 pounds and wait two hours before driving. But the conclusion drawn was different. It was that the 'two drink' limit, which is popularly supposed to be the legally acceptable limit, is too high, presumably on the confused grounds that, if in certain circumstances six drinks can be under the limit, the limit must be wrongly set. This is truly bizarre reasoning and it might more truthfully be said that it is an example of prejudice and ignoring the facts. *Ex hypothesi*, the facts would appear to be that, given food, size, and time, six drinks do not necessarily seriously impact a person.

There is an obvious difference between a sober person who says, 'I am going to drive dangerously', and a person who, due to alcohol, thinks that he can drive safely but cannot. The latter may be equally dangerous and, from a legal point of view, equally problematic. But he is not for these reasons immoral. Whether he can be accused of weakness of will by dint of the fact that he drinks too much, and, if so, whether that is a moral defect, are questions that need to be pursued much more fully than I have been able to do here. My initial response is that neither an instance of nor even a tendency to drink too much can be seen as weakness of will, which is a permanent characteristic pertaining to matters generally rather than a particular physical dependency, and, in any case, genuine weakness of will, though obviously detrimental to one's chances of behaving morally in a consistent manner, is not in itself a moral failing. It is not immoral to be weak and indecisive by nature, in the way that it is to be cruel, unkind, or untruthful by nature. However, I concede that this view is contentious. Aristotle distinguishes between profligacy or licentiousness (*akolasia*) and lack of restraint or weakness of will (*akrasia*) and provides a detailed study of the latter in the *Nicomachean Ethics* (Book Seven). My main point here is that not all admitted character defects should be seen as moral defects: haughtiness, coldness, arrogance, and conceit, for example, might all be said to be character defects without being regarded as moral failings. Weakness of will is something that through education we should seek to rectify, because it can lead to a lot of unfortunate and undesirable consequences, but a weak-willed person is not *ipso facto* a morally bad one.

Reference to the inconsiderateness of many cell-phone users raises the question of whether thoughtlessness is not itself a moral failing. The answer, as in the case of forgiveness, is surely that while being considerate or thoughtful about others is praiseworthy and very possibly useful to those who aspire to lead moral lives, it is not in itself a moral virtue. Forgiveness, thoughtfulness, imagination, determination, and strength of purpose are all valued and valuable qualities, but they are not inherently moral in the way that tolerance, kindness, compassion, and open-mindedness are. William Hare *Open-mindedness and Education* is relevant to this topic. Incidentally, the view presented here does not accord with Aristotle's famous disquisition on the subject in the *Nicomachean Ethics*, where he divides the virtues of the soul (*psyche*) into those of character (*ethos*) and intellect (*dianoia*), the former being also referred to as moral virtues.

Reference to the fact that some people may willingly choose to engage in, say, prostitution or casual sex raises questions about how free our choices are and related matters to do with our motivation. Plato maintained that no one willingly does wrong. His view appears to have been that if we knew what was morally good we would do it. That, though generally regarded as less than convincing, is to be distinguished from the dangerously false doctrine referred to in the text to the effect that everybody is guilty of false consciousness, in the sense that the reasons we give to explain our conduct are invariably false unless they conform to those of a given ideology. This view may perhaps owe something to the impact of Sigmund Freud's (1856–1939) stress on the workings of the subconscious, but it became a more particular tactic of Marxist writings: any claim concerning one's reasons for action that is at a variance with the ideological line that everything is determined by the material or economic structure of society is the product of false consciousness (material or economic determinism). In other words, there is no escaping the party line: either you say that your views are the product of the social order, and thereby preserve your credibility as a member of the party, or you falsely deny it and thereby reveal yourself as an enemy of the truth. It is a feature of ideologies that they dismiss as in some way deluded or inauthentic evidence that contradicts them. The fact is, however, that there are some people who enjoy being involved in the so-called sex trade and who are not deceiving themselves or anybody else on that score. (Incidentally, I ignore one line of argument in feminist theory to the effect that pornography etc. degrades women, because that begs the questions that I do raise in the text. If women are being exploited, if they ought not to act in ways entailed by pornography etc., then indeed they are being degraded; but such are the questions at issue.)

It does seem rather incredible that in many jurisdictions smoking has now been banned altogether from public places, including the open air. There are several pertinent questions to be raised in response to this: why, if it is so repugnant and detrimental to health or way of life, is it allowed at all, rather than made illegal, as is generally the case with dangerous drugs? Is the evidence relating to the dangers of second-hand smoke consistent and convincing? Given that such evidence as there is establishes far more clearly that, for example, those working at petrol stations face similar but more intense health risks from the fumes, why is something not done about that? Given that it is clear that our cars pollute our atmosphere in the same way, with the same detrimental consequences, and to a far greater extent, why is there not a ban on petrol-engine vehicles? Why is there not even a concerted effort to use rail rather than road for haulage? But the major concern that I would like to emphasize, apart from the point made in the text that whether it is a health hazard or not it is not immoral to smoke, is that a matter such as this is made the subject of draconian legislation. Why should not those who choose to risk death by smoking do so? What has happened to the idea of personal responsibility? I am ignoring the issue of secondary smoke here and focusing simply on those who wish to go to a pub, for instance, and join fellow smokers. The argument that a pub allowing smoking would be a place where those who wanted to avoid second-hand smoke could not find employment is stunning in its inadequacy. I cannot begin to list the jobs for which, for one reason or another, I am unable or unwilling to apply. Similarly, the argument that smoking costs the taxpayer money is one of the most unconvincing I have ever heard (notwithstanding the fact that, by chance, the day that I was making final corrections to this page the newspapers were full of a report in Canada claiming that smokers, drinkers, and gamblers cost the taxpayer billions of dollars a year). Allowing for the huge tax revenues from smoking, for the fact that those who would have died of cigarette-induced cancer will presumably live longer on pensions, social security, and other medical support, taking up the time of doctors, social workers, etc., and for the fact that many of them will still die expensively (to put it crudely but succinctly), the notion that there will be a net financial gain if smoking is banned, or that smokers are somehow costing the rest of us money, beggars belief in its implausibility. Such exercises in imaginary accounting more than prove the truth of the adage that one can prove anything with numbers.

In respect of personal responsibility, why is it that firemen, soldiers, and policemen now routinely find their jobs overwhelming and feel entitled to compensation for stress and danger? Is it that the soldiers of the past did not face danger, that they did not feel stress, or that they accepted them as part of the job? Or is it simply that the lawyers hadn't developed a lucrative line in claims for damages and compensation? Why is it that more and more people find other people's scent, aftershave, or mere presence unacceptable and demand that it be removed? Is it really the case that empirically we are less able to survive comfortably than our ancestors? Or is it that we have decided that we have a right to complain? If the latter, what are the grounds for this alleged right? On rights, see Chapter 4 above. On this topic generally, see Robert Hughes *The Culture of Complaint*.

The rather brief remarks on partial hiring practices, 'spin', and so forth may be supplemented slightly here. Partial hiring is, of course, a species of what used to be called 'reverse' or 'positive' discrimination. (It is interesting how quickly such catchphrases go in and out of fashion.) Such discrimination has never been well justified, despite the political support it briefly garnered. Yes, there are injustices that need to be redressed, but it is hard to see how discriminating against, say, men or white people will either make up for past discrimination against women and blacks or be morally justified. Two wrongs don't make a right. If we are to redress the balance of history, where and when are we to stop? Will the generation of whites who were deprived of job opportunities, promotion, and suchlike to atone for the sins of their parents, in the name of positive discrimination, be entitled to appeal for positive discrimination in favour of their children on the grounds that their parents were disadvantaged? The appeal to history in moral matters is something to be discouraged, for where do we stop or begin? Can I expect some compensation for the injustices my family suffered four generations ago? Why should I, who did not personally suffer at all, be a beneficiary of this historical claim? Why should you, who did not play any part in the injustice to my ancestors, have to pay a price to compensate me? How far back in history shall we go, indeed how far back can we go in any meaningful way, to determine who has a birthright to the land of Israel? There is a curious sense in which much of the argument on historical grounds seems in practice to attempt to revise the historical record: 'Six hundred years ago this land was taken from your ancestors and, sadly and no doubt wrongly, all but a handful of you were wiped out. Since then this other tribe or nation has created a civilization here. Ah, yes. But now we're going to pretend that never happened: this land is your land.' Unfortunately, the facts of history suggest that it is not.

The 'spin' that has become a cliché in reference to political life is part of a much broader problem. As George Orwell (1903–50) repeatedly argued, once language is distorted and debased we are all in very serious trouble. The rhetorical devices, the concern for sound and appearance rather than substance, that pervade almost all modern media communications and professional jargon, even the world of academia with its meaningless vision statements and often nearly incomprehensible argot and cant, are destroying not only credibility but also the chances of truly moral conduct. Talk and thought that are not clear and honest are themselves immoral, and a world in which communication itself is predominantly dishonest cannot enhance our chances of living the moral life.

Selling arms is wrong because it is done at the expense of others in order to make money, while the rhetoric justifying it is invariably false. It is also, of course, extremely dangerous, but my point here is that it is also dishonest to pretend that it is ever done for good motives, as vague allusions to peace, preserving the balance of power or maintaining the forces of good may suggest. It is done, whether by individuals or governments, to make money and/or to advance selfish political interests. The rhetoric may say that it is done to preserve or create democracy and some may sincerely feel that democracy is inherently preferable to any other political system, but the truth is that we do not have the knowledge to make this claim and we should, from a moral perspective, be more open-minded about how other people choose to live. There is certainly no clear argument to justify selling arms to one side in some other country's war on the grounds that they are 'democratic', even leaving out of account the fact that in practice such arguments stretch the meaning of 'democratic' and that the empirical record of success in such enterprises is dismal. Inasmuch as the motive (i.e. to make money) is generally more freely admitted, private arms sellers are perhaps marginally less venal than governments which, while espousing peace, stoke the flames of war. But it is still wrong for an individual to take advantage of the predicament of others, just as it is wrong for pharmaceutical companies to experiment clandestinely, or under the guise of providing help, on innocent and impoverished fellow human beings. In the past, a great deal of criticism of capitalism tried to suggest that the very idea of such an economy was immoral. There seems no good reason to make that claim, but there is every reason to say that at the present time corruption and hypocrisy – in short immorality – are rife in the practice of many corporations.

Oxford University Press has recently published a series of books on the seven deadly sins, including Simon Blackburn *Lust*. While some of the volumes are interesting and entertaining, it is not clear that the project as a whole does much to make a case for seeing this approach as useful to moral philosophy.

Perhaps this is the place for me to say that I do not happen to smoke, drive after drinking, possess a cell-phone, or gamble. I do like a drink and I shall keep my sexual proclivities to myself, but I wouldn't want any reader to assume that in denying that the various health and safety issues referred to in this chapter are moral issues, and that some of them are significant issues at all, I am grinding any personal axes. The nature of morality seems to me to indicate that these are not matters of moral concern, while the conduct of many of our leaders in government, business, the academy, and the media certainly is.

Part IV
Moral education

Part IV

Moral education

11 Moral questions in education

As with the field of morality and moral philosophy generally, it is necessary when considering moral education to begin by clearing away a number of misapprehensions, misconstructions, and misconceptions. The true enemy of understanding is not lack of understanding so much as misunderstanding. Again as with morality generally, a major mistake in respect of moral education is to define the subject too broadly and loosely, as if it covered everything from cultivating good manners to producing saints, from inculcating the habit of punctuality to instilling the courage of the martyr. It is necessary therefore to begin by getting our bearings; and, at the risk of disappointing those who do not see that clearing the ground of confused and confusing irrelevance is both an important and a necessary prerequisite to drawing positive conclusions, this chapter largely consists in outlining and explaining why there are some things that I am not going to be concerned with.

There are as many moral questions that may arise in the context of education as there are in any other setting. For example, is it morally acceptable to use corporal punishment? Is it ever justifiable to lie to a student or colleague? When should the interests of the majority limit the freedom of the individual? But there are also a number of questions which, though they are often described as 'moral', are not truly moral questions. Whether homosexual relationships should be condoned in a school context, for instance, is a legitimate educational question, but it is not on that account a moral question, for reasons already given in Chapter 9 above.

In addition to questions that, despite appearances, are not moral at all, there are those that, while they have a moral dimension, are only problematic for reasons that have nothing to do with morality. For example, the claim that all children should have equal access to education is a moral claim. But the difficulty with this claim is not primarily a moral one: the question is not whether the claim is correct, for nobody today argues that access to educational provision should be unequal in the sense that the children of the rich, say, should have greater access to quality education than the children of the poor. The problems are rather what constitutes fair or equal access to education and how in practice to ensure it. The latter is neither a moral nor a philosophical question, but an empirical one, and the former, while it is a philosophical question, is an educational rather than a moral one. It depends ultimately on what we understand the nature of education to be rather than on our view of fairness. The more general demand that all children should be treated fairly is a moral and uncontentious demand. The problem of working out what counts as fair treatment in regard to education is a question about education rather than morality.

This is not a mere quibble or a point about correct classification or terminology. I do not intend to pursue the question of equal educational access, but I am not justifying that omission simply on the grounds that, strictly speaking, it is not a moral question. The reason that the questions of equal access and fair treatment in education cannot be pursued here is that they are huge questions that depend upon a thorough exploration and understanding of the field of education. They are partly philosophical, but the expertise and background needed depend not on an understanding of the moral concepts of fairness and equality so much as on an understanding of what education is all about and of various empirical claims about children, such as whether or not there are innate differences in intelligence. So the first point to note is that many educational problems that seem on the surface to be moral problems are not going to be solved merely or even primarily through moral philosophy. Consequently, many interesting educational problems which may appear to be moral problems will nonetheless not be pursued here.

Professional ethics, which is sometimes seen as a branch of moral philosophy, is a confused area and one that I shall also ignore. Much of what passes for academic ethics is in fact concerned either with an issue that is genuinely moral or ethical, but not peculiar to the academic context, or with an issue that is particular to academic life but not specifically moral. For example, taking advantage of one's students is a genuine moral issue, but so is taking advantage of anybody in any context; and what constitutes taking advantage of students depends upon the nature of the academic context rather than upon morality. Conversely, the question of the appropriate relations between university professors and mature students is an issue for academic institutions, but not necessarily a moral one of any significance. To rape students or coerce them into sex by the threat of withholding grades is obviously morally wrong and would be in any context. This has nothing to do with the educational context therefore. By contrast, though friendship is intrinsically good, an academic institution may want to pursue the non-moral question of what forms and degrees of friendship are appropriate in an educational context, and that is primarily to be answered by reference to the nature of the institution and its purposes. In short, teachers' professional ethics, when we are not talking about moral demands that apply to us all, are, or should be, concerned with the norms of conduct that are appropriate to the role of a teacher in an educational setting; they do not hinge upon moral so much as educational philosophy. Questions of professional ethics, therefore, I shall also ignore.

There are some questions that are both specific to an educational context and truly moral. For example, is it morally acceptable to inculcate values in the young? Is it morally acceptable to provide differential education? Is it morally acceptable to punish children and, if so, in what ways? Punishment by definition involves a degree of pain or suffering, whether physical, psychological, or both. Other things being equal, it is of course morally wrong to make children or anybody else suffer and Dickens's Dotheboys Hall is indisputably an example of a morally repugnant institution. So much is hardly worth discussing. But whether a particular punishment, notwithstanding the fact that it involves some pain, may be morally justified in a specific educational context is a quite different matter. It is a moral question; however, it is still not one that can be adequately dealt with in the context of or by means of moral philosophy alone. To discuss the issue in a suitable manner would involve a thoroughgoing philosophical examination of the educational enterprise as well as empirical research relating to psychological concepts such as motivation and, more broadly, the educational practices of teaching and learning. But, since, despite my disclaimer above, some readers are bound to be restive at my insistence that such questions cannot reasonably be dealt with here, I will at least indicate my own position on this issue.

There are three prominent theories of punishment. The deterrent theory argues that punishment is justified by the fact that it deters people from doing wrong (whether the persons punished, other people, or both). The retributive theory sees justification in the fact of retribution and is often characterized in terms of 'an eye for an eye'; you are punished because you did wrong, regardless of the consequences of punishment. The reformative theory justifies punishment as a means to reform the wrongdoer. Needless to say, as with most theoretical divisions and categories, one can draw on any one or more of these theories to a greater or lesser extent. I draw on all three, taking the view that punishment is by definition retributive, that its prime justification is deterrence, and that we should seek to use modes of punishment that help to reform the wrongdoer. It is by definition retributive in that a given punishment only counts as punishment if it is administered in response to some act of wrongdoing. (This does not, incidentally, imply endorsement of the biblical call for a punishment that matches the crime in a literal or even symbolic sense; one can believe that a person should be punished because they took a life without believing that their life has to be the forfeit. But it surely does imply some notion of a punishment being proportionately related to the magnitude of the crime.) In saying that the main justification is deterrence, one is not committed to the view that if in particular cases there is reason to suppose that there will be no deterrent effect there is no justification for punishment. In the first place, it is arguable that it is the system of punishment rather than particular punishments that is justified by deterrence, and that particular punishments, while they should ideally take a form and a degree of gravity that take account of the deterrence value in the particular case, are also justified by appeal to both retribution and reform; in the second place, given that retribution is built into the concept, there is an element of retribution in any justification. But when it comes to imposing the most appropriate punishment, we would surely like to add particular reference to a form that provides some likelihood of reform on the part of the wrongdoer.

In the context of schools, there is no obvious reason to accept the view that punishment in all its forms is necessarily damaging either psychologically or educationally, or to deny that it can serve as a means to improvement and even as a type of motivation. But, because of the relative lack of foreknowledge and responsibility, combined with the relatively unformed and malleable nature of the young, retribution should probably play a lesser part in our thinking, apart from maintaining the broad attempt to make punishment relatively proportionate to the crime in the interests of fairness. However, there is no reason to abjure a system of punishment in schools in respect of social wrongs or academic wrongs (e.g. cheating); whether punishment is justified specifically in relation to poor academic performance or learning perhaps depends mainly on the empirical question of whether such things as keeping students in after class, setting them extra work, or making them clean the playground do or do not serve to motivate students or in some other way contribute to a better standard of performance. I suspect that we do not really know the answer to that question, and that it works in some cases and not in others. There is nothing very contentious about any of this, despite the fact that there have always been a few who argue that any kind of punishment is to be deplored (though it is not always clear if the grounds are that it is morally wrong or empirically ineffective). The interesting and more contentious question is whether corporal or any other form of physical punishment can ever be justified. I cannot myself see an argument for concluding that smacking is in itself always inherently morally offensive, though I am not a particular advocate of the practice and can see very real dangers arising out of sadism and the like in particular cases. Conversely, I do not accept that all punishment should be of the community service type.

I record these brief comments on punishment, without much in the way of argument, to remind readers that I am not ducking interesting questions because I do not have or do not want to reveal my position on what some might regard as controversial matters, but because, as even my brief remarks indicate, the questions cannot be settled on the basis of moral philosophy alone. Their resolution also requires a great deal of empirical research and a comprehensive philosophy of education.

There are a number of questions that are not unique to education, but have a particular importance in that context, such as questions relating to bullying. Bullying can take place in one form or another in virtually any context, but it is clearly a particular concern in schools. Similarly, certain issues may be thought to lack moral significance generally speaking, but to raise moral issues in the school situation. I have already argued that most aspects of sexual relations do not in themselves give rise to moral questions, but to say that sexual intercourse between two adults is not a moral issue is not necessarily to say the same about intercourse between two school children, or between the teacher and a young teenager. Here too I will make a comment, despite my wider point that an understanding of moral philosophy alone is insufficient to provide an answer to the question of whether such practices are variously morally unacceptable, morally wrong but justifiable, or even morally commendable.

There have recently been cases of young, occasionally middle-aged, teachers having love affairs with teenage students, of sexual activity among legally under-age students, and, at university level, countless instances of sexual relationships between student and professor, not infrequently involving alleged abuses of power. At the high school level there are also ongoing discussions about condom machines, keeping information from parents in the interests of confidentiality, and teaching in relation to matters of sexual orientation and practice. While not going as far as those who argue that loving relationships between student and teacher (including sex at the higher age levels) are a positive good, as witness, it may be said, Abelard and Heloïse, I believe that such relationships can sometimes be justified. There is certainly a need for us to rethink our assumptions about the age at which children can or should do this or that, for though psychological maturity notoriously lags behind physical maturity, the obvious fact remains that many of our attitudes are based upon an out-of-date view of what teenagers are like, both physically and psychologically. That said, in general, at the secondary level (and *a fortiori* at the elementary level), there is a moral responsibility on the part of the teacher to refrain from developing such relationships. It is not that there is anything intrinsically wrong with a love affair between a fifteen-year-old and a forty-year-old. But to some extent adults have control over whether they allow themselves to fall in love, certainly on how they act in response to their emotions, and we know that for all sorts of reason nine out of ten of the relationships we are talking about here end in disaster and are a great deal more trouble than they are worth, particularly for the student. It is therefore a form of taking advantage for the teacher to persist in developing any such relationship, whatever his or her immediate intentions. In the interests of well-being and respect (and perhaps even truth, since we know that the young very often get things wrong), I would conclude that there is a moral obligation on teachers to avoid forming passionate relationships with their students.

The extent to which gender issues are moral issues generally speaking is debatable. In the context of the school there would seem to be few serious and controversial moral issues arising out of gender considerations. There are of course those who see a moral issue in sex-role stereotyping, but it is hard to see on what grounds. There is no obvious link between the foundational moral principles and the practice of bringing up girls and boys in the conventional manner. It may be argued that if a child shows a clear inclination towards an unexpected role or stereotype, the claims of respect and well-being should lead us to go along with it. This is possibly true (it certainly isn't morally wrong to do so, though it is still unclear that this is really a moral issue), but it does not follow that there is anything morally wrong in parents from the outset acting in ways that will very likely contribute to moulding the child into the traditional gender role. (By the same token, it is not morally wrong to do the opposite, but there may be practical arguments against the wisdom of doing so.) I would conclude that the sensible way to proceed is to begin by bringing up boys and girls in traditional ways, but to look out for and respect differences or departures from the stereotype as they emerge. There is no good reason for feeling morally ashamed of influencing the shape of the development of one's children either in itself or in respect of following a stereotype.

As for some of the more familiar types of educational practice based on traditional views of gender difference, it is surely quite appropriate, for example, to teach boys and girls in mixed classes but to provide separate changing rooms. But, whatever one's views on this or any other particular example, it is not a moral issue so much as a question of what is reasonable given our conventions, our wider views about life and people in general, and, above all, the educational imperative. Those views may of course change, in a way that views of the fundamental moral principles cannot or should not change. So, while wanton cruelty was always and will always be wrong, the notion that boys and girls should have separate changing rooms may very well change over time; but that is not a moral problem, because it is not a moral issue.

The preceding paragraphs have distinguished between questions that, while they are commonly taken to be moral, are in fact variously and to a greater or lesser degree questions about education, professional norms, and empirical matters, and always, for that reason, impossible to answer in terms of moral philosophy alone, if they admit of an unequivocal answer at all. I shall illustrate the general point by reference to racism, which is seen by some as a major issue for schools.

Now, in the first place, one may question this premise. It is at least arguable that generally speaking schools are the least racist places in society, since they are institutions with a high degree of authority and control, exercised over relatively dependent individuals by people who are by and large particularly aware of, concerned about, and opposed to racism. This should be set against the picture painted by the sensationalism of the media, particularly the tabloid press, which by highlighting the exceptional and extreme cases gives a false impression, not necessarily of the awfulness of certain particular cases, but of the overall size and nature of the problem.

Nonetheless, racism is to some extent a problem in schools as well as society as a whole, and it is by definition immoral since it means 'treating people differently on grounds of race, when it is inappropriate to do so'. The clause 'when it is inappropriate to do so' is necessary, since it is not the case that it is always morally wrong to treat people differently on grounds of race. It does not, for example, even make sense to object morally to the fact that only Trinidadians can compete for the title of Miss Trinidad, and it is difficult to see much sense in objecting to a prize for the best European novelist. Likewise in the area of gender: there may be arguments for having male attendants in female lavatories, but they cannot plausibly be seen as moral arguments. It is a symptom of our confusion in the sphere of moral thinking that it can be supposed that it is always and necessarily morally wrong to act in the light of differences of race, sex, age, or anything else. Obviously many distinctions are invidious, but there is nothing in itself morally wrong with a distinction of treatment based on a distinction of classification. It all depends upon an argument in context to justify a particular act of differentiation. This is why those who object to so-called affirmative or positive discrimination have a *prima facie* case: they question what argument can possibly be strong enough to defeat the claim that such policies are racist or sexist, i.e. they favour certain people on grounds of race which, generally speaking, does not appear to be relevant to the jobs or careers in question. Different treatment *per se* is not the issue. The issue is inappropriate differential treatment or differing treatment for no good and relevant reason.

'Should racism be tolerated?' is, then, a moral question of very little interest since the answer is clearly 'No, it shouldn't'. The question of what constitutes or defines racism is interesting and important, but it is a conceptual question rather than a specifically moral one, albeit one's answer will be partially governed by moral considerations. But the conceptual question of what constitutes or what criteria define racism is different again from the question of what particular practices and policy meet the criteria. The crucial question is, 'Is this hiring practice justified?' rather than 'Is it racist?'; but to answer that question will involve, in addition to a clear understanding of morality and the concept of racism, a wide-ranging and deep understanding of the likely effects of various alternatives and the practical restraints on our choices and actions.

The questions in the context of schooling are not whether racism should be condemned (to which the answer is obvious), nor, by and large, what practices are racist (for, despite wild allegations of 'institutionalized racism', there is little evidence that either schools or teachers as such are racist), but what are the most effective ways to ensure that children do not develop racist attitudes or engage in racist acts, without resorting to indoctrination. The question of what racism means is for philosophers, not simply educationalists. The question for the latter, apart from considering whether there are aspects of the school situation that give rise to or provide opportunities for racist acts, is what to do to develop an antipathy to racism. My answer to that question, broadly speaking, is that we must educate children by providing understanding of other cultures, understanding of individuals' varying sensibilities, understanding of historical and other empirical facts, and, above all, but evidently not exclusively, understanding of moral philosophy.

Sadly, then, but for good practical reasons, I am not going to pursue these questions, interesting as they are, any further. 'What is indoctrination?', 'What counts as racism?', 'What, if anything, might justify a racist policy such as affirmative action?', 'When, if ever, is censorship permissible?', 'What should be done about teenage sex?', and 'What are morally justifiable and effective ways of curbing bullying?' are questions for another book or books, because they require immersion in specifically educational philosophy and empirical educational research. The prior task, and the task that follows most naturally and directly from an understanding of moral philosophy, is to consider in what moral education should consist. What, given the account of moral theory put forward here, follows in respect of bringing up the young? And that is the question that I am going to pursue in the remaining chapters.

Since the time of the Ancient Greeks, it has been widely held that education should be concerned with producing the *kaloskagathos* (literally, the 'noble and good man'), the person of moral character, the person of integrity, or the morally upright individual. This is still an important ideal, but it is one that needs some urgent attention. One way or another moral education has formally been on the agenda for a very long time, but it is far from clear that we are doing the appropriate things to develop the truly moral individual; in fact, sometimes it is not entirely clear that we are even trying to develop the moral person, as distinct from implanting automatic obedience to social rules, developing a fear of God, creating an uncritical reliance on certain rigid rules of conduct, indoctrinating, or, at the other extreme, preaching an incoherent relativism or substituting notions of caring and concern for moral understanding. But loving one's neighbour, for example, whether as a matter of religious commitment or of secular sentiment, is not essentially moral. As has been argued, respect for one's neighbours (or anybody else) in a particular sense is a fundamental moral principle, but actually feeling warm towards one's fellows, though it may well be something to be encouraged for a variety of reasons, is neither necessary nor sufficient for a moral life.

It is true that the majority of people grow up to abide by some standard moral rules, with the result that most of us do not kill, steal, or rob in a direct and blatant way very often. But, in the first place, it is far from clear that this has much to do with any formal moral education, as opposed to a more general enculturalization or social conditioning. In the second place, as I have tried to suggest, this is an inadequate understanding of morality. There is both more to morality than refraining from overt crime and, as one might say, less to it than treating all social rules as moral imperatives. Our world is shamefully lacking in morality in terms of integrity, regardless of the conduct of most individuals in their private lives, as the conduct of politicians, the business world, and the media makes clear on a daily basis. The vast majority of newspapers really don't give consideration to their responsibilities, let alone to what is morally appropriate. With their credo of 'If it bleeds, it leads', they sacrifice everything to sales. The corporate world likewise appears to feel no shame, even when their single-minded focus on profit leads directly to inadequate safety precautions and death, as in a series of rail disasters in Britain in the late 1990s. It is equally insouciant about 'rewarding' senior personnel who have done nothing other than fail in their jobs, in the form of pay-outs and settlements, while sacking, with little or no recompense, poorly paid workers who have given of their best and in most cases been successful in terms of their responsibilities. Politicians too often stop at nothing to gain their own selfish ends, whether it be by doctoring information about weapons of mass destruction, leaking salacious and often false information about rivals, or simply misleading the public. 'Spin', though sometimes criticized, is not often seen as a blatant moral wrong. Political culture is not 'in denial' on this matter. While some particular methods are from time to time condemned from a moral point of view, it is shamelessly accepted that a political party does what it has to do to retain or gain power. While we morally condemn those who abandon their children, even when they were obviously driven to such action by desperation, morally condemn twenty-four-year-olds for having sex with seventeen-year-olds, and morally condemn those who smoke, without recognizing the hypocrisy in doing this while driving around in an SUV – while, in other words, we still make moral judgements on a number of personal matters that are far from obviously unacceptable, we seem impotent to deal with the more blatant and true injustices. There seems to be no way, and perhaps no inclination, to prevent an innocent and by all accounts excellent employee from being suspended from his job for pointing out some serious health hazards in the hospital in which he worked. A teenager who wears a T-shirt with a picture of a nun in an erotic pose is punished by the law court because he has offended against a ban on religious insult, while nobody is held to account for the gas firm Transco's breach of health and safety regulations that led to the death of a middle-aged man. No action is taken against rogue cosmetic surgeons who openly carry on their practice, even as some of their patients find themselves disfigured rather than beautified. A prominent advertising mogul offers the opinion that women cannot rise to the top in his profession because success at the highest level is incompatible with bringing up children and running a home, and he feels obliged to resign in the face of the moral outrage this provokes, but still no charges have been brought against anyone in connection with the Potters Bar rail crash that killed seven and injured seventy, even though it is accepted that the crash was the result of negligence.

There is something very wrong with our moral priorities, in particular our unwillingness to treat institutional or corporate activity as a moral issue. The corruption, the self-serving, the hypocrisy, the double standards at the highest level in our society do not need me as witness. The evidence for the moral desert in which we live is to be found not in the murderers, thugs, and thieves in our midst, who are actually surprisingly few in number, but in the much wider lack of respect for others, in the lack of commitment to the other basic moral principles of fairness, truth, freedom, and well-being, and in the extent and degree of intolerance and dogmatism. It has been said that first-rate people choose first-rate people, while second-rate people choose third-rate people; and it has been said that all it takes (to frustrate the good) is for a few good men to fail to stand up. These maxims neatly highlight part of our problem: while the average middle-class citizen may assume that we live in an enlightened moral age, dedicated leaders of moral integrity have given way to second-rate managers or bureaucrats in all walks of life and they have surrounded themselves with the frankly servile, while manipulation and massage have replaced diplomacy and tact; meanwhile, the so-called silent majority of reasonable and honest people, whether in reality a majority or not, has conspicuously failed to stand up and oppose the substitution of moralizing for moral virtues, politically correct rules for moral principles, and 'street credibility' for moral character.

The prime question for education in relation to morality is what to do about this situation. How are we to improve the moral tone of society? What can we do to ensure that the next generation is a generation of people of moral integrity, which means people with certain principles and attitudes, particularly of tolerance and respect, rather than people who slavishly adopt and insist on absolute obedience to more and more social rules, or, at the other extreme, uncritically accept that there is no such thing as moral truth?

Commentary

The key text in philosophy of education, even forty years on, remains R.S. Peters *Ethics and Education*, and those who wish to become further involved with the broad question of the nature of education and some of the moral questions to which it gives rise are advised to begin there. Other related texts from the heyday of philosophy of education include James Gribble *Introduction to Philosophy of Education*, Paul H. Hirst and R.S. Peters *The Logic of Education*, and John Kleinig *Philosophical Issues in Education*. First published in 1975 but still in print and in some respects conceived of as a companion volume to this one is Robin Barrow and Ronald Woods *An Introduction to the Philosophy of Education*, 4th edition. In regard to fairness and equality in education, see David E. Cooper *Illusions of Equality* and Bryan R. Wilson (ed.) *Education, Equality and Society*.

Robin Barrow and Patrick Keeney (eds) *Academic Ethics* consists of papers on matters relating to academic ethics in higher education. Few of the papers are directly concerned with schools, but the issue of friendship and love between teacher and student, including specific reference to Abelard and Heloïse, is discussed by Cristina Nehring in 'The Higher Yearning: Bringing Eros back to Academe'. James Burge *Heloise and Abelard* is an excellent biography.

Dotheboys Hall is the infamous school introduced by Charles Dickens in *Nicholas Nickleby*. Equally noteworthy is his parody of a certain kind of fact-grinding education in *Hard Times*, as a result of which Gradgrind, the name of the teacher in question, has become a word in its own right depicting earnest and meaningless rote-learning.

H.B. Acton (ed.) *The Philosophy of Punishment* contains a set of standard papers on the topic. John Wilson *Preface to the Philosophy of Education* is useful on punishment in the educational context, as is R.S. Peters *Ethics and Education*. Relevant empirical studies include N.H. Azrin and W.C. Holz 'Punishment' in W.K. Honig (ed.) *Operant Behaviour*, K.D. O'Leary and S.S. O'Leary *Classroom Management*, and R.R. Sears *et al. Patterns of Childhood Rearing*. The use of punishment tends to be deplored by so-called 'progressive' educators such as Jean-Jacques Rousseau *Emile*, A.S. Neill *Summerhill*, and John Holt *Escape from Childhood*. Typically, the argument runs that children do not need to be punished because they will learn what is needed, right, and appropriate in time through experience (or 'by nature'). There is, however, a confusion commonly to be found in such writings between the empirical claim that punishment does not work and the evaluative claim that it should not be employed whether it is productive or not. Robin Barrow *Radical Education* offers a critique of progressive views and arguments.

It could be argued that a penalty for bad scholarly work, whatever its form, cannot be 'punishment' because bad work is not a moral offence and no 'wrong' has been committed. Strictly speaking, I think this is correct. But it still leaves us with the question of whether keeping students in or any other kind of penalty is either efficacious or morally acceptable.

Emphasizing the fact that most educational problems have an empirical aspect raises a most important point and that is that the empirical questions in general are a long way from being adequately answered. This may seem surprising to some: after all, we know how to conduct empirical inquiry in a scientific manner, we have invested years of research and huge amounts of money in the enterprise, and empirical questions are commonly supposed to yield clear answers in a way that evaluative questions are not, so surely we must by now know quite a lot about how most effectively to proceed? This is a major source of debate among educationalists today, but I have to say that my view is that we actually know very little of significance through such research, and that this is partly because of various logical weaknesses in much research to date, but mainly because it cannot in the nature of things be done. To put it simply, human beings are not inanimate matter, and there cannot be a science of human nature, given that humans act intentionally – the very phrase 'social sciences' is a misnomer. In support of this view, it can be said that most leading empirical researchers, when discussing the body of research in general, concede that there is much disagreement, inadequacy of conceptualization and failure to deliver, while critics point out that some of the apparent 'findings' are in fact necessary truths rather than empirical findings (for example, that a teacher should interest his students seems to arise out of what we mean by good teaching rather than to be something that needed to be discovered by observation). The issue is debated by Robin Barrow and Lorraine Foreman Peck in *What Use is Educational Research?*.

The real point that lies behind the issue of stereotyping is that as a parent or teacher one cannot avoid having an influence on, that is to some extent shaping, the development of the young. One is there and the child will react in one way or another to that fact. To refrain from any specific guidance, to present a bewildering variety of models, to do anything, is thus as much to influence as to present a consistent set of chosen values. The question, then, is not whether we should play a part in shaping our children's characters, but how we should do it, and, most important of all, in what direction. What kind of character should we seek to develop? There is no escaping that question.

On discrimination, see the Commentary on Chapter 9 above. On indoctrination, see I.A. Snook *The Concept of Indoctrination* and I.A. Snook (ed.) *Concepts of Indoctrination*. Diane Ravitch *The Language Police* is important reading on the subject of censorship in schools.

The examples of seemingly inane judgements as to what is and what is not morally significant that I throw out towards the end of the chapter are all taken from contemporary newspaper reports. I have not bothered to provide references as similar stories are to be found almost daily.

It was Edmund Burke (1729–97) who remarked: 'All that is necessary for the triumph of evil is that good men do nothing.' I'm afraid that, even with the resources of the internet at my disposal, I have failed to track down the origin of my other favourite aphorism ('First-rate people surround themselves with first-rate people; second-rate people surround themselves with third-rate people'). I cannot even recall where I first encountered it, but I think that it expresses a profound and disturbing political truth.

12 The question of moral education

The first question to ask about moral education is: what characterizes the morally educated person? What does a morally educated person look like? Only when we are clear about what we are trying to achieve can we intelligibly take up the question of how best to proceed.

There is a natural tendency to equate the morally well-educated person with the moral person, and consequently to assume that moral education is designed to produce moral people and that its effectiveness should be judged by its success in achieving that aim. But, importantly, this is not quite correct. Education in all its aspects is crucially about developing understanding: whatever else educated people are, they are people with some kind of understanding. In this respect, education differs from training, socialization, and other types of upbringing that do not necessarily imply any understanding of 'the reason why of things'. Moral education is a matter of developing understanding of the moral domain. Therefore, a morally educated person is not quite the same as a moral person, since it is possible to be moral without having experienced any kind of education and to be morally well educated but to fail to live one's life in a particularly moral fashion. A morally educated person understands the nature of morality and is committed to the standards and norms implicit in moral inquiry (such as consistency and truth), in the same way that the educated historian and scientist understand their subjects and are committed to the norms of their disciplines. But a morally educated person may nonetheless set the subject aside and declare no further interest in it, just as a good historian may turn his attention away from history; equally, a morally educated person may aspire to be moral but fail for a variety of extraneous reasons such as falling prey to temptation or being overwhelmed by fear or other external pressures. Conversely, a person may act morally without having received any formal moral education. So we cannot assume that the test of successful moral education is simply the extent to which students go on to lead moral lives, and we should not be assessing the quality of the moral education we provide by estimating the improvement or decline in moral conduct in society.

(It is only fair to point out here that according to one influential argument an educated scientist or historian must by definition be 'transformed' by their understanding, so that the historian, for example, necessarily lives his life and sees the world in terms that are to some extent affected by his historical knowledge. If that is accepted, it would seem to imply that the morally educated person must be transformed by his moral knowledge and that might be taken to mean that he must be moral. I am not sure whether I do or do not accept the premise that education necessarily involves transformation in this way. But, allowing that it may, I reject the inference that therefore the morally educated person must be moral. Perhaps the truly morally educated must be transformed in some manner by their understanding, but one can be transformed, affected, or altered by one's moral understanding in ways that do not guarantee that one's conduct will be moral.)

In any case, a further important consideration at this juncture is that improvement in the extent of moral conduct is not the kind of thing that is susceptible to measurement or any other plausible form of assessment. Crime figures, for example, are notoriously unreliable and heavily dependent on their interpretation, and anyway they are not the same as moral figures. We certainly do not have any way to measure, in the strict sense of the word, an increase or decrease in such genuinely moral qualities as honesty, kindness, and trust or the extent to which people are truly motivated by concern for fairness and truth, but, more than that, we cannot even gauge or estimate it in a coherent informal or impressionistic manner. It is idle to pretend that we are in a position to say, for instance, whether people are more or less moral today than in previous generations. We are not even in a position to say whether newspaper reports that corruption is currently rife in Russia reveal the truth that Russia is more corrupt than, say, the United States, let alone whether the average citizen of this or that country is more or less corrupt than his counterpart in another. In any case, just as a history programme may be judged a good one without necessarily producing an above average number of good historians (or even if it produces some bad historians, paradoxical as that may seem), so a good programme of moral education does not necessarily result in more moral behaviour (whether in the sense of better behaviour, more of it or both). There are too many other factors, besides education, that have an unavoidable and strong bearing on the ultimate moral quality of individuals, ranging from their genetic inheritance to powerful social pressures, by way of family and peer-group influence, for it to be reasonable to judge the success of an educational programme by reference to the ultimate moral conduct of its students alone.

But, despite the contemporary obsession with measurement and evaluation, the fact that we cannot determine the success of the moral education we provide in this way, or indeed estimate it with any degree of certitude in any other way, should not lead us to despair. A thing can be judged worth doing even when it is agreed that there is no way of estimating its benign effects, as many would say that art is worth having regardless of whether we can establish that it does or does not improve or benefit us. Friendship, love, beauty, and tranquillity are all generally recognized as worth having, regardless of the fact that we cannot demonstrate, let alone systematically prove or measure, the advantages they bring. Two courses in English literature can be critically compared and evaluated without recourse to misplaced attempts to measure or even estimate the sensibility they respectively engender in students. To recognize that we cannot judge our success in moral education by estimating the degree of moral behaviour that it induces is obviously not to say that we have no reason to engage in it. We probably are better off as a result of what we do in the name of moral education than we would be without it, and we would probably be better off still if we made some reasoned improvements. All that is being conceded is that we cannot prove or demonstrate this in some incontrovertible way. It does not follow that it is not the reasonable assumption. In fact it is the reasonable assumption, most particularly since, while moral education is not logically necessary to the development of a moral person, moral understanding *is* a necessary aspect of being moral (since truly moral conduct is conduct voluntarily engaged in in the light of commitment to certain principles), and it is hardly contentious to observe that the majority of people will not acquire this understanding of the nature of morality without the help and guidance that formal education provides. Being morally well educated is not the same as being moral, but being truly moral, as distinct from simply acting in a morally approved manner, necessarily involves moral understanding. Most people will not acquire an adequate moral understanding except through formal education, therefore moral education is desirable regardless of the fact that we cannot really estimate, let alone measure, the degree and extent of moral conduct in society.

Nor, in any case, should we be surprised, or automatically assume that our moral education is inadequate, even if we do have reason to believe that some people turn out to act immorally in spite of the moral education we provide. Some people may be genetically disposed towards the bad, some may be steered that way by circumstance (whether through need, fear, peer pressure, etc.), and some who recognize the good may nonetheless fail to do it through weakness of will. To know the good is not necessarily to do it, though it does provide some motivation towards doing it. If I understand morality then I understand that to betray my friend is intrinsically wrong, and that I ought not to do it, unless obliged to by some conflicting moral demand. But knowing that I should not and being sincerely committed to upholding moral principles cannot guarantee that I will not. Which of us knows how long we would hold out under torture, for example? Which of us can resist all temptation? We can say that those who do break down in extreme circumstances and betray their friends have done something that is bad or intrinsically wrong, and in such a case, even if we were sympathetic, we might not acknowledge that they were justified; but, even while we maintain that they did wrong and that, though their conduct was understandable, it cannot be justified, we may nonetheless on some occasions refuse to blame them or to heap moral reproach on them. It is true that knowing something to be good or right means, among other things, recognizing that it ought to be done; it is to see an intrinsic motivation. But human beings are what they are, and in part this means beings who are prey to temptation, fear, greed, and so forth. We must therefore temper our praise and blame with consideration of the human condition; morality demands of us, among other things, something that we could do fairly easily most of the time, and that is to show more tolerance and understanding. But it follows from the facts of human nature that we cannot under any system of moral education guarantee success. It is reasonable to say that any society that did succeed in bringing up all citizens in such a way that they always acted 'rightly' would not have produced moral agents at all, but must either have indoctrinated or in some other way coerced, manipulated, or terrified them into such a behaviour pattern. But in such a case we would not be faced with a truly moral society, which requires that individuals voluntarily act in certain ways because they see a moral obligation to do so.

What we can do is teach people what morality involves, what the various grounds for being moral are, and what some of the extrinsic advantages of being moral may be both for the individual and for society as a whole. Indeed, the extraneous advantages of a society in which people aspire to be moral, such as predictability, security, comfort, and even pleasure, while they may not in themselves be moral goods, do provide further reasons for being moral in addition to the argument that the fundamental defining principles are self-evidently and in some respects logically binding on us.

Moral education, then, cannot be qualitatively judged by its tendency to produce moral behaviour and its success cannot be quantitatively evaluated in any way. Nonetheless, we can and should seek to develop moral under-standing in the young. But to produce moral understanding is not only different from, it is also at a variance with, any mode of upbringing that insists on the acceptance of and adherence to a fixed set of rules or code of conduct. In particular, given our religious heritage, it has to be recognized that a strictly Christian upbringing has virtually nothing in common with a moral education, despite some overlap between the five fundamental moral principles and cer-tain values attributed to Christ in the New Testament. Certainly, an upbringing that consisted in instilling obedience to the Ten Commandments as set forth in the Book of Common Prayer, or any other similar set of injunctions, is not simply inadequate but actually unacceptable as a form of moral education. The objection to this form of moral education is therefore worth spelling out, but it should be noted that while I shall use the example of the Commandments there are many other examples, including non-religious ones of an ideological or political kind, of the same form. The Ten Commandments are:

1 Thou shalt have none other Gods but me.
2 Thou shalt not make to thyself any graven image.
3 Thou shalt not take the Name of the Lord thy God in vain.
4 Keep holy the Sabbath.
5 Honour thy father and mother.
6 Do no murder.
7 Thou shalt not commit adultery.
8 Thou shalt not steal.
9 Thou shalt not bear false witness against thy neighbour.
10 Thou shalt not covet they neighbour's wife . . . nor anything that is his.

It has often been remarked that this is a very negative code, with eight don'ts to two dos. Less often remarked is how very thin it is as a summary of the moral sphere. Even though it has been part of my argument that typically the sphere of morality is construed too widely and that many issues that people tend to think of as moral issues are not, the pared-down moral realm that I have outlined covers a considerably greater area than do the Commandments. But in any case the list of Commandments is clearly not an account of morality or a moral theory, as the complete absence of any reference to first-level principles and to the need to act on principle (as distinct from out of fear of God or in obedience to the Law) shows. This is a code of behaviour, most of the values being social rather than moral and in some cases owing the value they do have to being universally accepted rather than to any intrinsic merit, as driving on the left-hand side of the road is important in countries that adopt that custom but is not in any way intrinsically superior to driving on the right-hand side. (It will be recalled that I have argued that a large part of so-called 'sexual morality' falls into this category: if a society adopted a coherent pattern of relationships that did not disapprove of what we call 'adultery', as some have done, then adultery would be an accepted practice. Either way it is not intrinsically immoral in the way that unkindness, intolerance, or killing are, for all that they may on occasion be justified.)

The first four Commandments are purely religious and have nothing to do with morality at all. It may be a sin to take the name of the Lord in vain and it may be unwise, but it is not immoral. Nor is it morally right, good, or justified to take it in vain. It is a non-moral issue, and that remains true even if one believes in a specifically Christian God. (It is of course a sin in Christian terms, but we should remember that sin is properly speaking a religious concept. It is true that, thanks to our extensive religious past, we retain the word 'sin' in common parlance and sometimes use it as if it were akin to 'morally wrong', as in 'It's a sin to tell a lie', but the fact remains that it is primarily a religious term.)

One could argue that honouring one's father and mother is a moral requirement, i.e. something that morally one ought to do regardless of faith; if so, one would presumably argue that it is a second-order principle deriving from and subservient to the first-order principles of treating others with respect and beneficence or well-being. But this is not very convincing. Certainly one should honour one's parents, as one should honour anyone else in the sense of respecting them. But there is no obvious reason to honour them in the more specific and demanding sense that I take to be implied by the fifth Commandment. (For instance, I take the Commandment to imply obeying and following all behests of parents.) And it is not clear that one should honour them in any sense (including respect) *more* than others. (One might happen to love them more, and one might as a child have reason to pay more heed to them than to other people, but that appears to be different from what is meant by 'honouring' them in Christian terminology.) My point, as on previous similar occasions, is not to argue in favour of dishonouring parents or to denigrate those who do honour them, but to argue that there is no moral obligation to treat one's parents with more respect than anyone else, simply because they are one's parents, and no apparent argument to support the contention that we have a specifically moral obligation (as opposed perhaps to a filial obligation) to honour them in any other sense.

There is a textual problem in connection with the sixth Commandment. The book of Exodus has God ordering Moses to inscribe 'Thou shalt not kill' as part of the Decalogue, but Jesus, according to Matthew (19:18), interpreted this to mean 'Thou shalt not murder' (as I have rendered it, in line with the Book of Common Prayer). 'Murder' is, by definition, always bad: it means the unacceptable killing of a fellow human. (We do not, for example, call killing as an act of war 'murder' unless we are making the very point that we think a given war immoral.) 'Do not murder' can be conceded, then, to be a legitimate moral command, rightly admitting of no exceptions. (But it gives us no help in determining when a killing constitutes murder. Does the householder defending his family and killing an armed intruder, for instance, commit murder?) The injunctions against killing and stealing are recognized second-order principles. Killing and stealing are intrinsically bad, though they might conceivably be morally justified by circumstance. Here then are recognizably moral prescriptions, but the objection to direct and inflexible commands such as these is that no allowance is made for circumstance or a clash of first-order principles. 'Thou shalt not kill' either denies that any killing can ever be justified or fails to take account of complex and threatening situations when it may be a morally justifiable choice. Killing a traitor in time of war or killing a psychopathic burglar may conceivably be justifiable, and while in general one shouldn't steal, there may be circumstances where it is morally justified.

I have already argued that committing adultery cannot be classified as a moral wrong *per se*, although that is neither to condone nor encourage it. There may be good reason to promote the institution of marriage and along with it the value of fidelity even unto death. There are certainly some instances of adultery, perhaps the majority, that are morally reprehensible because the manner in which the adultery is carried out involves moral failings. But it is not intrinsically moral wrong, even if it is a sin.

As with the fifth Commandment, there is a problem with precisely what is meant by the injunction not to bear false witness. It is widely taken to mean 'Never tell a lie', though it seems fairly clearly to mean more specifically 'Never give false testimony against anyone'. Either way, not bearing false witness is subservient to the principle of truth and as such another reasonable second-order principle (with due allowance for the archaic language). What we say about 'covetousness' depends very much on what we mean by it. Desiring one's neighbour's wife, lusting after her, even having an affair with her, are, as I have argued, not necessarily morally wrong (although, equally, the last at least may be). It seems most plausible to assume that the argument is that covetousness often leads to admittedly wrong acts such as theft, but that, though it may be true, does not make the act of covetousness immoral, however unattractive it may be.

It is arguable, then, that the Ten Commandments give us only three plausible moral imperatives, and even these (if 'murder' is read as 'kill') give us only second-order principles that may be overridden by circumstance or by the clash of claims from conflicting first-order principles. Most of the Decalogue is not concerned with genuinely moral issues. It is wrongly inflexible in its demands. It does not constitute a moral theory or provide an adequate account of, even a summary of, the nature of morality. To think that morality consists in obeying these rules (or any other set of similarly inflexible rules, especially when they do not relate to any of the fundamental principles of morality) is entirely mistaken. More to the immediate point, it is clear that promulgating this or any similar list of commandments does not constitute a moral education. Most of the rules are not moral rules. The few that are cannot serve as unqualified and dogmatic guides to conduct and owe their significance, as generalizations, to one or more of the first-order principles; to present them as unqualified injunctions admitting of no exception is to provide a wholly erroneous guide to moral conduct, let alone moral theory. The fact that a society that adheres to some such set of rules might, for example, conceivably be more stable and predictable should not mislead us into thinking that it would be more moral; indeed, in so far as conduct is based on blind obedience to the rules, it would not be moral at all, since there would not be the freedom to act out of a sense of moral obligation that is necessary to moral conduct. Finally, an upbringing based on inculcating commitment to such rules would not be recognizable as a species of moral *education* at all. Education is to be distinguished from other forms of upbringing such as training, indoctrination, and socialization, by reference to the fact, among other things, that it implies developing understanding. Instilling obedience to various rules may count as a type of training, but it cannot count as *bona fide* education.

If we focus on the nature of morality itself and the nature of moral education, as distinct from moral training, moral conditioning, or moral indoctrination, we see that there is less difficulty with moral education than has often been thought – not less difficulty in terms of determining effective means or guaranteeing success, but less difficulty in terms of determining what it is appropriate to do, regardless of how effective it may prove to be in respect of producing a more moral society. The desire to wrap the topic up in terms of certainties (dogmatic rules, inflexible prescriptions, and demonstrable effects) is born of confused thinking. As we have seen, numerous so-called moral issues are not moral issues at all, and many issues that are indeed moral nonetheless do not allow of unequivocal solutions. It is the essence of the moral sphere that there are not only difficulties and problems, but also dilemmas. There are many situations in which, though in principle there may be an answer or a right and a wrong, we cannot establish it. This is a fact about the moral domain. It is no good bewailing it, trying to get round it, or ignoring it. It is in the nature of the beast and we must acknowledge it, which means that in practice we must leave individuals to make up their own individual minds in such cases. Relativism is quite wrong if it means that there is no grounding for moral rules at all or that all rules of conduct are merely social rules or conventions; but it is quite right if it means that in many cases particular situations give rise to varying judgements at different times and places, and sometimes to no clear directive at all. Abortion and euthanasia, as we have seen, are clear examples of issues where we are not in a position to decree whether they can be morally justified or not, and therefore it would be wrong, because an obvious infringement of freedom, to force an individual to act in line with one view or the other.

There are many issues that are important, perhaps, but are not moral issues, such as concern for the environment, recycling, manners, and many aspects of sexual relations. Quite apart from very real disagreements over the facts of the matter in such examples, and regardless of how prudent, sensible, or wise it might be to act in one way rather than another, these are not moral issues. (A far better case could be made for regarding the carrying of guns as immoral, but even in this case it would be better to say that it should be illegal.)

So what should a person of integrity do and refrain from doing? And what, therefore, should we be teaching the young in the name of moral education?

First, we need to teach the young the meaning and nature of morality. Morality is not to be confused with law, religion, prudence, social value, custom, or mere efficacy. It is a set of first-order high-level abstract principles that should ideally govern all human interaction at all times and places, although, of course, in practice they cannot. They are the principles of freedom, fairness, well-being, respect, and truth. We know these to be desirable, as we may put it, by intuition or self-evidently. These principles are inherently, intrinsically, or in themselves good.

Second, we should teach them that a moral person, a person of integrity, acts in accordance with these principles for their own sake, not for praise, from fear, or under compulsion, and regardless of apparent or real personal advantage. Even keeping a promise or acting kindly, if done in order to curry favour with another or under threat, for example, does not constitute acting with integrity.

Third, by reasoning from first-order principles we can be more specific and show students that there are a number of more particular second-order principles that generally speaking hold good, although they are not absolute: keep promises, be loyal, cultivate friendship, speak out in defence of the good, show tolerance, defend freedom of speech, do not steal or cheat, and avoid using people as means by, for example, kidnapping, raping, or mugging them, but also by taking advantage of them in more domestic settings such as failing to return what you have borrowed, ignoring them, or failing to come to their aid. The goodness of second-order principles can be recognized in some cases by reference to first-order principles and in some cases by reference to consequences.

But the qualification 'generally speaking' must be clearly understood. Even freedom of speech may have to be curbed in time of war. It is difficult to see how rape or mugging as usually understood could ever be justified, but all the other rules may sometimes rightly be broken, if only because either the rules themselves or the principles from which they derive clash. Keeping a promise is not always possible if one is also bound to tell the truth; cultivating friendship is not an obvious good if it is done for personal gain, out of fear, or with a thoroughly bad person. Circumstances or the claims of one or more first-order principles may sometimes justify even disloyalty or intolerance. Working out when it is appropriate to break a second-order rule must therefore involve taking account of circumstances and be conducted by reference to the first-order principles. Thus, the third element in moral education may be summarized as developing understanding of second-order principles and the appropriate ways in which to weigh these claims in the case of competing demands. It should also be stressed that the fact that in certain cases there is no right way to proceed should not be confused with the erroneous claim that there is no moral truth or no objectivity in morality.

Fourth, moral education must also involve teaching people to see that discussion and decision-making in the light of principles also very often involve conceptual work, as well as reference to likely consequences. Emphasis should be placed on the need to explore and develop understanding of key moral concepts such as loyalty, friendship, and tolerance, as well as concepts that are central to moral theory and debate such as objectivity and subjectivity. Whether one should remain loyal on a particular occasion can only be determined by one who has a good idea of what counts as loyalty and of what being loyal or not being so will lead to in a given instance. Consideration of truth in morality can only come from those who have a grasp of concepts such as truth, knowledge, objectivity, and subjectivity.

Fifth, there are certain moral dispositions, such as kindliness and tolerance, which need to be developed and which we should therefore exemplify for the young, draw attention to, and encourage. Notwithstanding the emphasis that I have placed on understanding (an emphasis which is necessary both because moral understanding is crucial to moral conduct and because contemporary fashion tends to underplay, even resist, it), there is an affective side to morality. This is more a matter of caring about morality itself than anything else: a moral person feels that it is important or obligatory to act in certain ways and cares passionately about this, which is why moral concern tends to be expressed as moral indignation or anger. Of course moral people care about others too, but it is not clear that we are morally required to 'love our neighbour' in the sense of forming strong emotional attachment to others; the moral requirement would be better characterized as that concern that is the hallmark of respect for persons. But in this sense we need to develop moral sentiment as well as moral understanding.

Sixth, the same process of reasoning that affirms that there are *bona fide* second-level principles equally clearly shows that some putative moral issues are not moral at all (e.g. recycling, being drunk). Of course, any activity can be made to look like a moral issue by linking it to consideration of harm or freedom. But it is a confusion to assume that therefore every act is either moral or immoral. Being drunk and boorish may lead to unfortunate consequences that cause distress to others: since it is bad to cause distress to others, on a particular occasion you may be said to have behaved badly. But that does not make drinking in excess immoral in itself, although it is certainly, generally speaking, anti-social. What characterizes the second-order principles (apart from the fact that they derive from first-order principles) is that they refer to behaviours that tend in themselves to have either desirable or deleterious consequences; breaking promises by its nature tends to lead to confusion, uncertainty, and other undesirable consequences; kindness, though a particular act may have unfortunate consequences, is itself a balm. By contrast, drinking too much doesn't necessarily lead to good or bad consequences, and in itself it is neither; failure to recycle has no necessary moral consequences and no inherent moral value one way or the other.

Seventh and finally, intention is another vital ingredient in conduct of integrity. Why one does what one does is what turns a behaviour into an action: it is my intention that makes my hand-waving a cry for help, a greeting, or a secret signal. Moral conduct can only be so if behaviour is engaged in for a certain kind of reason. It has been suggested that Eichmann did not intend to destroy the Jews, but that he was nonetheless immoral. Quite apart from the question-begging premise (did Eichmann really not 'intend' to implement the 'final solution', even allowing for the fact that his prime motivation may have been to follow orders, gratify the Fuehrer, or whatever?) there is another major confusion here. What one intends to achieve, what one sees as a reason for what one is doing, and what one is in fact doing (let us say, obeying orders in order to gain promotion) may all indeed be irrelevant. But the intention to act on moral principle or not is a different matter. Eichmann acted immorally because he did not 'intend' to abide by any moral principles; whatever his precise motivation, he chose to eschew morality. In opting to do anything, whether obey orders or something else, in place of showing concern for the fundamental principles of morality, he revealed a lack of moral integrity.

To promote understanding of the seven points summarized here is one and the same thing as to provide moral understanding. As we have seen, moral understanding does not guarantee moral behaviour, but it is nonetheless the essence of moral education. A person without such understanding might conceivably act in ways that are regarded as morally desirable and might have beneficent sentiments, but he could not act with moral integrity, which implies acting in certain ways because one recognizes the distinctively moral obligation to do so. Persons with such understanding, notwithstanding the fact that they might fail to act morally on occasion, are generally more likely both to desire and to be able to pursue the moral path, just as generally speaking the historian is likely to be more inclined and more able than others to look at the world through his historical understanding.

Commentary

Meriel Downey and A.V. Kelly *Moral Education* provides a basic introduction to both theory and practice in this area, while Roger Straughan *Can
We Teach Children to be Good?* is an introduction to the philosophical
questions. See also Robert E. Carter *Dimensions of Moral Education*. Paul
Hirst *Moral Education in a Secular Society* is particularly good on the relationship between morality and religion. R.S. Peters *Psychology and Ethical
Development* is an extensive collection of his papers relating to moral
education and, as the title implies, gives critical attention to the place of
psychology. D.B. Cochrane *et al.* (eds) *The Domain of Moral Education* and
Ben Spiecker and Roger Straughan (eds) *Philosophical Issues in Moral
Education and Development* are both useful collections of philosophical
papers, while Nancy F. and Theodore R. Sizer (eds) *Moral Education: Five
Lectures* and W.R. Niblett (ed.) *Moral Education in a Changing Society* are
important multi-disciplinary collections. Richard Pring *Personal and Social
Education in the Curriculum* and Patricia White (ed.) *Personal and Social
Education* are, as their titles indicate, not strictly focused on moral education
as I understand it, but they have obvious relevance. Advertised to appear
in late 2006 is Colin Wringe *Moral Education: Beyond the Teaching of Right
and Wrong* which, according to the advance publicity, argues, as does this
book, that both 'fashionable relativism and recent moves towards inculcatory
authoritarianism' are to be 'firmly rejected'. It appears that it may be more
sympathetic to religion as contributory to moral education and is structured
around consideration 'of a range of ethical theories'.

J. Wilson *et al. Introduction to Moral Education* is a particularly interesting
book, being the work of a philosopher, a sociologist, and a psychologist
who worked together on a research programme on moral education at the
height of the era that believed that educational problems were best tackled
by bringing together expertise from the foundational disciplines of philosophy, history, psychology, and sociology. This view has unfortunately been
superseded by the incoherent idea that education is a *sui generis* discipline
of inquiry. Other books on moral education, that are not specifically philosophical, include Peter McPhail *et al. Moral Education in the Secondary
School*, William Kay *Moral Education*, Alan Harris *Teaching Morality and
Religion*, and P.W. Musgrave *The Moral Curriculum*. A classic text in the
sociology of moral education that deserves mention is Emile Durkheim
(1858–1917) *Moral Education*.

The view that education is conceptually linked with understanding is
widely accepted among philosophers of education, even those of otherwise
differing viewpoints, and has been since the time of Plato. Some such as Glenn
Langford *Philosophy and Education* have argued against understanding being

BISHOP BURTON COLLEGE
LIBRARY

seen as the central feature of the concept; many others have been concerned about too strong or exclusive an emphasis on rationality; and, of course, there is a great deal of argument about what it is that educated people should understand. But few, if any, seriously deny that to be educated is at least partly to acquire understanding. This view has become a commonplace in my own work, e.g. Robin Barrow *The Philosophy of Schooling*, but the classic argument for this position is to be found in the works of Paul Hirst and Richard Peters, particularly their joint work *The Logic of Education*. The phrase 'the reason why of things' is introduced by Peters in *Ethics and Education*. It should be added that it is Peters also who seems to imply, though perhaps unintentionally, that if you turn away from, for example, your historical knowledge in later life, you somehow become that much less educated.

The following excerpt from Elizabeth Taylor's *At Mrs Lippincote's* has some pertinence to the distinction between education for its own sake and training for some further particular end:

> 'They will try to stuff her head with Virgil and Pliny and Greek irregular verbs.'
>
> 'All Greek verbs are irregular,' Julia murmured.
>
> 'I think it nonsense. What use will it be to her when she leaves school? Will it cook her husband's dinner?'
>
> 'No, it won't do that, but it will help her to endure doing it, perhaps. If she is to cook while she is at school, then there will be that thing less for her to learn when she's grown up: but if she isn't to learn Greek at school, then she will never learn it afterwards. And learning Greek at school is like storing honey against the winter.'
>
> 'But what use is it?' he persisted.
>
> 'Men can be educated; women must be trained,' she said sorrowfully. ... 'My mother,' Julia went on, 'begged me to look upon my education as a luxury, never to think of it as a way of getting a good job, nor a good husband either, but only as a means of lessening my boredom if I did.'
>
> (pp. 107–8)

The complex issue of weakness of will is well explored by Roger Straughan *I Ought to, But . . .*

For discussion of social values, see above, Chapter 9. Chapter 8 above, on second-order principles, includes a discussion of killing. It does not explicitly mention stealing, but this is clearly another inherently wrong act that could only be justified in circumstances where the claims of some other first-order principle(s) are equally or more compelling. Thus, stealing might be justified, if, for example, one was starving and on the run from the Gestapo. Some prefer to say that, in such an example, taking a loaf of bread or whatever does not constitute or should not count as stealing. But it comes to the same thing: defining a term is another way of determining limits and boundaries. Adultery is considered in Chapter 9 above. For discussion relating to abortion and euthanasia, see Chapters 7 and 8 above.

13 Forms of moral education

The question of whether virtue can be taught is a very old one. Whether it is taught or caught, innate or acquired, is of perennial interest because, whereas if we set out to teach students history by and large they gain some historical understanding, when we set out to bring people up to be moral it is a far more hit and miss affair. Predictions as to which of our students will turn out to be moral do not have the accuracy that predictions as to who will progress as historians do. It may also be said that arguably some historical understanding is better than none, while it is not so clear that a partially successful moral education is of much use or even that the idea of it makes sense.

Nonetheless, the answer to the question of whether virtue can be taught may be less obscure than frequent attempts to grapple with it through the centuries and some current major research projects suggest. The problem of whether one's moral self should be seen as innate, given by nature, or as being developed by nurture or one's surroundings, at any rate, seems now to be clearly answered in the only way that ever made sense: one's moral character is the product of both and the interplay between them. But now we do not need to talk vaguely of 'nature' and 'nurture'. There is now fairly incontrovertible evidence that in relation to our moral and all other aspects of our identity what can develop is constrained or made possible in the first place by our genetic inheritance. One's inherited gene pool puts limits on what one can become. However, it is equally clear that within those bounds experience, including, very significantly, education, makes a major difference, even to the extent that our genetic make-up can itself be modified by circumstance. Hence the phrase 'nature via nurture' has been coined to set against the old and unnecessary polarization of 'nature vs. nurture', meaning that who we are as adults is the outcome of the effect that our upbringing in the widest sense, but certainly including schooling, has on our innate, inherited characteristics (instantiated in our genes).

The classical observation that, while we can pick out teachers of history, carpentry, mathematics, and so on, we cannot pick out teachers of morality, and that time and again highly moral parents, who one would expect both to know something and care about morality, fail to raise moral children, has some truth. And it is indeed obviously not possible to ensure that every child will grow up to be moral, or to predict accurately who will turn out to be less or more moral, or to guarantee success with any particular individual by any particular method of upbringing. But it is possible to take those steps that are most likely to develop the three distinct elements that go to make up the moral person: first, an understanding of the nature of morality; second, a commitment to morality; and third, the ability to act on that commitment. Not only are these distinct, they are also of a different order from each other, the first being a matter of mind or intellect, the second a matter of attitude or will, and the third a combination of character, intellect, and practical wisdom; for those who have an understanding of and a commitment to virtue do not necessarily have the strength or the ability to act on it in practice. Nonetheless, different as these elements are, we know something of what it is appropriate to do to raise people with moral integrity in this sense.

To achieve a true moral education, it is first necessary to sweep away, in both theory and practice, the various irrelevant and misguided things that we currently do that are based upon unacceptable notions of morality or being human, or both. In particular, we have to dispense with all variants of value clarification programmes, with preaching or condoning a superficial adherence to various types of relativism or subjectivism (often in the guise of postmodernism, or post-something else no doubt by the time you read this: the name changes, but the thesis remains essentially the same), and, at the other extreme, with drilling a set of particular contingent rules into the young, whether in the name of religion, the state, ideology, or morality.

There is no hard evidence on the extent to which parents and teachers today still treat moral education primarily as a matter of inculcating a list of dos and donts and demand practice in accordance with these precepts. But we should not dismiss or ignore this model just because it may be outside our own experience. This model of moral education is to be found extensively among fundamentalist religious groups of all persuasions and denominations, as well as throughout the many ideological totalitarian regimes that still flourish. Fanaticism is merely the most obviously visible sign of this type of moral upbringing. But for every individual whose morality is so simple and dogmatic that he is prepared to kill and die in its name, there are thousands, perhaps millions, whose minds are equally closed and inflexible, though their actions may be less extreme. Not only is such an approach unjustified, as we have seen, in that the specific rules, whatever they are, cannot be shown to be valid, but, more than this, though some of them might be acceptable as rules of thumb, none are valid as absolute and unqualified rules. Even the injunction to 'keep promises' cannot be treated as an absolute rule; even the first-order principles of truth or freedom may occasionally have to be honoured in the breach. It should also be recognized that in so far as such an approach 'works' on its own terms (i.e. results in consistent following of the rules), it necessarily leads to inflexibility and intolerance and an inability to think for oneself and to make moral judgements; but this dogmatism and inability to think for oneself are both counterproductive in terms of contributing to a more moral community and incompatible with genuine morality, which logically requires freely chosen activity rather than activity that is rule-bound or the outcome of indoctrination. Third, such an approach seldom does 'work' on its own terms, except within extremely closed groups; a type of upbringing that can work in a small, strongly religious community of very fixed and decided views is exceedingly vulnerable when practised in the polyglot, polycultural, polypolitical societies that most of us are familiar with today. Thus, drilling a set of moral rules into the young is unwarranted, leads to certain kinds of immorality or amorality in so far as it succeeds, and generally won't work anyway, even on its own terms. And it is important to stress the objections to moral upbringing of this type because, while it is not the prevailing orthodoxy in educational circles in Western liberal democracies, it is still the approach that is adopted in closed religious and political communities, is still the approach of a number of sects within liberal democracies, and is possibly the type of 'moral' upbringing that the majority of the world's inhabitants currently experience.

More fashionable in educational theory and practice in liberal democracies are species of moral upbringing that exemplify the other two approaches I have mentioned. Value clarification programmes and exercises had a vogue in the 1960s, and the phrase is now out of fashion; but a great deal of the spirit, the underlying theory, and to some degree the practice associated with such approaches is still very much alive. The basic approach involves encouraging students from an early age to 'share', as we might now say, their values, the presumption being that this will help them to articulate those values, to think about reasons for holding them, and to recognize diversity and differences of opinion. It is the antithesis of the dogmatic approach that I have just criticized. In general, teachers using such an approach deliberately avoid commenting on, let alone evaluating, the values to which the children subscribe. There is, for instance, little evidence that in value clarification programmes in the past teachers differentiated between different kinds of value or assessed the quality of the arguments or reasons given for or against holding them. In other words, this is an approach focused on the importance of expressing oneself rather than on any criteria of quality. (Again, studies of value clarification programmes suggest that little or no consideration was given even to the quality of the individual's articulation of her values, let alone the putative reasoning behind it.) This, then, is very much education as therapy, where the presumed value of 'expressing oneself' or 'sharing' outweighs all other considerations. Paradoxically, some research suggested that such an approach, far from being therapeutic in all cases, sometimes caused considerable anxiety and grief, as a consequence of people not being at ease with each other's very different views and not being comfortable with unburdening themselves in what was felt to be a private and personal area. But there are other stronger grounds than its potential to unsettle for objecting to such an approach to moral upbringing.

First, as has been argued in Part I of this book, it is important that people should come to recognize that there are different kinds of value, and that assessing the reasonableness of value judgements involves distinguishing between these different kinds. It will not do, for instance, to treat a moral judgement as though it were a prudential or aesthetic judgement. In failing to focus on such distinctions, value clarification programmes are seriously misleading. Second, it is not sufficient to be able to explain one's values or judgements; one needs also to attempt to justify them in a reasonable fashion. Explanation and justification are quite distinct activities, the former providing the reasons why one values this rather than that, the latter providing reasons as to why one should value this rather than that. It is a most important part of basic moral understanding to recognize and appreciate the difference. Overall, the practice in value clarification courses in their heyday tended to be varied, with some teachers being blithely unconcerned about whether students had or could have had good reason to hold the views they did, and others attempting to evaluate or accept and reject various particular judgements. The former method of teaching is unhelpful in the extreme (if it can be considered 'teaching' at all), since it purveys the false idea that all that matters is that you hold your views sincerely, regardless of what they are, how you acquired them, or what good reasons there may be to support them. But the latter is not acceptable either, unless, as is seldom the case in such programmes, attention is paid to the nature and quality of the reasoning behind judgements (paying particular attention to the relevance of certain kinds of reason to certain kinds of value), rather than simply to whether the judgements do or do not conform to a list of acceptable and unacceptable or correct and incorrect responses. This is the nub of the objection to this kind of approach to moral upbringing: it ignores the question of reasoned justification, which must involve reference to the particular nature of morality if it is to be done adequately. One cannot, for example, justify a moral value by appeal to legal facts. There is something to be said for encouraging students to articulate their views, but there is more that needs to be done if we are to provide a real moral education, and there is nothing to be said for promulgating the idea that all that matters is that one should know what one likes and be prepared to assert it, or for confusing explanation with justification, especially when one does not even bother to distinguish between good explanation and poor explanation.

Interest in value clarification programmes is not the necessary outcome of any particular moral position, but it perhaps tends to grow out of and certainly reinforces a rather facile relativism. But relativism is far more widely preached, implied, and assumed in relation to moral upbringing than merely through such programmes as these. Whether as a result of an unwillingness to make clear intellectual demands on students and to assert and argue for certain values and against others, or of a reluctance to challenge the current orthodoxy, a great deal of schooling clearly fails to stand up on this issue. Yet, as has been argued throughout this book, the moral sphere is not anything you choose to make it. It has its boundaries and its defining elements. There are many and various truths in this domain, ranging from the fact that fairness is a moral good to the fact that one cannot establish beyond reasonable doubt whether euthanasia is morally justifiable or not. Of course there are practical difficulties in maintaining and demanding certain moral standards, and it is difficult to get away from the common perception that such judgements are just a matter of opinion. But the first prerequisite of an adequate approach to moral education is the recognition that one certain truth is that not everything in this sphere is just a matter of opinion, and that the school in particular, through its ethos, examples, and rules, its expectations and above all its teaching, should both represent and argue for that truth. Just as the schools' job, in the long run, is to identify, articulate, justify, and pass on the norms and procedures of good science, good history, good athletics, and so on, and to point out the differences between them, so it is their job to distinguish, articulate, justify, and pass on the norms and processes involved in moral reasoning and conduct.

Finally, in briefly reviewing popular but nonetheless inadequate approaches to moral education, mention must be made of developmental theories. A psychological developmental theory seeks to establish maturational levels of development, as distinct from levels of ability or achievement that may be acquired as a result of environmental factors, including in particular teaching. Any such theory seeks to locate definable stages, to label them, and to relate them to chronological age. In the nature of things, such a programme of research is difficult given the problems inherent in separating what is due to innate maturation and what is due to external factors. In the event some aspects of any developmental theory turn out to be arguably at least partly a matter of logical necessity, while the truly empirical claims remain broad and tentative. Thus the stages of moral development through which theorists and researchers conclude that children pass can only be taken as a very rough and ready guide. Consequently, notwithstanding the popularity of such theories, perhaps occasioned by the quite mistaken view that anything that is the product of observation must be both reliable and of practical value, the sad truth is, not that such research is necessarily mistaken, but that it is actually of very little use to the practising teacher. The theory will tell the teacher, for example, that at about the age of twelve most children will have an increasingly critical attitude to rules and will begin to think in terms of fairness. But in the first place this is already (and inevitably) heavily qualified (e.g. 'at *about* the age', '*most* children', 'an *increasingly* critical attitude'), so that the teacher still has to establish the reality of his or her classroom; in the second place, though explicit programmes of moral teaching have been based on such theories, there is no obvious reason to suppose that they indicate any particular way or approach to moral education, other than the obvious point that it is futile to teach children what they are too young to understand (whether in terms of maturation or in terms of their social and educational background).

There are a variety of contexts in which moral education can take place and a number of different ways of approaching it, for example through literature, through discussion of school rules, through history, science, or sports, or by engaging with actual moral problems, whether vicarious or experienced at first hand. But, if we want to provide genuine moral education, by some means or other, at some stage, we must introduce students directly to the concepts and argument of morality, and we must evaluate the quality of contributions to the moral debate. Different subject matters admit of different degrees of certainty and have to be approached in different ways. The certainty of the mathematical proposition that $2 + 2 = 4$ is greater than the certainty of the literary judgement that Shakespeare was a great dramatist, and the manner of establishing the truth in each case is quite different. Morality is an area or subject where it is more difficult to arrive at clear-cut arguments for definitive specific judgements than it is in, say, science or even history. But that is no excuse for pretending that we cannot aim for that degree of reasonableness that the case allows or for failing to try to attain it. We do not conclude that any historical judgement is as good as another, despite the undeniable fact that a historical judgement such as that Mussolini was a bad leader is quite different from and harder to justify or disprove than a typical scientific proposition. The moral judgement that Mussolini was a bad man may be even more complex and harder to establish as unequivocally true or false than the historical claim that he was bad leader, but it is nonetheless not just a matter of opinion. It is a matter of understanding and making coherent sense of both the facts of the matter and the moral argument.

Moral people or people of moral integrity cannot be defined solely in terms of their behaviour or what they do. Whatever one's behaviour, one is not acting morally unless one does what one does freely, on the basis of specifically moral reasoning. But moral education, though it should be far more concerned with moral understanding than seems generally to be recognized, is not only about understanding. Even if one acts in a certain way because one recognizes a moral duty to do so, a person of integrity is not only sincere but also consistent and determined in acting in this kind of way; one needs to care in the sense that one acts not simply out of obedience to moral rules, but out of concern for and commitment to the moral order. To keep a promise is inherently a good thing; it is generally the right thing to do, though exceptions can sometimes be morally justified. But merely to keep a promise is not to be moral. Even to keep promises generally is not in itself to be moral, if one is simply following a rule or acting out of habit, in the way that most of us keep the (non-moral) rule about looking both ways before crossing a road. A moral person keeps promises because he understands and accepts the need to do so in terms of such principles as truth and well-being, and he is concerned about or has a positive sentiment towards them.

This means that as well as developing the moral understanding which has been the focus of this book, we need to cultivate in people a moral sentiment or a sympathy, and a kind of courage, will-power, or moral determination. The nature of a moral sentiment, as distinct from other kinds of sentiment, is to be discerned in the nature of morality, in particular the fact that the object of morality is to bring comfort and security to all and that all persons count equally. Given that this is the point or purpose of morality, moral sentiment must involve some degree of compassion or concern for others, not in the sense of personal affection addressed to particular individuals, but in the sense of recognition of others as beings like ourselves, capable of experiencing suffering and happiness. There has been some interest shown in the concept of imagination in respect of education in recent years, but that does not capture the kind of imaginative sympathy that is referred to here; nor does the distinction sometimes made between sympathy and empathy really help, while much of the work on 'caring' argues that we should have an emotional commitment to people which goes far beyond what is required in terms of our moral attitude to others. What is needed is not so much a focus on the imagination in the abstract, as if 'the imagination' could be located, worked on, and developed like a physical muscle, but a focus on imaginative history, imaginative science, or imaginative photography; similarly, we need to cultivate a moral imagination – a tendency and an ability to consider and act towards others as persons and not simply to recognize them as such in a formal sense. It is the ability to put ourselves in the place of others that needs to be cultivated, rather than the ability to feel or share their pain or joy: an ability to recognize that given the circumstances a person is likely to be feeling jealous, rather than the ability to empathize or feel the jealousy vicariously.

'Will-power' is not a particularly fashionable term these days. But being moral clearly requires a lot of strength and determination, not necessarily because we are prey to great temptation, but simply because it is generally easier to ignore moral imperatives than to respond to them. Weakness of will is a very common failing – something that we surely all experience to some degree at some time or another. Many of the worst moral outrages in history take place as much because the majority do not stand up to be counted, do not resist the wrongdoing, as because a few instigate the wrong. This is not, incidentally, to suggest that I or anyone else would necessarily have shown the requisite moral courage in Nazi Germany, in the face of the genocide in Cambodia, or Rwanda, or Yugoslavia; it is merely to stress that one characteristic of those who acted in a truly moral manner in such situations was that they had the necessary courage to act on their moral views. On a more parochial or domestic front there is far less excuse for the failure to live up to our principles and to act as we should, yet it is surely the case that all too often we take the line of least resistance and look away, rather than take the risks involved in confronting moral issues.

To an extent that is not perhaps sufficiently appreciated, the development of understanding in itself contributes to the development of both moral sentiment and moral will-power. To understand all may not be quite to forgive all, but it is a lot easier to care about the plight of the political prisoner, or feel for the pregnant teenager facing abuse and hostile criticism for choosing to have an abortion, if you are clear in your mind on the moral issues, and it is easier to stand your ground against opposition when you are sure of your ground. Understanding of other things besides morality further contributes to one's ability to feel and express moral sympathy. Having some understanding of teenagers, for example, would help in this case, as would some understanding of biology. More generally, understanding of history and culture often helps to sharpen and inform our moral perception.

It is clear that to some extent what does move us and what we are prepared to stand up for are determined by inner convictions that are partly formed from a very young age by example, illustration, and encouragement. To this end, there cannot be any doubt that the stories that we tell matter immensely, whether we are referring literally to children's stories or to the more sophisticated stories of history, literature, and morality itself. This is not an argument for indoctrination or censorship. It is an argument for selection of material on educational grounds. There is a vital difference between banning the works of the Marquis de Sade, and simply saying that his works are not a priority for teachers or school libraries. This is an argument for accepting the view that educators should to some extent, particularly in the early years, impose their views and seek to influence and form the embryonic views of students. It is an argument, specifically, for telling stories to the young that celebrate the moral. While nobody pretends that this age-old approach to early moral education is guaranteed success, one cannot reasonably deny that cultivating the seeds of will-power and sentiment in this way is both desirable and justifiable.

But ultimately a true moral education must consist of coming to understand morality, and in particular in seeing through some of the common confusions and heresies in moral thinking, and in coming to understand and appreciate moral exemplars. To that end, we need to continue moral education after the early years of moral habituation through the study of the humanities generally and moral philosophy in particular. (Let it not be forgotten that as things stand there is no moral philosophy or any other kind of philosophy in the curriculum, and furthermore that, extraordinarily, a philosophy degree is one of the few degrees that does not count towards qualification as a teacher in many jurisdictions.) That, after all, is what the humanities and philosophy are for: to enlarge a certain kind of understanding and sympathy so that we may improve our character, develop our integrity and inspire our moral courage and determination.

In conclusion, I shall outline the moral education that seems to be demanded and justified by the overall argument of this book in schematic and summary form. The first and most important point is that moral education is a process that continues throughout the school years and should not be conceived of in terms of a course or a programme; one does not teach moral education as one might say one teaches chemistry, languages, or a sport. Becoming morally educated is a matter of learning a variety of things in a variety of contexts. At different stages of schooling the appropriate contribution to moral education takes different form.

In the early years, parents and teachers should both exemplify and encourage moral behaviour. They should themselves act in accordance with the first- and second-order moral principles and exhibit the fundamental virtues or moral characteristics of, for example, kindness and fairness. They should encourage such behaviour in children and endorse it through praise and blame. The question of whether certain forms of punishment or reward are effective is an empirical one that goes beyond the scope of philosophy, though I will venture the suggestion that, despite all the research that has been conducted into such matters, we are not really in a position to say much of a categorical nature: we simply don't know whether reprimands, physical punishment, withdrawal of treats, and so forth are effective procedures or not, probably because it depends a great deal on the individuals and the particular circumstances in question. We are not in a very strong position to be categorical about the moral acceptability of various types of reward and punishment either: we cannot, for example, claim to have categorically established that paying out money for good behaviour or administering physical punishment for bad are always either morally acceptable or unacceptable.

Common sense, however, and an understanding of what truly moral behaviour involves suggest that ideally we should aim to foster moral acts by the time-honoured means of simple praise and blame, avoiding as much as possible material reward and physical penalty, primarily because we want people to be motivated by a sense of honour and shame, and don't want them to be motivated by fear or self-interest.

The young should be told, and encouraged to read, stories that enshrine moral values. It hardly requires philosophy to make a point that has been accepted throughout the ages, but it is unfortunately necessary to make this point as against those who confuse this with indoctrination or who wrongly think that to provide the young with material that is in keeping with our values is in itself in some way immoral. Closing a child's mind, intending to implant unquestioning allegiance to some set of values, and rooting out any capacity for critical thought, as certain types of religious and political regime seek to do, are indeed all morally (and educationally) objectionable. Openly declaring one's values to the young, however, is not. Let the young be introduced to a world in which goodness is respected and ultimately rewarded, and badness is barren. Let the foundations be laid securely. Time and the development of critical thought and autonomy through education will more than balance the situation and teach adolescents that life is not in fact like a fairy tale, but will allow them still to feel that we should strive to make it so.

Discussion of moral values can and should be carried on, on a limited level, with the young. They ask the question 'Why?' and it usually makes sense to reply in terms that are essentially moral in that they invoke the basic principles: 'We don't do that because it hurts people'; 'You wouldn't like them to do that to you'; 'We try to mean what we say and say what we mean'. Young children can also learn to appreciate that making decisions and choices must partly be governed by getting the facts of the situation right, by knowing something about the consequences of our actions. And of course, without anybody overtly talking about it, and without having any of the vocabulary, young children can quickly come to appreciate that hypocrisy is the antithesis of moral integrity.

In short, there isn't any problem about the early stages of moral education, provided that we have the sense not to be intimidated by ill-founded educational fads, such as the absurd idea that we shouldn't be doing any of the above. Secondary education, reasonably enough, needs to continue to provide a moral climate and to extend opportunity for individuals to exercise moral responsibility and to make moral decisions. At this later stage, however, there is more of a problem than people seem to realize, because the two elements that are crucial are, in their different ways, right out of fashion: philosophy, including moral philosophy, is never formally regarded as a useful school subject and does not figure seriously in any national curriculum in the English-speaking world, while the humanities, though they survive and have their powerful supporters, nonetheless tend to have to work overtime to be regarded as an educational priority in this materialist and mechanistic age. But it is the study of moral philosophy, literature, and history that must form the basis of a true moral education.

What is to be avoided at all costs is the idea that moral education should itself be a subject. To think otherwise is to be a victim of the same kind of fallacy that lies behind the critical thinking movement. Thinking critically is something that all educationalists rightly approve of and regard as a key educational objective. But critical thinking is not a skill or a set of skills like ball control in a sporting context, to be practised and developed in itself without concern for different subject matter. A person who is noted as a critical thinker in the context of politics may prove a duffer in the context of sports. This is not simply to do with difference of interest or a lack of factual information in one or other context. It is because, although there are a few general strategies that may be said to be common to any kind of critical thinking, what constitutes critical thinking, what the rules and standards that the critical thinker needs to appreciate are, varies from subject to subject. Critical thinking in any context must avoid contradiction, for example, but to recognize a contradiction in science you need to know science, and the fact that you can recognize one there doesn't mean that you will recognize one in a debate on art. So the only plausible way to teach for critical thinking is to emphasize a critical approach to whatever subjects one chooses to teach for other reasons. Even philosophy can be taught in an uncritical way, and the only way to produce a critical philosopher is by teaching philosophy in a critical manner. In much the same way, the way to produce moral thinkers or people who tend towards the moral is to teach them by emphasizing the moral aspects of everything they study and do. But here there is another reason for doing this: morality does have a content, which critical thinking does not. Questions about the ethics of research on animals, about fraudulent scientific research, about the morality of historical events and people, and about the moral dimensions of certain biological matters, all need to be addressed.

The humanities have a particular role to play. In literature we encounter what are among other things studies of human morality which feed both the imagination and the understanding; they are also studies of human psychology. Of course, not all books are equally good, but part of the reasoning that leads to classifying great literature as such is that it is regarded as particularly penetrating, acute and plausible in its depiction of people and their way of living. To study literature, meaning here to read it rather than to discuss technique, is the surest way I can think of to come to grips with erudite explorations of human and in particular moral sensibilities, problems, and challenges. One could of course substitute lessons devoted to discussing the students' own moral concerns. But contrary to the fashionable view that this is what should be done, it is unclear that it is actually of interest to most students; they do not have the richness of experience or the imaginative capability to tell the story, and they do not have the solutions. It is also often easier to have an unheated but penetrating debate at one remove. History, of course, provides countless examples of and opportunities for moral argument, sometimes explicitly sometimes obliquely. Literature and history have their prime educational value as repositories of material that is tailor made for learning about morality.

But for any of this to be of any use in contributing ultimately to moral education, the debate, the discussion, and the thinking all have to be of a certain sort. As has repeatedly been said, the facts of the matter have to be known and to be right, and to that end almost all school subjects may contribute: you have to understand quite a lot of science, particularly biology, to talk intelligently about abortion, cloning, animal rights, and so on, and quite a lot of history to talk intelligently about political questions. Morality is also predicated on a commitment to truth and rationality, education as a whole being, one hopes, geared towards their development. But still we lack the final ingredient. This is of course moral philosophy. In order to have a meaningful debate, in addition to the other factors, one has to have some philosophical *nous*; one has in particular to understand something of the nature of moral theory and of key moral concepts. This book has been written in the hope that it may make a small contribution towards developing a critical understanding of the basics of the requisite moral philosophy.

Commentary

'Can virtue be taught?' was a question that exercised Plato. See, for example, *Protagoras*; but his interest in the question pervades many of the dialogues. Plato also had what must surely be essentially the right answer to the nature vs. nurture debate: our moral character is the result of the interplay between our innate nature and our circumstances, including, most importantly, our education. For an excellent summary of this interplay in terms of contemporary genetic understanding, see Matt Ridley *Nature via Nurture*. Finally, it is Plato yet again who first observed that while we can pick out those who are the best teachers of music, architecture, science, and so on, we cannot pick out the teachers of virtue. On Plato's philosophy of education generally, see Robin Barrow *Plato*.

Perhaps to claim that 'drilling a set of moral rules into the young . . . leads to a certain kind of immorality' is too strong. Such an approach may lead both to an inappropriate dogmatism, causing one sometimes to do what is actually wrong, and it would seem likely to work against the individual choosing to act in a certain way because she sees it as her duty, which, as we have seen, is one aspect of true moral behaviour. But it might be better to end the sentence: 'makes true moral conduct difficult, if not impossible'. Be that as it may, the practice is not dead. At the time of writing there are reports in the press that the British government wants to introduce compulsory classes on 'core British values'. It is not entirely clear what such classes would involve, but, on the face of it, this approach is at odds with the one argued for in this book, notwithstanding the fact that one could claim that the five fundamental principles of morality are also core British values (as well as the core values of many other peoples).

Louis Raths *et al. Values and Teaching* was a seminal book in the positioning of values clarification; S.B. Simon *Meeting Yourself Halfway* and S.B. Simon and J. Clark *More Values Clarification* both seem to condone extreme and untenable forms of subjectivism. For those interested nonetheless in examples of practical strategies, see S.B. Simon *et al. Values Clarification*.

Lawrence Kohlberg is one of the more prominent moral development theorists. See *The Philosophy of Moral Development* and 'Education for Justice: a Modern Statement of the Platonic View' in N.F. Sizer and T.R. Sizer (eds) *Moral Education: Five Lectures*. Other notable developmental theorists, not necessarily focusing on specifically moral development, include Jean Piaget, Susan Isaacs, Jerome Bruner, and Erik Erikson.

On imagination, see Mary Warnock *Imagination* and K. Egan and D. Nadaner (eds) *Imagination and Education*. See also Nel Noddings *Caring*. In a number of places, specifically in 'The Generic Fallacy' and *Understanding Skills*, I have argued against the idea that such things as imagination, creativity, critical thinking, and intelligence are generic skills.

Reference to moral courage or the courage to stand up and be counted should not be taken to imply that such courage is in itself a moral virtue. Just as weakness of will is not a moral failing, so courage or determination, though necessary to enable one to act morally on many occasions in today's world, is not in itself a moral virtue any more than the exercise of free choice is. There are obvious echoes of Plato's division of the soul into three parts (intelligence, will, and appetite or desire) here.

The idea of education as story-telling is another cliché: a headline grabbing gimmick that has more to do with rhetoric than substance. Teaching isn't story-telling. Education isn't to be based simply on stories. But in a more limited and literal sense, as stated in the text, it does matter what stories we tell to the young, because to some extent in most cases they will be affected in one way or another by the stories.

The fallacy that lies behind the critical thinking movement is precisely the generic fallacy referred to above. It is also fallacious to see mental abilities as skills. John McPeck *Critical Thinking* remains one of the most sensible texts on this topic. See also Harvey Siegel *Educating Reason: Rationality, Critical Thinking and Education.*

I should say, perhaps, that advocating the study of moral philosophy in schools is not necessarily the same thing as advocating philosophy for children. That is to say, there are a number of specific programmes designed to introduce relatively young children to philosophical thinking in various non-traditional ways. I do not have a particular view on the idea of such programmes in general, but here I am referring to the straightforward traditional study of moral philosophy by older students.

Bibliography

Acton, H.B. (ed.) (1969), *The Philosophy of Punishment*, London, Macmillan.

Anscombe, G.E.M. (1958), 'Modern Moral Philosophy', *Philosophy* 33, pp. 1–19.

Archambault, Reginald D. (ed.) (1965), *Philosophical Analysis and Education*, London, Routledge & Kegan Paul.

Aristotle (1955), *Nicomachean Ethics*, Harmondsworth, Penguin.

Aristotle (1962), *Politics*, Harmondsworth, Penguin.

Ayer, A.J. (1936), *Language, Truth and Logic*, London, Gollancz.

Barrow, Robin (1975), *Plato, Utilitarianism and Education*, London, Routledge and Kegan Paul.

Barrow, Robin (1978), *Radical Education*, Oxford, Martin Robertson.

Barrow, Robin (1980), *Happiness*, Oxford, Martin Robertson.

Barrow, Robin (1981), *The Philosophy of Schooling*, Brighton, Wheatsheaf.

Barrow, Robin (1982), *Injustice, Inequality and Ethics*, Brighton, Wheatsheaf.

Barrow, Robin (1990), *Understanding Skills: Thinking, Feeling and Caring*, London, Ont., Althouse Press.

Barrow, Robin (1991), 'The Generic Fallacy', Educational Philosophy and Theory 23(1), pp. 7–17.

Barrow, Robin (1997), *Utilitarianism: a Contemporary Statement*, Aldershot, Edward Elgar.

Barrow, Robin (1999), 'The Need for Philosophical Analysis in a Postmodern Era', *Interchange* 30(4), pp. 415–32.

Barrow, Robin (2007), *Plato*, London, Continuum.

Barrow, Robin and Foreman-Peck, Lorraine (2006), *What Use is Educational Research? A Debate*, London, Philosophy of Education Society.

Barrow, Robin and Keeney, Patrick (eds) (2006) *Academic Ethics*, Aldershot, Ashgate.

Barrow, Robin and Woods, Ronald (2006) *An Introduction to Philosophy of Education*, 4th edition, London, Routledge.

Bavidge, Michael and Ground, Ian (1994), *Can We Understand Animal Minds?*, Bristol, Bristol Classical Press.

Beardsmore, R.W. (1971), *Art and Morality*, London, Macmillan.

Beckerman, Wilfred and Pasek, Joanna (2006), *Justice, Posterity and the Environment*, Oxford, Oxford University Press.

Benn, S.I. and Peters, R.S. (1959), *Social Principles and the Democratic State*, London, Allen and Unwin.

Bentham, Edward (1999), *An Introduction to Moral Philosophy*, Bristol, Thoemmes Press.

Bentham, Jeremy (1948), *The Principles of Morals and Legislation*, New York, Hafner.

Billington, Ray (2003), *Living Philosophy: an Introduction to Moral Thought*, 3rd edition, London, Routledge.

Blackburn, Simon (2002), *Ethics: a Very Short Introduction*, Oxford, Oxford University Press.

Blackburn, Simon (2004), *Lust*, New York, Oxford University Press.

Blackburn, Simon (2005), *Truth: a Guide*, Oxford, Oxford University Press.

Blum, Lawrence A. (1980), *Friendship, Altruism and Morality*, London, Routledge and Kegan Paul.

Boyd, Neil (2004), *Big Sister*, Vancouver, Greystone Books.

Bradley, F.H. (1967), *Ethical Studies*, Oxford, Clarendon Press.

Braybrooke, David (2004), *Utilitarianism: Restorations; Repairs; Renovations*, Toronto, University of Toronto Press.

Brown, Montague (2002), *The Quest for Moral Foundations: an Introduction to Ethics*, Toronto, Scholarly Book Service.

Burge, James (2003), *Heloise and Abelard*, San Francisco, Calif., Harper.

Butler, Christopher (2002), *Postmodernism: a Very Short Introduction*, Oxford, Oxford University Press.

Butler, Joseph (1950), *Five Sermons*, New York, Bobbs-Merrill.

Campbell, Robert (1988), *Ending Lives*, Oxford, Basil Blackwell.

Carter, Robert E. (1984), *Dimensions of Moral Education*, Toronto, University of Toronto Press.

Cavalieri, Paolo and Singer, Peter (1993), *The Great Ape Project*, London, Fourth Estate.

Chang, Iris (1997), *The Rape of Nanking*, Toronto, HarperCollins.

Chappell, V.C. (ed.) (1962), *The Philosophy of Mind*, Englewood Cliffs, NJ, Prentice-Hall.

Chisholm, Roderick (1966), *Theory of Knowledge*, Englewood Cliffs, NJ, Prentice-Hall.

Chomsky Noam (1967), *Syntactic Structures*, New York, Mouton.

Clark, Stephen R.L. (1977), *The Moral Status of Animals*, Oxford, Oxford University Press.

Cochrane, D.B., Hamm, C.M., and Kazepides, A.C. (eds) (1979), *The Domain of Moral Education*, Toronto, Paulist Press.

Cooper, David E. (1980), *Illusions of Equality*, London, Routledge and Kegan Paul.

Cooper, David E. (1983), *Authenticity and Learning*, London, Routledge and Kegan Paul.

Cranston, Maurice (1973), *What Are Human Rights?*, London, The Bodley Head.

Crofton, Ian (1988), *A Dictionary of Art Quotations*, London, Routledge.

Cross, R.C. and Woozley, A.D. (1964), *Plato's Republic: a Philosophical Commentary*, London, Macmillan.

Curry, Patrick (2005), *Ecological Ethics: an Introduction*, Cambridge, Polity Press.

Damasio, Antonio (2003), *Looking for Spinoza*, Toronto, Harcourt.

de George, Richard T. (ed.) (1966), *Ethics and Society*, London, Macmillan.

d'Entreves, A.P. (1951), *Natural Law*, London, Hutchinson.

Devettere, Raymond J. (2002), *Introduction to Virtue Ethics: Insights of the Ancient Greeks*, Washington, DC, Georgetown University Press.

Downey, Meriel and Kelly, A.V. (1978), *Moral Education*, London, Harper and Row.

Downie, R.S. and Telfer, Elizabeth (1969), *Respect for Persons*, London, Harper and Row.

D'Souza, Dinesh (1991), *Illiberal Education*, New York, Free Press.

Dunant, Sarah (ed.) (1994), *The War of the Words*, London, Virago.

Durkheim, Emile (2002), *Moral Education*, New York, Dover Publications.

Dworkin, Ronald (1993), *Life's Dominion*, London, Harper Collins.

Egan, K. and Nadaner, D. (eds) (1988), *Imagination and Education*, New York, Teachers College Press.

Encyclopedia of Philosophy (1967), New York, Macmillan.

Enright, D.J. (2003), *Injury Time: a Memoir*, London, Pimlico.

Ewing, A.C. (1947), *The Definition of Good*, London, Routledge and Kegan Paul.

Ewing, A.C. (1953), *Ethics*, London, English Universities Press.

Feinberg, Joel (ed.) (1973), *The Problem of Abortion*, Belmont, Calif., Wadsworth.

Feinberg, Joel (1980), *Rights, Justice and the Bounds of Liberty*, Princeton, NJ, Princeton University Press.

Foot, Philippa (1978), *Virtues and Vices*, Oxford, Basil Blackwell.

Frey, R.G. (ed.) (1984), *Utility and Rights*, Oxford, Basil Blackwell.

Fulford, K.W.M. (1989), *Moral Theory and Medical Practice*, Cambridge, University of Cambridge Press.

Gallie, W.B. (1955), 'Essentially Contested Concepts', *Proceedings of the Aristotelian Society, 1955–6*, pp. 167–98.

Glendon, Mary Ann (1991), *Rights Talk*, New York, The Free Press.

Glover, Jonathan (1977), *Causing Death and Saving Lives*, Harmondsworth, Penguin.

Gray, John (1983), *Mill on Liberty: a Defence*, London, Routledge and Kegan Paul.

Gregory, I.M. and Woods, R.G. (1971), 'Valuable in Itself', *Educational Philosophy and Theory*, pp. 51–64.

Gregory, Richard L. (ed.) (1987), *The Oxford Companion to the Mind*, Oxford, Oxford University Press.

Gribble, James (1969), *Introduction to Philosophy of Education*, Boston, Mass., Allyn and Bacon.

Ground, Ian (1989), *Art or Bunk?*, Bristol, Bristol Classical Press.

Hampshire, Stuart (1977), *Two Theories of Morality*, Oxford, Oxford University Press.

Hampshire, Stuart (ed.) (1978), *Public and Private Morality*, Cambridge, Cambridge University Press.

Hare, R.M. (1952), *The Language of Morals*, Oxford, Clarendon Press.

Hare, R.M. (1963), *Freedom and Reason*, Oxford, Clarendon Press.

Hare, R.M. (1981), *Moral Thinking: Its Levels, Method and Point*, Oxford, Clarendon Press.

Hare, William (1979), *Open-mindedness and Education*, Montreal, McGill-Queen's University Press.

Hare, William (1985), *Controversies in Teaching*, London, Ont., Althouse Press.

Harris, Alan (1976), *Teaching Morality and Religion*, London, Allen and Unwin.

Harris, John (1985), *The Value of Life: an Introduction to Medical Ethics*, London, Routledge and Kegan Paul.

Hart, H.L.A. (1963), *Law, Liberty and Morality*, Oxford, Oxford University Press.

Hayman, Ronald (1997), *Nietzsche: Nietzsche's Voices*, London, Phoenix.

Hentoff, Nat (1992), *Free Speech For Me – But Not for Thee*, London, HarperCollins.

Herodotus (1954), *Histories*, Harmondsworth, Penguin.

Hick, John (1964), *The Existence of God*, London, Macmillan.

Hick, John and McGill, Arthur (1968), *The Many-faced Argument*, London, Macmillan.

Hirst, P.H. (1974), *Moral Education in a Secular Society*, London, University of London Press.

Hirst, P.H. (1974), *Knowledge and the Curriculum: a Collection of Philosophical Papers*, London, Routledge and Kegan Paul.

Hirst, P.H. and Peters, R.S. (1970), *The Logic of Education*, London, Routledge and Kegan Paul.

Hobbes, Thomas (1914), *Leviathan*, London, Dent.

Holt, John (1974), *Escape from Childhood*, Harmondsworth, Penguin.

Honderich, Ted (ed.) (1973), *Essays on Freedom of Action*, London, Macmillan.

Honig, W.K. (ed.) (1966), *Operant Behaviour*, Englewood Cliffs, NJ, Prentice-Hall.

Horace (1979), *The Satires of Horace and Persius*, Harmondsworth, Penguin.

Horace (1983), *The Complete Odes and Epodes*, Harmondsworth, Penguin.

Hospers, John (1946), *Meaning and Truth in the Arts*, Chapel Hill, University of North Carolina.

Hospers, John (1961), *Human Conduct: an Introduction to the Problems of Ethics*, New York, Harcourt Brace.

Hudson, W.D. (1967), *Ethical Intuitionism*, London, Macmillan.

Hudson, W.D. (ed.) (1969), *The Is/Ought Question*, London, Macmillan.

Hudson, W.D. (1970), *Modern Moral Philosophy*, London, Macmillan.

Hughes, Robert (1993), *The Culture of Complaint*, New York, Oxford University Press.

Hume, David (1911), *A Treatise of Human Nature*, London, Dent.

Hume, David (1953), *Political Essays*, Indianapolis, Bobbs-Merrill.

Hume, David (1957), *An Inquiry Concerning the Principles of Morals*, Indianapolis, Bobbs-Merrill.

Hursthouse, Rosalind (1987), *Beginning Lives*, Oxford, Basil Blackwell.

Hutcheson, Francis (1994), *Philosophical Writings*, London, Dent.

Ignatieff, Michael (2000), *The Rights Revolution*, Toronto, Anansi.

Jones, Peter (1995), *Rights*, St Louis, Mo., Vhps Distribution.

Kant, Immanuel (1934), *Critique of Pure Reason*, London, Dent.

Kant, Immanuel (1948), *Groundwork of the Metaphysic of Morals*, translated and analysed by H.J. Paton as *The Moral Law*, London, Hutchinson.

Kay, William (1975), *Moral Education*, London, Allen and Unwin.

Kleinig, John (1982), *Philosophical Issues in Education*, London, Croom Helm.

Kleinig, John (1985), *Ethical Issues in Psychosurgery*, London, Allen and Unwin.

Kluge, Elke Henner W. (1992), *Biomedical Ethics in a Canadian Context*, Scarborough, Ont., Prentice Hall.

Kohlberg, Lawrence (1981), *The Philosophy of Moral Development*, Toronto, HarperCollins.

Kupperman, Joel J. (1983), *The Foundations of Morality*, London, Allen and Unwin.

Lacey, A.R. (1976), *Dictionary of Philosophy*, London, Routledge.

Ladd, John (ed.) (1979), *Ethical Issues Relating to Life and Death*, Oxford, Oxford University Press.

Langford, Glenn (1968), *Philosophy and Education*, London, Macmillan.

Leahy, Michael P.T. (1991), *Against Liberation: Putting Animals in Perspective*, London, Routledge.

Lillie, William (1948), *An Introduction to Ethics*, London, Methuen.

Locke, John (1950), *A Letter Concerning Toleration*, Indianapolis, Bobbs-Merrill.

Lockwood, Michael (1985), *Moral Dilemmas in Modern Medicine*, Oxford, Oxford University Press.

Lyotard, Jean-François (1984), *The Postmodern Condition*, Minneapolis, University of Minnesota Press.

Mabbott, J.D. (1966), *An Introduction to Ethics*, London, Hutchinson.

Machiavelli, Niccolò (1961), *The Prince*, Harmondsworth, Penguin.

MacIntyre, Alasdair (1967), *A Short History of Ethics*, London, Routledge and Kegan Paul.

Mackie, J.L. (1977), *Ethics: Inventing Right and Wrong*, Harmondsworth, Penguin.

McPeck, John (1981), *Critical Thinking*, Oxford, Martin Robertson.

McPhail, Peter, Ungoed-Thomas, J.R., and Chapman, Hilary (1972), *Moral Education in the Secondary School*, London, Longman.

Masson, Jeffrey and McGarthy, Susan (1994), *When Elephants Weep: the Emotional Lives of Animals*, London, Jonathan Cape.

Melden, A.I. (ed.) (1970), *Human Rights*, Belmont, Calif., Wadsworth.

Midgley, Mary (1979), *Beast and Man: the Roots of Human Nature*, Brighton, Harvester Press.

Midgley, Mary (2005), *The Owl of Minerva: a Memoir*, London, Routledge.

Miethe, Terry and Flew, Antony (1991), *Does God Exist?*, London, HarperCollins.

Mill, John Stuart (1968), *Utilitarianism; On Liberty; Representative Government*, London, Dent.

Mitchell, Basil (ed.) (1971), *The Philosophy of Religion*, Oxford, Oxford University Press.

Montefiore, Alan (1958), *A Modern Introduction to Moral Philosophy*, London, Routledge.

Montefiore, Alan (ed.) (1975), *Neutrality and Impartiality*, Cambridge, University of Cambridge Press.

Moore, G.E. (1903), *Principia Ethica*, Cambridge, Cambridge University Press.

Moore, G.E. (1912), *Ethics*, Oxford, Oxford University Press.

Morris, Thomas V. (ed.) (1987), *The Concept of God*, Oxford, Oxford University Press.

Murdoch, Iris (1992), *Metaphysics as a Guide to Morals*, London, Chatto and Windus.

Musgrave, P.W. (1978), *The Moral Curriculum*, London, Methuen.

Nehring, Cristina (2006). 'The Higher Yearning: Bringing Eros back to Academe', in Robin Barrow and Patrick Keeney (eds), *Academic Ethics*, Aldershot, Ashgate.

Neill, A.S. (1962), *Summerhill*, Harmondsworth, Penguin.

Niblett, W.R. (ed.) (1963), *Moral Education in a Changing Society*, London, Faber.

Nietzsche, Friedrich (1961), *Thus Spake Zarathustra*, Harmondsworth, Penguin.

Nietzsche, Friedrich (1973), *Beyond Good and Evil*, Harmondsworth, Penguin.

Noddings, Nel (1984), *Caring*, Berkeley, University of California Press.

Noddings, Nel (2003), *Happiness and Education*, Cambridge, University of Cambridge Press.

Norman, Richard (1988), *The Moral Philosophers: an Introduction to Ethics*, Oxford, Oxford University Press.

Nowell-Smith, P.H. (1954), *Ethics*, Harmondsworth, Penguin.

Nozick, Robert (1993), *The Nature of Rationality*, Princeton, NJ, University of Princeton Press.

O'Connor, D.J. (1967), *Aquinas and Natural Law*, London, Macmillan.

O'Leary, K.D. and O'Leary, S.S. (1977), *Classroom Management*, New York, Pergamon.

Osborne, Harold (ed.) (1972), *Aesthetics*, Oxford, Oxford University Press.

Palmer, Donald (2005), *Why It's Hard to be Good: an Introduction to Ethical Theory*, New York, McGraw Hill.

Pascal, Blaise (1961), *Pensées*, Harmondsworth, Penguin.

Paton, H.J. (1948), *The Moral Law*, London, Hutchinson.

Peters, R.S. (1966), *Ethics and Education*, London, Allen and Unwin.

Peters, R.S. (1974), *Psychology and Ethical Development*, London, Allen and Unwin.

Phillips Griffiths, A. (ed.) (1967), *Knowledge and Belief*, Oxford, Oxford University Press.

Pinker, Stephen (2002), *The Blank Slate*, New York, Viking.

Pitcher, G. (ed.) (1964), *Truth*, Englewood Cliffs, NJ, Prentice-Hall.

Plato (1954), *Phaedo* in *The Last Days of Socrates*, Harmondsworth, Penguin.

Plato (1956), *Protagoras* and *Meno*, Harmondsworth, Penguin.

Plato (1974), *The Republic*, Harmondsworth, Penguin.

Pring, Richard (1984), *Personal and Social Education in the Curriculum*, London, Hodder and Stoughton.

Quinton, Anthony (1973), *Utilitarian Ethics*, London, Duckworth.

Rae, Scott B. (1995), *Moral Choices: an Introduction to Ethics*, Toronto, HarperCollins.

Raths, Louis, Harmin, Merrill, and Simon, S.B. (1966), *Values and Teaching*, Columbus, Ohio, Merrill.

Ravitch, Diane (2003), *The Language Police*, New York, Alfred A. Knopf.

Rawls, John (1972), *A Theory of Justice*, Oxford, Oxford University Press.

Regan, Donald H. (1980), *Utilitarianism and Co-operation*, Oxford, Clarendon Press.

Regan, Tom (2003), *Animal Rights: Human Wrongs: an Introduction to Moral Philosophy*, Lanham, Md., Rowman and Littlefield.

Regan, Tom and Singer, Peter (eds) (1976), *Animal Rights and Human Obligations*, Englewood Cliffs, NJ, Prentice-Hall.

Reiss, Michael J. and Straughan, Roger (1996), *Improving Nature?*, Cambridge, University of Cambridge Press.

Ridley, Matt (2003), *Nature via Nurture*, London, HarperCollins.

Roberts, T.A. (1973), *The Concept of Benevolence*, London, Macmillan.

Ross, W.D. (1923), *The Right and the Good*, Oxford, Clarendon Press.

Ross, W.D. (1939), *Foundations of Ethics*, Oxford, Clarendon Press.

Rousseau, Jean-Jacques (1913), *The Social Contract*, London, Dent.

Rousseau, Jean-Jacques (1972), *Emile*, London, Dent.

Ryle, Gilbert (1949), *The Concept of Mind*, Harmondsworth, Penguin.

Scarre, Geoffrey (1996), *Utilitarianism*, London, Routledge.

Schauer, Frederick (1982), *Free Speech: a Philosophical Enquiry*, Cambridge, University of Cambridge Press.

Scruton, Roger (1983), *The Aesthetic Understanding*, London, Methuen.

Scruton, Roger (2005), *Gentle Regrets*, London, Continuum.

Searle, John (1984), *Minds, Brains and Science*, Cambridge, Mass., Harvard University Press.

Searle, John (1995), *The Construction of Social Reality*, Harmondsworth, Penguin.

Searle, John (2004), *Mind*, Oxford, Oxford University Press.

Sears, R.R.T., Maccoby, E.E., and Levin, H. (1957), *Patterns of Childhood Rearing*, Evanston, Ill., Row, Peterson.

Sellars, Wilfred and Hospers, John (eds) (1970), *Readings in Ethical Theory*, Englewood Cliffs, NJ, Prentice-Hall.

Sen, Amartya and Williams, Bernard (eds) (1982), *Utilitarianism and Beyond*, Cambridge, University of Cambridge Press.

Sidgwick, Henry (1963), *The Methods of Ethics*, London, Macmillan.

Sidgwick, Henry (1988), *Outlines of the History of Ethics*, Indianapolis, Hackett.

Siegel, Harvey (1988), *Educating Reason: Rationality, Critical Thinking and Education*, London, Routledge.

Sim, Stuart (ed.) (2005), *The Routledge Companion to Postmodernism*, London, Routledge.

Simon, S.B. (1974), *Meeting Yourself Halfway: Thirty-one Values Clarification Strategies for Daily Living*, Niles, Ill., Argus Communications.

Simon, S.B. and Clark, J. (1975), *More Values Clarification*, San Diego, Calif., Pennant Press.

Simon, S.B., Howe, L.W., and Kirschenbaum, H. (1972), *Values Clarification*, New York, Hart.

Singer, Peter (1977), *Animal Liberation*, St Albans, Paladin Books.

Singer, Peter (1979), *Practical Ethics*, Cambridge, Cambridge University Press.

Singer, Peter (ed.) (1991), *A Companion to Ethics*, Oxford, Basil Blackwell.

Singer, Peter (1994), *Rethinking Life and Death: the Collapse of our Traditional Ethics*, New York, St Martin's Press.

Sizer, Nancy F. and Sizer, Theodore R. (eds) (1970), *Moral Education: Five Lectures*, Cambridge, Mass., Harvard University Press.

Smart, J.J.C. and Williams, Bernard (1973), *Utilitarianism: For and Against*, Cambridge, University of Cambridge Press.

Smith, Page (1990), *Killing the Spirit*, New York, Viking.

Snook, I.A. (1972), *The Concept of Indoctrination*, London, Routledge and Kegan Paul.

Snook, I.A. (ed.) (1972), *Concepts of Indoctrination*, London, Routledge and Kegan Paul.

Spiecker, Ben and Straughan, Roger (eds) (1988), *Philosophical Issues in Moral Education and Development*, Milton Keynes, Open University Press.

Straughan, Roger (1982), *Can We Teach Children to be Good?*, London, Allen and Unwin.

Straughan, Roger (1982), *I Ought to, But . . .*, Windsor, NFER.

Sumner, L.W. (1987), *The Moral Foundation of Rights*, Oxford, Clarendon Press.

Swinburne, Richard (1979), *The Existence of God*, Oxford, Clarendon Press.

Tanner, Michael (2000), *Nietzsche: a Very Short Introduction*, Oxford, Oxford University Press.

Tarnas, Richard (1991), *The Passion of the Western Mind*, New York, Balantine Books.

Taylor, Elizabeth (1988), *At Mrs Lippincote's*, London, Virago.

Telfer, Elizabeth (1980), *Happiness*, London, Macmillan.

Thompson, Mel (2000), *Ethics*, London, Hodder and Stoughton.

Tilghman, B.R. (1984), *But is it Art?*, Oxford, Basil Blackwell.

Trigg, Roger (1973), *Reason and Commitment*, Cambridge, University of Cambridge Press.

Urmson, J.O. (1968), *The Emotivist Theory of Ethics*, London, Hutchinson.

Waldron, Jeremy (ed.) (1984), *Theories of Rights*, Oxford, Oxford University Press.

Walsh, Jill Paton (2006), *Debts of Dishonour*, London, Hodder and Stoughton.

Warnock, Geoffrey (1967), *Contemporary Moral Philosophy*, London, Macmillan.

Warnock, Geoffrey (1971), *The Object of Morality*, London, Methuen.

Warnock, Mary (1960), *Ethics since 1900*, Oxford, Oxford University Press.

Warnock, Mary (1976), *Imagination*, London, Faber.

Warnock, Mary (1998), *An Intelligent Person's Guide to Ethics*, London, Duckworth.

Waugh, Alexander (2004), *God*, London, Review.

Wheelwright, Philip (2005), *A Critical Introduction to Ethics*, Whitefish, Mont., Kessinger Publishing.

White, Patricia (ed.) (1989), *Personal and Social Education*, London, Kogan Page.

Whyte, Jamie (2003), *Bad Thoughts: a Guide to Clear Thinking*, London, Corvo.

Wilde, Oscar (1999), *Complete Works of Oscar Wilde*, Glasgow, HarperCollins.

Williams, Bernard (1972), *Morality: an Introduction to Ethics*, New York, Harper and Row.

Williams, Bernard (1985), *Ethics and the Limits of Philosophy*, Cambridge, Mass., Harvard University Press.

Williams, Gerald J. (1998), *A Short Introduction to Ethics*, Lanham, Md., University Press of America.

Wilson, Bryan R. (ed.) (1975), *Education, Equality and Society*, London, Allen and Unwin.

Wilson, John (1966), *Equality*, London, Hutchinson.

Wilson, John (1979), *Preface to the Philosophy of Education*, London, Routledge and Kegan Paul.

Wilson, J., Williams, N., and Sugarman, B. (1967), *Introduction to Moral Education*, Harmondsworth, Penguin.

Windschuttle, Keith (1996), *The Killing of History*, New York, Free Press.

Wollheim, Richard (1968), *Art and its Objects*, New York, Harper and Row.

Woozley, A.D. (1949), *Theory of Knowledge: an Introduction*, London, Hutchinson.

Wringe, Colin (2006), *Moral Education: Beyond the Teaching of Right and Wrong*, London, Springer.

Index